MISTRUST

Sara Miller McCune founded SAGE Publishing in 1965 to support the dissemination of usable knowledge and educate a global community. SAGE publishes more than 1000 journals and over 800 new books each year, spanning a wide range of subject areas. Our growing selection of library products includes archives, data, case studies and video. SAGE remains majority owned by our founder and after her lifetime will become owned by a charitable trust that secures the company's continued independence.

Los Angeles | London | New Delhi | Singapore | Washington DC | Melbourne

GLYNIS M. BREAKWELL

MISTRUST

Los Angeles | London | New Delhi
Singapore | Washington DC | Melbourne

Los Angeles | London | New Delhi
Singapore | Washington DC | Melbourne

SAGE Publications Ltd
1 Oliver's Yard
55 City Road
London EC1Y 1SP

SAGE Publications Inc.
2455 Teller Road
Thousand Oaks, California 91320

SAGE Publications India Pvt Ltd
B 1/I 1 Mohan Cooperative Industrial Area
Mathura Road
New Delhi 110 044

SAGE Publications Asia-Pacific Pte Ltd
3 Church Street
#10-04 Samsung Hub
Singapore 049483

Editor: Amy Maher
Assistant Editor: Esmé Carter
Production Editor: Prachi Arora
Copyeditor: Solveig Gardner Servian
Indexer: Caroline Eley
Marketing Manager: Camille Richmond
Cover Design: Wendy Scott
Typeset by: C&M Digitals (P) Ltd, Chennai, India
Printed in the UK

Library of Congress Control Number: 2021932189

British Library Cataloguing in Publication data

A catalogue record for this book is available from the British Library

ISBN 978-1-5297-3210-8
ISBN 978-1-5297-3207-8 (pbk)
eISBN 978-1-5297-6558-8

At SAGE we take sustainability seriously. Most of our products are printed in the UK using responsibly sourced papers and boards. When we print overseas we ensure sustainable papers are used as measured by the PREPS grading system. We undertake an annual audit to monitor our sustainability.

To Colin Rowett – Invaluable informant and Interlocutor

CONTENTS

About the Author

xi

Preface

xiii

1 The Nature of Mistrust

1

The Importance of Mistrust

1

Trust, Distrust and Mistrust

3

Why Mistrust?

6

Identity Processes and Social Representations

7

2 Risk and Mistrust

13

What is Risk?

13

Making Decisions in Uncertainty: Representativeness, Availability and Anchoring

14

Weighing Up Prospects and Subjective Values

16

Cumulative Prospect Theory and Mistrust

18

Biases in Estimating Risk and Attributing Mistrust

19

Risk Reactions

26

Rationality and Mistrust

27

3 Shared Uncertainty

29

An Age of Uncertainty

29

No Uncertainty Lives Alone

31

Absolute Uncertainty

34

Shared Mistrust

36

4 Identity, Emotions and Mistrust

39

Expressions of Mistrust

39

Mistrust and Emotion

39

Being Mistrusted, Self-efficacy and Helplessness

43

Self-doubt and Mistrust

45

Extreme Mistrustfulness

47

Identity Resilience and Mistrust   49
Practical Relevance of Modelling Identity, Mistrust and Emotion   53
Influences on Behaviour: An Example
Navigational Aids   53

5 Images of the Mistrusted_____**55**
Prototypes, Stereotypes and Caricatures   55
Ranking Untrustworthiness   59
The Mistrusted in Popular Culture   62
Images and Social Representations   64
Images of People, not Institutions   64
Methodological Limitations   67

6 Leadership and Mistrust_____**71**
The One Thing that Changes Everything   72
Types of Leadership   72
Leadership Style, Trust and Efficacy   75
What do You do to be Less Mistrusted?   77
Leader Personality and Mistrust   79
Gender, Leadership and Mistrust   84
Life Cycles of Mistrust in Leaders   86
Identity Processes, Social Representations and Leader Mistrust   90

7 Communication Channels for Inciting Mistrust_____**93**
Gossip   94
Rumour   100
Social Media   104

8 Weaponising Mistrust: Disinformation and Propaganda_____**115**
The Concepts of Disinformation and Propaganda   115
Propaganda Techniques and Processes of Persuasion   118
The Disinformation Crisis   124
The Disinformation Spreader   128
Defending against Disinformation   131
Is Mistrust Weaponised?   132

9 Conspiracy Theories_____**135**
What is a Conspiracy Theory?   135
Characteristics of Conspiracy Theories   138
Conspiracy Theories are Social Representations   139
Resistant to Refutation   141
Why Believe in Conspiracy Theories?   143

Identity, Emotions and Conspiracy Beliefs   147
Channelling Mistrust   149
Roots of COVID-19 Conspiracies   151
COVID-19 Conspiracies   152
Mistrust: The Allure of Conspiracy Theories   156

10 Modelling Mistrust Processes   **157**
Mistrust is Normal   157
A Model of Mistrust Processes for the Individual in Social Context   158
Limitations and Elaborations of the Model   166
Things to Remember and to Question   169

References   173
Index   195

ABOUT THE AUTHOR

Glynis M. Breakwell is a psychologist whose research focuses upon the psychology of risk perception, communication and management; leadership; and identity processes. Her work has included studies of policy responses to BSE, HIV/AIDS, pandemic respiratory diseases and bio-terrorism.

She received her PhD and LLD (Hon) from the University of Bristol and her DSc from the University of Oxford. She is a Fellow of the Academy of Social Sciences, an Honorary Fellow of the British Psychological Society and Principal Fellow of the Higher Education Academy.

In 2014, the UK Science Council named her as one of the 100 leading practising scientists in the UK. She was made Dame Commander of the Order of the British Empire in 2012 for her contributions to higher education.

From 2001 to 2018, Glynis was President and Vice Chancellor of the University of Bath and is an Emeritus Professor there. She holds Visiting Professorships at Imperial College, the University of Surrey and at Nottingham Trent University.

PREFACE

Many influences shape mistrust. This book explores some social psychological processes that explain how mistrust develops, and the effects that it has upon those who are mistrustful and those who are mistrusted. This requires an examination of some key issues: the distinction between trust, distrust and mistrust; the bases of risk estimation in cognitive biases and heuristics; the impact of societal shared uncertainties; the effects of identity motives and emotion; the role of social representation processes in erecting the images of the mistrusted; the importance of mistrust for leaders and organisations; the ways gossip, rumour and social media operate to create and channel mistrust; the use of disinformation and propaganda to weaponise mistrust; and the intimate relationship between mistrust and conspiracy theories. Each of these issues is discussed as a precursor to presenting a model of mistrust processes experienced by the individual in social context. The model encompasses the cognitive and affective processes occurring in individuals that are either mistrusted or mistrustful. It includes the routes through which the social context influences the mistrust responses of individuals, directly and through identity resilience. The prime routes are through the societal representations of risk and uncertainty when associated with danger. The theoretical framework throughout the book relies upon Identity Process Theory (IPT) and Social Representations Theory (SRT).

CHAPTER 1
THE NATURE OF MISTRUST

The Importance of Mistrust

This book describes a social psychological analysis of the dynamic processes that generate and maintain mistrust. It also considers whether understanding these processes can be used to mitigate some of the adverse effects of mistrust. Writing in a time of a global pandemic, the nature of mistrust has become of vital importance. The role of mistrust in dictating thought, feelings and behaviour in response to health hazards should never be ignored. Mistrust is fundamentally about feeling doubt, suspicion or scepticism about someone or something. It is thus closely associated with uncertainty and with risk. Mistrust involves not being sure whether to trust or distrust. Knowing who or what can be trusted when trying to protect yourself and your family from a fatal disease becomes an existential issue. Mistrust will affect choices that change the course of new diseases, as it has done with others in the past. The reasons for, and targeting of, mistrust need to be understood now more than ever.

Yet mistrust is hardly a new phenomenon. Mistrust has always been a source of intergroup conflict and a foundation for international relations and negotiations. Mistrust has hampered acceptance of the evolution and discoveries of science and medicine. Mistrust has characterised public responses to politics and politicians. Mistrust has been common in business and, of course, in interpersonal relationships. Mistrusting oneself is an experience catalogued throughout history.

Now, mistrust has emerged explicitly in the 21st century as a major societal concern, associated with questioning the motives and competences of established institutions. Governments, media, banks, academia, health professionals, and, inevitably, big business and the very wealthy, as well as leaders in general, all fall under the shadow of mistrust. In many societies traditional family and friendship networks are breaking down, and interpersonal and intergenerational mistrust is increasing. Mistrust matters because it has implications for the wellbeing and behaviour of individuals, communities and whole nations. Mistrust has consequences for the people who feel it and for the people or organisations that are mistrusted. In recent times, mistrust has been used as a rather nebulous explanation for changes in broad-ranging social processes (reflected in protest movements, enhanced violence, and political disengagement) and for shifts in the cognitive or emotional condition of individuals.

Mistrust is rife, it could be said to be unlimited. It is something that we all live with, all of the time. We typically can learn to navigate a route through it – charting a course through our mistrust of others and their mistrust of us, and, indeed, of our mistrust of ourselves. However, the route can be circuitous and difficult. It is easy to lose the way.

Mistrust is a powerful force because, once present, it shapes how we interpret information, the emotions we feel, and the actions we are willing to take. It is not only being mistrustful that has an impact, being mistrusted also has its consequences. This broad spectrum of effects will be explored later in this book. At this point, it is worth acknowledging that mistrust can have positive as well as negative effects. The capacity to mistrust is a platform for self-defence. Active suspicion of some person or thing can lead to the avoidance of danger or reduction of risk. Equally, avoiding premature decisions concerning trustworthiness can reduce the likelihood of missed opportunities. Either way, the capacity for mistrust could be said to offer an evolutionary edge – as long as not taken to extremes. Examination of the costs and benefits of mistrust is a common thread throughout this book.

Given that mistrust is rife and that it has adaptive advantages, it is unlikely to be eradicated soon. Nevertheless, because it is such a powerful force, it is a prime target for manipulation. Influencing or re-directing, if not controlling, mistrust has been a prime goal in most types of conflict in recorded history. This includes conflicts between nations, ideologies and religions, as well as those between individuals or between social groupings. The strategies and techniques used to arouse, channel and deflect mistrust have been increasingly objects for social psychological analysis in recent years. Models of the genesis of conspiracy theories and the promulgation of disinformation and propaganda have been developed. Analyses of how 'fake news' is produced and what impact it has are available. Antidotes, like fact-checking, with their variable efficacy have also been studied. At the heart of all these phenomena is the manipulation of mistrust. Findings from some of the studies of them are considered in later chapters.

The main message of this book is that we ignore mistrust at our peril – no matter who we are – and there are some useful things we can learn about how mistrust processes work. Thinking about the dynamics of mistrust can be an analytical frame of reference; a way of orienting yourself when interpreting your experience and coming to decisions. Some people will want to use the insights from this book to try to reduce mistrust or to minimise its negative consequences. Others may be seeking knowledge to ignite and fan the flames of mistrust. Manipulating mistrust is an important tool – for good or ill. It would be wrong to shun the possibility of deliberately using what we know about the dynamics of mistrust sometimes to arouse mistrust. The debate that must be examined in this book is centred on the pragmatic, moral and ethical justifications that might be mounted for acting to promote or enhance mistrust. And, if you can justify to yourself arousing mistrust, how you go about doing it most efficiently.

Trust, Distrust and Mistrust

The thorny task of differentiating between definitions of trust, distrust and mistrust cannot be avoided here. Trust is a topic that has been examined from every social science perspective and from levels of analysis at the systemic (Sztompka, 1999) through to the neurophysiological (Kosfeld et al., 2005). While sociologists focus on the position and role of trust in social systems (e.g. Giddens, 1984) and psychologists have been concerned with the development of the capacity to trust with its implications for personality and wellbeing, social psychologists have examined the role of trust in social influence, group membership and identity processes (Tanis & Postmes, 2005). The concept of trust, as a form of social capital and factor in decision making, is also central to many models in economics. With the advent of the 'post-truth' world (McIntyre, 2018) the significance of trust may have changed. There is a shift to encompass a situation where 'objective facts' or 'evidence' are less influential in shaping individual or public opinion than appeals to emotion and personal belief. Of course, it can be argued that 'truth' has always (and long before the label 'post truth' was coined) been viewed through the lens of emotions and beliefs. Nevertheless, in a time even less concerned than previously with verified or verifiable facts, trust, or its absence, becomes even more important because it can act as a filter that limits the effect of appeals to emotion and belief. It can also bolster the impact of those appeals, heightening their emotional resonances and their belief relevance.

So how is trust defined? The word itself actually has rather more definitions than can possibly be good for it. They range from the legal (a trust is an arrangement whereby a person – a trustee – holds property as its nominal owner for the good of one or more beneficiaries), to the archaic (where to trust is to give financial credit to someone or to express a hope or expectation). Commonly, it is used to refer to holding a firm belief in the reliability, honesty, strength or ability of someone or something. According to the compilers of the Oxford English Dictionary the word *trust* was more used in publications in 2020 than it had been any period since 1850. The definition of *distrust* is more unidimensional: the feeling that someone or something cannot be relied upon to be truthful or to behave as they are supposed to. The use of distrust is at its lowest level now since 1850. In contrast, *mistrust* (like trust) has been used more recently than at any time since 1850. The definition of mistrust focuses upon being suspicious of someone or something, upon being doubtful, wary or full of misgivings. Mistrust, in this sense, is about being actively suspicious about whether to trust a person or thing but without having actually decided. This definition of mistrust is used in this book. Mistrust is a state of active uncertainty that may be fleeting or prolonged. Mistrust is not just about cognitions, it is also often embedded in emotional responses (i.e. fear, anger, love). Mistrust is of particular interest when considering how people respond to hazards where the estimates of risk are themselves uncertain. This is examined in Chapter 2.

The difference between distrust and mistrust is subtle. Sometimes they are used in common parlance as if they were synonymous or interchangeable. However, they are not. The subtle difference in definition matters. Distrust is used more frequently in the context where the basis for removing or refusing trust has been established or decided. Mistrust is used when there is still uncertainty about whether trust is justified: the suspicion is there but the decision has not yet been made. The concept of mistrust captures this essential ingredient: uncertainty.

If trust is defined as a firm belief in the reliability, honesty, strength or ability of someone or something and mistrust is defined as uncertainty about those features of the person or thing, then it is interesting how trust comes about and, more particularly, what happens when uncertainty is aroused. From a social psychological perspective, trusting someone or something can be viewed as a process of evaluation. This process is not necessarily based on facts, reason or logic. It may also be based on habits, beliefs or emotions and upon the broader purposes or needs of the evaluator. This process is embedded in and influenced by its social context. What constitutes being worthy of trust is socially negotiated and varies across cultures and over time. Societal institutions (professions, religions, political parties etc.), besides deciding who and what they will trust themselves, have a pivotal role in erecting the framework used for trust evaluation by others. The individual evaluates trust in terms determined by norms and expectations established by her or his group memberships, history and future objectives.

At its most basic, the trusting process might be argued to involve three logically possible outcomes: trust, distrust or mistrust. In reality, the process is not so simple. Judging trustworthiness involves ongoing cognitive and emotional activity that may entail in quick succession (and in any order) mistrust, distrust and trust but will not necessarily produce a single stable outcome. The stream of incoming information will shift the needle back and forth on the trust barometer. Illustrations from what happens in friendships and romance are common. A partner is totally trusted, then some incident occurs (e.g. discovering s/he is meeting someone secretly) and suspicions begin, mistrust emerges, and then the suspicions are independently corroborated, resulting in confirmed distrust. This direction of movement from trust to distrust is rather more common and easier to envisage than the reverse. However, it does happen. Consider how evaluations of politicians can change. A candidate during a political election campaign promises to improve national health services, but her past performance indicates that this promise will not be kept. Distrust would be a common response. However, in the run up to the election, she explains her plans in detail and significant health practitioners argue that the strategy could work. The assumption that she must be distrusted may be displaced by doubt and suspicions. Mistrust of her replaces distrust. Within months of her election, she introduces legislation and budgetary allocations that can deliver her planned reforms. She has lived up to her promises. Mistrust gives way to, at least, temporary, probationary trust. This illustration immediately suggests that the move from distrust to trust may be more likely to be conditional.

Both trust and distrust may be temporary resting places in the trusting process. Mistrust is less a resting place and more a state of unrest, characterised by suspicion, doubt and ambivalence, and, sometimes, anxiety or fear. It is typified by being uncertain about what to believe. However, mistrust is more than just a matter of uncertain belief, it is typically linked to an emotional state. The emotion can be anxiety, or fear, or anger, or hatred. This is not an exhaustive list of affect that accompanies mistrust, what they have in common is that they are all what would be called 'negative' emotions in most societies. The subjective uncertainty that mistrust involves and its emotional concomitants would in many contexts (though not all, as we see later in this chapter) result in it being regarded as undesirable. Of course, just because it has its downsides does not mean that it has no advantages. Mistrust can be a strong pillar in self-protection, and we will come back to that later.

Mistrust can be a situationally specific response to a particular piece of information or person, like in the case of the person who suspects a partner of having an affair because evidence is discovered. But it can also be a chronic state. The individual may be habitually suspicious, doubtful, ambivalent, lacking in conviction, anxious and sceptical. At this level, mistrust is a cognitive and emotional trait of the person, having stability over time. Erikson (1963), in his theory of psychosocial development, argued that experiencing mistrust very early (birth to 12–18 months) in life shapes the subsequent personality. Mistrust can also be a preferred and regularly deployed coping strategy for dealing with threats to identity, acting as the basis for effective denial of evidence that would otherwise be damaging to self-efficacy, self-esteem, continuity or distinctiveness (Breakwell, 2015a). It is interesting that viewed, in this light, mistrust may be less involved in precipitating a search for the resolution of uncertainty and more about allowing uncertainty to remain because it acts as a defence against what might be understood or known should doubt be eliminated. These issues are addressed further later.

Mistrust is not just an individual state, trait or coping strategy. Just as some societies are said to be based on the presumption of trust, others are depicted as based on mistrust. Ethnographers have described societies dominated by cultures of mistrust. In early studies, Banfield (1958) characterised them as 'backward' plagued by solitude, anomie and pitiless mutual predation. More recently, Carey (2017) studying contemporary European communities (e.g. the Ukraine) where mistrust is considered to be widespread has argued that it does not need to be corrosive and can have utility. Simmel (1950: 318–19) describes trust as 'a hypothesis regarding future behaviour, a hypothesis certain enough to serve as a basis for practical conduct'. Carey suggests the same is true of mistrust – 'it is an alternative hypothesis and one that gives rise to social forms of its own' influencing practices of communication, co-operation and politics (p. 3). Cultures adapted to pervasive mistrust will deal with novel uncertainty differently to those founded on assumptions of trust. Obviously, this begs the question: if we now live in an age of societal uncertainty (as Galbraith, 1977, claimed), are we already a culture of pervasive mistrust? We will return to this question.

Why Mistrust?

There are two sorts of answer to the question: why mistrust? The first describes the circumstances when mistrust appears. The second describes the purposes mistrust serves.

The circumstances capable of sowing or germinating the seeds of mistrust are myriad. Most cluster into three identifiable types:

- unfulfilled expectations
- being warned
- history repeats

The cluster involving *unfulfilled expectations* is possibly the most common. When people or things fail to behave in the way you expect, mistrust can grow. It is most likely if you consider the breach of expectations to be a bad thing – either by failing to do something or by doing something. Nice things that challenge expectations tend to be less fertile ground for mistrust – though not always. Even things that are intrinsically nice that are unexpected may raise suspicion (such as the gift given without apparent rationale). Why are our expectations about the behaviour, thoughts and feelings of others so important? They are important primarily because they are fundamental to our capacity to predict and anticipate the future. They are part of how we plan what we should do. When our expectations are met we are more likely to feel secure and in control – even when we are expecting bad things. Correctly anticipating the bad thing may allow us to deal with it more effectively when it arrives. Even when anticipation does not allow us to handle the bad thing better, we can still feel good about having been right! People or things that undermine our confidence in this ability to predict because they do not fulfil expectations are natural candidates for mistrust.

The cluster involving *being warned* is wide-ranging. Being told that we should mistrust someone or something is pretty much a daily occurrence. We can be told we should mistrust a specific individual or particular thing. We can be told that we should mistrust a whole category of people or objects. We can even be told that we should just mistrust everyone and everything. These warnings may be influential in some respect or they may fall on deaf ears. That depends on many factors. For instance, it depends who gives the warning; how, when and where they give it; and, especially, on the individual they give it to. Mistrust instigated in this way is particularly interesting. It is not a direct product of someone's personal observations and evaluations of events. The evidence, at least initially, is second-hand, a social product. Complex social psychological processes direct mistrust that has been stimulated in this way. Some of these are described later in this chapter – they concern identity processes and social representations.

The cluster involving *history repeats* revolves around generalisation and habit. People use many shortcuts when interpreting information. They generalise from one experience to another, allowing themselves to come to conclusions about what is happening faster. They use what they know has happened in the past to interpret the present. If novel experiences echo a previous pattern, generalisation offers a pre-packaged interpretation of their meaning. Mistrust in a new person or thing can be triggered when generalisation processes tie them to an earlier experience of mistrust. For generalisation to happen there needs to be some perceived – not necessarily objective – similarity between the earlier and the new experiences. Habit will also play a part in history repeating itself. Individuals may repeatedly place themselves in the same type of situation – it is their habit. They do this for all sorts of reasons that we will not examine here but come back to them later. The point is that some people habitually find themselves in situations where they feel mistrust – either that they are mistrusted by others or that they mistrust others. Mistrust itself becomes a habit – something that is practised regularly and hard to give up.

These clusters of circumstance will be revisited later, particularly in considering the effects of rumour, gossip, disinformation and conspiracy theories, and then some of the social psychological theories that explain what happens are presented. In examining the explanations for what is underlying the emergence of mistrust when these circumstances occur, answers to the second meaning of the question 'why mistrust?' will become evident as we start to address what mistrust achieves and what purposes it serves. But first, as mistrust is a dynamic psychological process, to understand how it works it will be important to understand it within appropriate theoretical frameworks.

Identity Processes and Social Representations

While numerous hypotheses about the manifestations of mistrust will be described later, throughout this book two main social psychological theoretical frameworks are used to show how mistrust processes in general can be understood. These are Identity Process Theory (IPT) (Breakwell, 1983, 1992, 1996, 2014a; 2015a; Jaspal & Breakwell, 2014) and Social Representations Theory (SRT) (Breakwell, 2001a, 2011, 2015b; Breakwell & Canter, 1993; Moscovici, 1988; 2001; Jodelet, 2008; Sammut et al.,

2015). These two theories are chosen in preference to others for a number of reasons. Neither are micro-models built specifically to explain mistrust. They are broad theories used to explain a wide range of psychological and societal phenomena. Used in conjunction, they provide a comprehensive interpretation of the intra-psychic, interpersonal and societal dynamics of mistrust. Both these theories are primarily concerned with how people adapt to change and uncertainty. Such adaptation is a core feature of mistrust. Since IPT and SRT are used throughout the book, they are each described here in outline and, where needed, greater detail is presented later.

Moscovici (1988), in SRT, described how people give meaning to novel social realities, things and situations that they have not seen before and are unexpected. Moscovici showed how 'anchoring' and 'objectification' processes come into play when a community is facing something new. These processes involve social communication and negotiation that give meaning to what is new (Abric, 1996) and often what is newly understood to have been present but previously unknown (Marková, 2012). Both processes contextualise the novel and by doing so make it part of an intelligible set of meanings: anchoring ascribes meaning to a new phenomenon by linking it to pre-extant understandings or explanations; objectification gives it substance by associating it with material examples, translating innovative ideas in terms of palpable things. New or changed phenomena thus become manageable by being reconceptualised, normalised or identified within the pre-existing system of societal understandings – often by reference to existing social representations of comparable phenomena. For instance, cybercrime, which came to public attention as online activities grew, is now recognised as a major societal risk, yet it is an amorphous concept that spans an enormous range of activities. Making the phenomenon meaningful to a public unversed in the technicalities of digital systems has required the development of a dynamic social representation of many aspects of what it can involve, such as hacking, identity theft or scamming. This has shown how the new virtual reality frauds and the gangs that employ them are similar to old-fashioned cons and thieves. Cybercrime has been anchored and objectified by linking it to past incarnations based in earlier technologies. This social representation has to be dynamic because the nature of cybercrime changes. As it changes, the anchors and objects used will also change, building always upon the foundations laid in earlier iterations of the representation.

IPT (Breakwell, 1986; 2015a; Jaspal and Breakwell, 2014) is concerned with how people construct a unique identity for themselves. Such an identity will have many components (or facets). Components will include self-images derived potentially from any type of psychological, social or physical experience. IPT proposes that identity is not static but is dynamic – a work continually in progress. IPT argues that individuals are motivated to develop and maintain (through active processes of assimilation and accommodation) configurations and evaluations of the components of their identity that will satisfy or achieve four primary principles or goals: self-esteem, self-efficacy, distinctiveness and continuity. They may use many sorts of coping strategies at the intra-psychic, interpersonal and intergroup levels whenever these principles that guide identity construction are threatened or somehow undermined (Breakwell, 1988). The range of coping strategies deployed will differ according to social context and constraints. Identity-threat coping strategies also often involve social engagement and shared action with others. Threat to identity continuity elicited by political changes have been shown to stimulate involvement in new groups and in social protest. Breakwell (1996) showed this in relation to activism associated with the expansion of the European Union (EU) to include new member states, where for some individuals' identity continuity was challenged by perceived loss of national sovereignty. It is notable that this sense of identity continuity loss can linger long after the event that initiates it and can result in continuing efforts to reverse the consequences of that event. The exit of the UK from the EU in 2020 springs to mind, even though many other reasons beside identity processes explain that.

The two theoretical frameworks link together since social representations have a fundamental role to play in creating and sustaining identities. They provide the raw material from which many identity elements are crafted. They provide the medium through which identity is expressed. They provide avenues for influence that allow coping strategies to be conceived and deployed. They translate the physical reality into the social reality in which all identities reside. While their role in identity construction is fundamental, it is not determinist. The individual is agentic, engaging with social representations and social representational processes actively and purposively.

IPT has been elaborated to explore how identity processes influence the individual's engagement with social representations (Breakwell, 1993; 2001a & b; 2010; 2011). SRT states that objectification and anchoring are not individual processes. They are processes that normally involve social interaction and the establishment of shared meaning and consensus through communication among people. However, this does not mean that everyone coming into contact with a social representation will retain an absolutely identical version of it. Breakwell (2001a) distinguished between 'personal representations' and social representations. To the extent that a social representation is present in an individual's cognitions, emotions or behaviour, it has a parallel existence as a personal representation. This is not to suggest that the personal representation is a complete reproduction of the social representation. Quite the opposite, it will be partial and selective. The facets of the social representation that appear in the personal representation will be predictable based on the requirements of identity processes. The individual will prefer to adopt aspects of the social representation that fit the requirements of the identity principles. For instance, an individual will be unlikely to accept all aspects of a social representation of immigrants if it threatens their self-esteem or their positive distinctiveness. Timotijevic & Breakwell (2000) found that migrants to the UK from former Yugoslavia following the outbreak there of civil war encountered a social representation of refugees from such major conflicts that caused them great distress. The social representation not only included a stereotype of them that undermined their self-esteem and self-efficacy, it also gave them a heightened sense of negative distinctiveness. They did not accept the attributions that the social representation made about themselves but, equally, they recognised it as a thing that shaped their social experiences. The study highlighted how social representations do not have to be accepted to be powerful influences upon identity.

Individuals do have scope for selectivity in their adoption of social representations. The range of extant social representations is complex and dynamic. Moscovici (1981), in moving away from the Durkheim's notion of collective representation, emphasised the multiplicity of social representations that exist in modern societies and their capacity for change. No individual has access to all of the existing social representations and only a few might have access to a single social representation in its entirety. Individuals will have different roles in the social process of construction, elaboration and sharing of the representation. They differ in their exposure to and awareness of the representation; their understanding of it; their acceptance of it; their assimilation of it into pre-existent systems of personal representation; and the salience they attribute to it at any one time and over time. In part, these differences across individuals are a function of the requirements of the identity processes outlined above.

In addition, engagement with a social representation will depend upon what type of representation it is. Moscovici (1988) identified three types: hegemonic, emancipated and polemical. The three types of social representation offer differing freedoms for the individual to construct a personal representation. The hegemonic representation supposes little individual variation. The emancipated representation supposes individual variation based upon differential exposure within group contexts. The polemical representation supposes individual variation based upon participation in prevailing intergroup conflict.

The scope for personalising representations emerges when emancipated or polemical representations prevail about an object. Indeed, this is one of the necessary conditions for innovation and change. This assertion is not meant to trivialise or ignore the real differentials between individuals in their power to maintain or to proselytize their personal representations. This perspective emphasises that personal representations will be perpetually under pressure to change from the social representations that surround them. Individuals that are personally powerful (through position, expertise or some other route) are more likely to be able to retain their own personal representations and to be able to influence the development of social representations.

Any examination of the freedoms available to the individual in deriving a personal representation begins to highlight the need to understand the role of the individual in constructing a social representation. Since a social representation is defined as a set of understandings shared by a number of people then, to the extent that any individuals in the relevant communities demure from the shared understanding, the status of the social representation changes. It may be that the social representation itself changes in content. It may be that it simply changes its adherents (moving from one set of people to another). It may be that it changes its significance – becoming less used and less prominent. The important thing here is that the processes encircling the creation of personal representations also flow back to influence the construction and perpetuation of social representations. The intimacy of their relationship cannot be overestimated.

Furthermore, some social representations seem to have a greater tendency to attract and retain adherents (what Breakwell, 2014c, calls 'stickiness'). This can depend upon who promulgates the social representation (e.g., if it is emanating from a community that is mistrusted, it may have low stickiness). It can be associated with how the social representation is transmitted (some transmission routes are more mistrusted than others). It can be tied to how far the social representation has already achieved saturation in the particular social environment – for example in terms of the number of people accepting it, the length of time it has been active, the number of channels through which it is communicated, or how many times it has been presented. Additionally, stickiness could be associated with the extent to which the social representation is capable of triggering, or is aligned with, emotional arousal.

The stickiness of a social representation probably matters when it comes to the way identity processes interact with it. The interaction with a sticky social representation might still be purposive in terms of identity construction but may result in any resistance or reactance to it being lower or less effective. The penetration of the social representation into personal representation and then into identity structure would seem likely to be greater if the stickiness is greater. It may also be linked to its permanency or intransience in the identity structure. IPT proposes that individual responses to social representations are linked to the ways in which the representation may threaten or support the operation of the identity principles. It is notable that coping strategies that manage identity reconstruction frequently entail the manipulation of personal representations and their relationship with social representations. In later chapters, we see how important this is for manipulating mistrust.

The analysis of the dynamics of mistrust permits us to examine further how identity processes and social representation processes interact. In the context of mistrust, it is particularly important to explore the role of emotion in their relationship. Affect is often an integral part of a social representation. For instance, in social representations of hazards, fear and anxiety are often an integral part of the narrative attached to the risk. Affect also has a role to play in the social communication process that produces the social representation. Emotions influence the willingness of people to participate in developing and communicating the representation. Heightened arousal – whether through fear or joy – may encourage engagement with the social representational process. There is evidence that social representations are more likely to be reproduced and communicated) when they arouse fear (e.g., the social amplification of risk model illustrates this – Pidgeon, Kasperson & Slovic, 2003).

The emotional content of a social representation is also important in determining how it is integrated into personal representations and, thereafter, how it impacts upon identity at the individual level.

IPT and SRT can contribute a lot when they work together. SRT assumes that social representations have an impact on individuals and assumes individual actors have a role to play in evolving, promulgating and reproducing the representation. IPT assumes not only that social representations frame the realm of the possible identity content and evaluation, but also that the identity principles will determine at least in part the nature of the individual interaction with the social representation. Social representations provide the interpretative framework for identity construction and maintenance. Identity processes navigate the individual through the engagement with social representations. The two theories will be used in conjunction in later chapters to analyse mistrust.

However, it is important to use other cognitive and social psychological models when trying to understand mistrust. For instance, there is a significant body of evidence about the way people react when faced with uncertainty and the possibility of harm that has been collected from research on perceptions and decision making about risk. Chapter 2 focuses upon this work.

CHAPTER 2
RISK AND MISTRUST

Risk and mistrust are intimately interlinked. Mistrust emerges most often when people feel that there is the possibility that they will suffer some harm. That is to say, it becomes manifest most clearly when people feel at risk. Of course, the perceived risk may actually initiate mistrust because it can present the evidence or clues that trigger suspicion or the fear of betrayal. Furthermore, feelings of mistrust may exist before a particular risk is perceived but it becomes a more important influence on thoughts, feelings and action once that risk is evident. For instance, a person may mistrust the effectiveness of vaccines. That mistrust is likely to have profound effects on decision making and behaviour if the person is faced with the risk of contracting a disease that might be mitigated by a vaccine. Mistrust becomes the filter through which the potential for harm is interpreted because it affects what or who is considered a reliable source of information about the hazard. Frequently, it also suggests who might be likely to be responsible for the harm. Trying to analyse mistrust without considering the cognitive and social psychological processes that underlie risk perceptions and reactions would be a mistake. Risk perception and reactions are important influences upon the genesis and effects of mistrust, just as they are influenced by mistrust.

What is Risk?

Risk refers to the possibility that harm will occur. Two dimensions of the construct 'risk' are distinguishable: probability and effect. Risk refers to the *likelihood* of occurrence of some specific event or combination of events (the 'hazard') that could lead to harm. Risk also refers to the degree of harm the hazard might cause – its *effect*. The probability and effect of the hazard can vary independently. Estimates of probability and effect will differ in the levels of certainty attributed to them. The levels of uncertainty associated with these estimates can also vary independently of each other. So, when thinking about the risk of a hazard it is always important to remember both perceived likelihood and perceived effect.

Social science debate has frequently centred on whether risk can ever be objectively assessed or whether it is inevitably a social construction (Burgess, 2015). It has led to some stunningly good social analysis of risk assessment and cultures of uncertainty (Wynne, 1982, 2001; Wynne & Dressel, 2001). As a result, it may be reasonable to say that whether or not a risk can be objectively assessed in some hypothetical social vacuum is not actually the main question. What matters is how the features of the hazard and the information about it are interpreted and given social meaning. Not only the character and significance of the hazard's effects are constructed through the social representation processes described in Chapter 1. Even the reality of the hazard and the likelihood that it will indeed cause harm are subject to these same processes. Social representation processes will influence the level of uncertainty attached to any estimate of probability or effect. In some cases, they will militate for certainty – for instance, on some occasions where strong hegemonic representations are in play. In other cases, where conflicting polemical representations, emanating from different sources are involved, uncertainty may be heightened.

Levels of uncertainty in the estimates of probability and effect of a hazard are one determiner of reactions to it. However, uncertainty can emerge in another guise. Faced with the possibility of harm, responses are at least partly shaped by the information available about its origin, form and the opportunities for its avoidance, mitigation or removal. The degree of certainty attributed to this information (either by its source or by its recipients) is crucial in predisposing responses, especially if certitude levels fluctuate over time (Gaspar et al., 2014). In fact, the behavioural, physiological, cognitive, emotional and motivational effects of information uncertainty on individuals can be significant. Uncertainty about the probability and effects of a hazard can induce anxiety, act as a stressor, and alter decision making and the use of information (de Berker et al., 2016). However, people vary in their reactions to uncertainty. Crucially, responses to risk and to uncertainty in risk estimates are determined by the way that individuals actively interpret risk information. Prior mistrust of the source of that information is fundamentally important. Indeed, mistrust may be the basis for personal uncertainty in the face of risk.

Making Decisions in Uncertainty: Representativeness, Availability and Anchoring

Individuals can differ in the way they perceive the same message about the same risk estimate, so they may respond differently to what is ostensibly the same level of uncertainty about a hazard. This means that, while social representational processes will set the frame for the appreciation of risk and may determine the information available, the individual is not a passive consumer or conduit of the risk message or its image of the risk.

Psychological research on the factors affecting individual responses to risk and uncertainty came to the fore in the 1970s (Fischhoff and Kadvany, 2011) and subsequently has clustered around modelling certain key issues. The first cluster of work describes information processing in conditions of uncertainty and showed judgements reveal consistent biases and that these can be partly predicted on the basis of the heuristics that people employ. While any one individual may regularly use a particular heuristic, the use of it across people may vary considerably.

Essentially, heuristics are systematic guesses or strategies that are based on experience and emotional responses. They guide information gathering and interpretation and can be used to accelerate decision making. Heuristics could be regarded as the basis of 'jumping to a conclusion'. They cut out the perceived need for rigorous search for and evaluation of data and this can be particularly useful where the data are patchy or unverified. Instead, they deploy preconceived assumptions about what the data should look like and might mean. Heuristics are akin to a cognitive 'rule of thumb'. They do not necessarily result in the right or most optimised decisions. They are reflected sometimes in recognisable biases in judgement.

Many heuristics that direct probability judgements if information is incomplete have been described. Notably Tversky and Kahneman (1974) and Kahneman et al. (1982) reported that a number of heuristic principles are often used when we assess the probability of an event or the probability that an object will possess certain characteristics. These heuristics concern representativeness, availability and anchoring.

Representativeness affects the perception of the probability that an object (A) belongs to a class of objects (B), people typically assume that the probability is greater if A resembles B in some fashion. It is helpful, when thinking about heuristics, to construct an example of how you use them yourself. So, for instance, if you had to estimate the probability that someone who has a cough (Object A) actually has COVID-19 (Class B) you may rely upon the extent to which the coughing resembles the sort of coughing characteristic of coronavirus sufferers. The fact that coughing can be associated with cancer or the side effects of medication may not enter your considerations because the representativeness of the symptom is a dominant focus for you.

Availability comes into play where asked to estimate the frequency of an event or the probability of an event; typically, people assume that the probability is greater if they can easily remember an instance of such an event. So, for instance, at the height of a coronavirus pandemic it may seem unremarkable that a cough might be thought a probable signal of COVID-19. If an event is associated with more remembered (retrieved) instances, its probability will be over-estimated. Retrieval from memory of relevant instances is itself a process riddled with biases and highly dependent upon motivations and emotion. For example, a man who has just lost his wife to COVID-19 could be more or could be less likely to see someone suffering a fit of coughing as probably a victim of the disease. Choice of memories to retrieve will depend very much on the needs of the individual. Not thinking about COVID-19 may be a prime need of the new widower. Knowing that availability will lead to higher probability ratings is valuable. Predicting what will be available and when availability will occur would be even more valuable. To get to that point needs a bit more work.

Anchoring (not to be confused with the use of the word in SRT) is a phenomenon that occurs where people are asked to estimate the value of some object (in principle it could be something or someone). On the basis of whatever information they originally have, they make a guess at the value. This initial guess is said to be the anchor. People will adjust their initial guess as they receive more information. However, the adjustments made tend to be too small – as if the initial anchor is constraining movement. Explanations for anchoring effects on adjustment of estimates are contested and not proven. There are individual differences in the anchoring effect. Experience or expertise reduces the likelihood of the effect but does not eradicate it (Wilson et al., 1996). Personality traits are thought to have an effect (Furnham, Boo & McClelland, 2012).

It is evident that these three heuristics that drive probability estimates will have significance for risk perception and decisions made about risk. They are also important in the manufacture and maintenance of mistrust. It is worth just delving a little into what these three heuristics mean for the process of evaluating the trustworthiness of an individual. Suppose he is called Max and you have just met him. How might the operation of these three heuristics result in you mistrusting him? Max says things that echo the slogans of a particular protest group. The representativeness heuristic suggests that Max is probably a member of the group. You have many vivid and easily retrieved recollections of the actions of this protest group but especially of one occasion when they blatantly lied about their reasons for taking action. The availability heuristic leads you to expect that the group will lie again. Your initial evaluation of the group is that you should be suspicious of the honesty and reliability of it and its members. You mistrust it. Max, as a putative member or ally of the group therefore is also suspect and merits mistrust. You have made an evaluation. It may be based on slender evidence about Max but it is now what you think. Max is pinned to your personal frame of reference. Anchoring processes will mean that shifting your assessment of Max is likely to occur only in small adjustments – if at all. The illustration, evidently contrived, is designed only to suggest that thinking about the way the three heuristics interact to shape mistrust estimates is worthwhile. But it is also important always to remember that individuals differ in the degree to which they use these heuristics.

Weighing Up Prospects and Subjective Values

Establishing how representativeness, availability and anchoring operated led Tversky and Kahneman (1981) to develop Prospect Theory. This explains the decision processes involved when people make comparisons between options. A seminal model in behavioural economics, it proposes that people do not make decisions in keeping with the predictions from Expected Utility Theory (which assumes people mirror rational agents in their choices). Indeed, Prospect Theory states that people base their decisions on the *potential* value of losses and gains which they assess using the three heuristics described above. In coming to their decision, they are likely to place greater weight upon their potential losses than on their potential gains. Essentially, individuals tend to exhibit loss aversion more than gain attraction.

However, people differ in how they show this asymmetry in the way they attach value to losses and gains. Each individual makes subjective judgements of value. These judgements are lodged in a personal frame of reference based on information available. The frame of reference when used in Prospect Theory refers to the introduction of a reference point that represents the position where the value of the potential gains and losses entailed in the outcome of a choice are equivalent (the neutral point). Below the reference point, outcomes are considered losses, and above it, they are considered gains. People differ in the reference points that they establish even when given the same information. They appear to use heuristics in different ways – even on the same data.

However, the way information is presented will influence where reference points are set. For instance, an option framed positively may shift its perceived value, effectively making it easier for it to reach the reference point and become accepted as a gain. A common example used to illustrate framing effects comes from the presentation of statistical data on medical interventions. Data could be presented in a positive frame: 35% of those treated with a particular drug will be saved. It could be presented in a negative frame: 65% of those treated will not be saved. The drug is more likely to be regarded as more valuable when presented in a positive frame. Framing effects have been shown to be empirically very robust across a wide range of decision-making contexts (Levin et al., 1998).

Kahneman and Tversky proposed that an outcome of a decision is associated with a subjective value (or utility) that is expressed as deviations (gains or losses) relative to the neutral reference point. They also argued that as the objective value of the gain associated with an outcome increases above the reference point, the rate of increase in the subjective gain decreases and flattens as the gain gets much larger. In contrast, as objective loss increases, the rate of increase in subjective loss is initially faster and continues longer before flattening. The subjective value function that passes through the reference point is S-shaped and asymmetrical. Apparently, losses create more pain subjectively than gains create subjective satisfaction.

It is a puzzle why this should be so. It could be as simple as loss continues to be more relatively disadvantageous as it gets greater, whereas gain gets relatively less advantageous as it gets bigger. This is actually unsatisfactory as a complete explanation since the relative advantage of gain as it gets bigger will depend upon where the reference point is set. If the reference point is very low in terms of the objective value, the shape of the subjective function might change – with increases in objective gain continuing to increase subjective gain to much higher levels.

Prospect Theory includes an additional premise. This is that people attribute unjustified weight to events with low probabilities and not enough weight to events with high probabilities. Events with low probabilities consequently can influence decisions unjustifiably. The interaction of overweighting small probabilities and the shape of the subjective value function was hypothesised to lead to predictable patterns in relation to risk attitudes. It leads to risk-seeking when losses have moderate probabilities or gains have small probabilities. It leads to risk-aversion when gains have moderate probabilities or losses have small probabilities. It is as if moderate probabilities, whether of gain or loss, are relatively discounted in coming to a decision or formulating an attitude. However, this may not be generally true, and this was recognised by Tversky and Kahneman.

Various critiques of Prospect Theory have resulted in its extension. Tversky and Kahneman (1992) produced Cumulative Prospect Theory. The two are similar except that Cumulative Prospect Theory recognises the importance of both the probability of an outcome and the significance of the effect it has. Prospect Theory said that people tend to overweight unlikely events when making decisions. Cumulative Prospect Theory says people tend to overweight *extreme*, but unlikely, events, and underweight events that are merely average. This modification is important since it predicts the greater significance in decision making of extreme events that occur with small probability, rather than all types of event with low probabilities. This makes intuitive sense and seems to fit the empirical evidence from risk research. The model is a powerful way of interpreting choice made under conditions of uncertainty.

Cumulative Prospect Theory and Mistrust

It comes as no surprise that Cumulative Prospect Theory can be used to analyse some of the aspects of mistrust. There are two arenas where the interface with mistrust occurs: in the genesis of mistrust, and in the impact of mistrust upon subjective value judgements. We already considered how the representativeness, availability and anchoring heuristics might come into play when deciding to mistrust someone (Max – the putative protest group member). A particular significance of the bias in importance attributed to extreme events with low probabilities emerges when considering why mistrust of someone or something may occur initially. Take as an illustration: you have known someone for several years, you have regarded her as reliable and honest and you have had no reason to doubt her, however one day, completely without warning, you learn that she has trashed/maligned you badly on social media. Will this single event, even if hurtful, outweigh the evidence of her friendliness over years? All things being equal, mistrust would creep into the relationship. The low probability but extreme event, in all likelihood, would lead you to re-evaluate her and you would become more suspicious and be on the lookout for more breaches of trust. This is, in part, because the extreme and low probability event makes you more risk-averse. However, not all things may be equal. She may explain her online outburst – it was a complete error, she was drunk, it will not possibly happen again, someone hacked her account and so on. It is important to acknowledge that the interpretation and valuation of an event in the real world is typically negotiated and subject to reconstruction.

Yet the fact that mistrust is initially aroused will have its own consequences for subjective value judgements. First, pre-existent mistrust may influence whether an event is considered to have a low probability. If you are suspicious of some people because they have let you down once, you may believe they are more likely to do so in the future. If they do then let you down, you would not regard this event as having had a low probability. Mistrust actually changes the probability estimate. Second, pre-existent mistrust may influence how serious or extreme an event is regarded to be. An event may have less impact if it merely confirms prior suspicions. The negative event may entail less subjective loss if mistrust makes it more predictable and less hurtful. Mistrust, in this way, can be a form of insurance against hurt. Third, more generalised, rather than specific, mistrust can have a role in creating the frame of reference within which any information is used when making decisions. Cultures or communities that are characterised by high levels of mistrust will differ in the salience that they give to empirical evidence, to past relationships, or to the possibility of gain or loss. General levels of uncertainty and associated mistrust can operate through the 'focusing effect' or 'focusing illusion'. Shared mistrust can result in people focusing excessively upon one aspect of an event or information set and disregarding others, causing errors in their estimates of future outcomes. This could be seen as mistrust channelling attention or filtering data. We will come back to the role of mistrust in creating frames of reference, particularly when dealing with risk. At that point, it will be useful to consider how far the channelling and filtering effects of personal or shared mistrust are deliberate and purposive.

Biases in Estimating Risk and Attributing Mistrust

Individuals differ in their use of heuristics when making decisions in conditions of uncertainty. Individuals also differ in the biases that they manifest when estimating risk. Not all biases are derived from heuristics. While a heuristic is a strategy for problem solving that offers a short cut to a judgement which is 'good enough', a bias is a systematic distortion that prejudices what judgement is made. Heuristics may cause bias, but biases do not typically provide useful heuristics.

There are rather a lot of biases that have been identified in one way or another and then labelled. Some labels are less empirically defensible than are others. Three biases that bear on mistrust are singled out here for description:

- optimistic bias
- hindsight bias
- self-serving bias

Optimistic Bias or Unrealistic Optimism

People believe that they are personally less likely to experience negative events and more likely to experience positive events than other people. In the context of threat, this is sometimes known as 'perceived invulnerability' or 'subjective immunity'. This bias has been found to occur in myriad contexts (from perceived risks of bungee jumping, contracting cancer, surviving hurricanes or being attacked by terrorists) (Trumbo et al., 2011; Caponecchia, 2012) and in most age and cultural groups (though not in all, i.e., the bias seems absent in Japanese). Recently, it has been implicated in refusal to comply voluntarily with self-protection measures against COVID-19 (Clark et al., 2020). It also appears in behaviour online (Miller, 2018) motivating greater risk-taking in virtual environments.

However, the way the bias manifests itself can be subtly graduated – the point at which the line is drawn between oneself and others is dependent on many factors. Shared perceived invulnerability does come into play. In this, I believe not only am I less likely to be harmed by other people similar to me, or associated with me, but also less likely to be harmed than others. The boundary for this subjective shield of perceived invulnerability is flexible.

Of course, the problem is that it is *unfounded* optimism, based on a false premise. It leads to poor risk assessments and to bad decisions. On occasion, an individual may be correct in estimating his or her own risk to be smaller than that of others. It is the fact that it is a majority effect – most members of a sample will say that they are less at risk than the average person – that makes it a noteworthy phenomenon. In reality, in purely statistical terms, a majority cannot be less at risk than the average because if they were, then the average itself would reduce. This is the paradox of the optimistic bias.

Weinstein (1989) proposed that optimistic bias has two types of source: motivational and cognitive. The motivational may involve seeking to enhance or maintain one's self-esteem – the exercise of comparing one's own risk levels with those of others is seen as an opportunity to achieve positive distinctiveness; to show one is better than others. Indeed, IPT would predict people are motivated to enhance self-esteem, self-efficacy, distinctiveness and continuity when called upon to compare their own level of risk with that of others. In motivational terms, the optimistic bias is also a form of defensive denial – a type of psychological avoidance strategy – perceiving yourself to be less at risk than others allows you to downgrade the significance of the threat you face. Research on coping strategies against threats to identity has shown how ubiquitous denial can be and how it acts as a mediator for other psychological responses to danger (Napier et al., 2020; Jaspal & Cinnirella, 2012).

The cognitive source of optimistic bias has three elements:

- *egocentrism* – inability to adopt the perspective of the other (and thus inability to understand that the same factors that affect others will affect oneself);
- *availability of information about the risk* – lack of information is associated with seeing oneself to be less at risk (though increasing knowledge does not necessarily eliminate optimism) but the origin of the information seems of paramount importance, that drawn from personal experience of any threat seems influential in reducing bias as does the vicarious observation of the experiences of friends and family;
- *stereotype salience* – comparing themselves against their stereotype of a high-risk individual and feeling at lower risk.

Riskiness of behaviours associated with one's own groups is usually underestimated and that associated with other groups is overestimated. Campbell and Stewart (1992) claimed this originates in the desire to achieve a positive social identity for one's group and oneself through the social comparison. Where the comparator group is already negatively stereotyped this tendency is magnified. Weinstein pointed out that, typically, when asked to compare oneself with some unspecified 'other', people conjure up a 'fuzzy stereotype' – not an image rich in detail – which is a loose amalgam of risky features. Of course, the use of a fuzzy stereotype can also serve motivational ends. Comparing oneself with a stereotypical 'other' who is riskier allows identity motives such as self-esteem and distinctiveness to be satisfied. In fact, individuals who conjure strong negative stereotypes for their comparators also perceive themselves as more in control of their relationship with the risk (Weinstein, 1980). This explanation fits with predictions from IPT concerning the importance of asserting self-efficacy.

Optimistic bias is a major concern because if people see themselves to be at less risk than others, they may not see the need to defend themselves. Fortunately, it does not always have that effect. If people are very worried about the risk (or fearful of the hazard), optimistic bias is unlikely to affect behaviour so much (if at all). Also, optimistic bias is not found for all hazards or for all people. For instance, even schoolchildren realise that they are just as likely to catch the flu or experience the bad effects of air pollution as other children of their age (Whalen et al., 1994).

Optimistic bias is not ubiquitous, but it does have its ecological niches. Generally, optimistic bias is more likely when the risk is thought to be in the control of the individual. For instance, Bernardes and Lima (2005) argued that optimistic bias was a product of believing oneself more capable or likely than others of taking measures to protect oneself against the risk. They found that when people were allowed to include the effects of self-protection measures within their risk estimates the optimistic bias was reduced. Optimistic bias seems to be enhanced when the risk is seen to be under personal control. In fact, Dolinski, Gromski and Zawisza (1987) found that the absence of control leads to unrealistic pessimism. Van der Velde, Hooykaas and van der Joop (1992) concluded that if their control is perceived to be insufficient to surmount obstacles to using preventive measures, then people become pessimistic rather than realistic or optimistic about their risk relative to that of other people.

Consistent with this, optimistic bias is less likely when the individual has already had personal experience of the hazard. People showed less optimistic bias with respect to earthquakes just after they had lived through one, even though they still displayed optimistic bias with respect to other hazards (Helweg-Larsen, 1999). People who had experienced salmonella food poisoning were less likely to show optimistic bias about contracting it again than those who had not had it (Parry et al., 2004). However, there is some evidence that this de-biasing effect of personal experience depends on just how injurious the experience was. Lower severity tends not to diminish optimistic bias. Moreover, the bias becomes less evident when people compare their own risk with that of others who they know. Familiarity with the comparator appears to make it more difficult to claim superior immunity. Some studies have also suggested that whether or not optimistic bias occurs is dependent on exactly what method is used to elicit or measure it. Optimistic bias is sensitive to contextual changes. As a result, it is difficult to predict how it might work over time in directing an individual's decisions about risk in very complex environments where many comparisons between the self and others can be made iteratively and are often based on rich information.

The idea of the optimistic bias has become part of pop psychology. It has penetrated public awareness and is now a label that tends to be used indiscriminately. In fact, it is a bias that occurs sometimes but not inevitably. Discovery of the optimistic bias, despite the complexity of its manifestations, has given rise to various attempts to find ways to reduce it. These include:

- Providing information designed to heighten understanding of the relevance of the risk factors to the self – this has not proven effective in most contexts.
- Challenging egocentrism by giving more information about the comparators – this has also not proven effective.
- Making the unpredictability and uncontrollability of the risk salient – this tends to reduce optimistic bias.

When it does occur, the bias seems to show a certain resilience to attempts to curb it – except where modification in expectations of risk control is involved. Perceived controllability does seem to be important. This resonates with the significance of self-efficacy that IPT proposes.

The optimistic bias can influence the mistrust process through several routes. Mostly, as long as it is operating, the optimistic bias serves to diminish mistrust because:

- it changes your interpretation of any available uncertain evidence. Faced with hints of dishonesty or glimpses of unpredictability, optimistic bias suggests that those hints are unlikely to be confirmed or correct. You would rather rationalise or dispute reports of the bad behaviour in order to maintain your own sense of invulnerability.

- it limits how far you are willing to generalise from other people's experiences concerning whether someone or something should be mistrusted. You feel immune even when you know others definitely have been affected.
- It leads you to feel that you are more able to control or predict the potential the person or thing has to do you harm.

Mistrust is not precipitated because an optimistic bias subdues doubt and suspicion – and thus limits concomitant aversive emotions. The optimistic bias makes the development of mistrust less likely. Since an assessment affected by optimistic bias, once established, is resilient to deflection by corrective information, it is possible that mistrust will not develop even when evidence accrues that it is justified. The exception might be where the unpredictability and uncontrollability of the candidate for mistrust is highlighted in a way that cannot be ignored or contested. The possibility of being the victim of betrayal – just like others – is then less easy to deny. It is not so simple to say 'it could never be me in that situation or treated that way' when the potential culprit has a proven and publicly acknowledged history of unpredictability and uncontrollability. Thinking about the potential culprit as a hazard whose risk has to be assessed is useful. It focuses upon the process of mistrust as a process of risk perception. The perception of the risk can be changed by eliminating or diminishing the bias.

There is a question about whether optimistic bias is normally beyond the individual's control, a process driven by complex needs and motivations. By training, it is possible to stop the bias being manifested in some situations – for example, in relation to estimates of probability of failure on particular tasks. Limiting the automaticity of the bias has benefits. People are less likely to take unjustified risks. This could be said to be an incontestable benefit of controlling the bias. The opposite could also be argued; taking unjustified risks comes to be justifiable when it leads to a gain rather than a loss. It may be that sometimes the optimistic bias that prevents or assuages mistrust leads to a gain rather than a loss. This is just to acknowledge that evading mistrust – even if only with the aid of an uncontrolled bias – might sometimes be useful.

Hindsight Bias

Hindsight bias (Fischhoff, 1975) is the label given to the tendency that people have to say 'I knew that all along' – foresight claimed after the event. Typically, people given information about an event after it occurs will say (and think) that they could have (or did) predict it. Fischhoff et al. (2005) examined the evolution of cognitive and emotional responses to terror risks for a nationally representative sample of Americans between late 2001 (post–9/11) and late 2002. Respondents displayed hindsight bias, changing their memories of their earlier risk judgements to fit the changing data available to them.

Interestingly, when people are not allowed to reconstruct their memories because the evidence of what they thought earlier is still before them, they will modify the significance of their previous predictions by re-estimating the degree of certainty that they attributed to the predictions (Bradfield and Wells, 2005). Therefore, they admit that their estimates were inaccurate but make it clear that they had never been very certain that the estimate was correct anyway.

There have been many hypotheses to account for hindsight bias. Dekker (2004) argued that hindsight bias creates a greater sense of control over the future by making us feel we predicted the past. Indeed, there is some association between the strength of the bias and the individual's level of field dependency or need for favourable self-presentation (e.g., Campbell & Tesser, 1983; Musch, 2003). Tykocinski, Pick and Kedmi (2002) suggested that hindsight bias is a part of retroactive pessimism that people introduce in self-defence to regulate disappointments – predictions of the undesirable outcome are in retrospect changed to make it appear more inevitable and, since it was inevitable, self-blame and disappointment are not deemed appropriate.

Cognitive explanations for hindsight bias include a proposal that it could be a product of memory encoding and retrieval processes (Villejoubert, 2005). It is suggested that, after an event, memory is probed in a detailed and selective way for evidence of what one thought about the event prospectively. The probe unearths support for the conclusion that one had expected the outcome all along. Effectively, the prior judgement is reconstructed as knowledge is updated and probabilities of particular outcomes are modified (Blank & Nestler, 2007).

Hindsight bias happens selectively. It occurs differentially for events that are attitude-consistent (Hölzl & Kirchler, 2005). Basically, in retrospect you are more likely to say that you predicted things that have happened if they are what you would have wished to happen. Hindsight bias seems stronger for more recent or more 'surprising' events. The tendency to claim to have predicted an outcome is reduced with the passage of time and, possibly, with the fading of the surprise. However, it could be that this is an artefact of the research designs used. Repeatedly asking people if they had predicted an event might encourage them to be more conservative in their estimates of their predictive powers after a while. Cultural differences in the expression of this bias have been reported, but the evidence for these differences is limited and inconclusive.

People still reveal hindsight bias even after they have been informed that it happens (Pohl & Hell, 1996). Reducing its occurrence is therefore no simple matter. One suggestion that has been made repeatedly is that hindsight bias can be reduced by making the cost of indulging in it greater for the individual (Arkes et al., 1988). It may not be evident initially why it is necessary to bother with controlling hindsight bias. One reason is that it is thought to be associated with overconfidence (Merkle, 2017) and this leads to poor risk decisions. Thinking you are good at predicting what happened in the past misleads you into thinking you can predict what will happen in the future (Bernstein et al., 2016). Hindsight bias can cloud judgements in any area of life, including legal decisions, medical diagnoses, consumer satisfaction, sporting events and election outcomes. Ironically, expertise has been found to exacerbate hindsight bias (Knoll & Arkes, 2017). Knowing you know presumably makes you think you must have known. Hindsight bias and its link to overconfidence seems particularly important when it comes to investment decisions: being persuaded that you could predict the past makes you expect to predict the future and this tends to precipitate sub-optimal risk-taking (Mittal, 2019). There is another reason for thinking the hindsight bias needs to be contained: it has been shown to impede learning (Mahdavi & Rahimian, 2017) essentially because people, misled by hindsight bias, come to regard themselves to be more expert than they actually are and resist instruction thus failing to assimilate new information.

The role of hindsight bias in the mistrust process depends on the extent to which mistrust has developed. If mistrust is mature, embodied in long-lived suspicion or doubt, the hindsight bias can work to confirm those beliefs. Some unpredicted, unpleasant event happens, the hindsight bias kicks in, and you think 'I knew that would happen, I suspected it might, I guessed it all along'. In quick succession comes the thought 'I was right to suspect'. Hindsight bias affirms your existing preconceptions. A mature system of mistrust beliefs about someone or something is very likely to be supported by hindsight bias because the bias is less likely to emerge if events occur that challenge the mistrust. Other biases are more likely to come to the fore – such as the self-serving bias described later.

When mistrust is nascent, fresh and incompletely formed, when it is merely the scintilla of a query about the purposes or actions of someone or something, hindsight bias effects are more unpredictable. At this stage, hindsight bias could derail the progress of mistrust. Some unpredicted, pleasant event occurs, hindsight bias kicks in and you think 'I knew that would happen, I suspected it might, I guessed it all along'. In quick succession comes the thought 'I was wrong to doubt'. Hindsight bias affirms the insecurity of the platform for your mistrust. If the platform for mistrust subsequently is reinforced in some other way, later instances of hindsight bias will be less likely to be interpreted as justifying any diminution of mistrust.

Self-serving Bias

This is not specific to interpreting risk. This bias describes the tendency to attribute positive events and successes to our own abilities and actions, but blame negative outcomes on external factors (whether people or things). We do the opposite when making attributions about other people – when they do something wrong it is explained in terms of their personal characteristics, when they do something good it is said to be a result of circumstances. This is sometimes labelled a 'fundamental attribution error'.

The origins of the self-serving bias could be related to the optimism bias. However, explaining one bias with another is never good practice. IPT would suggest that the self-serving bias is one way of improving or preserving our self-esteem, illustrating our self-efficacy, promoting distinctiveness and preserving continuity of self-image. However, as a coping strategy, it has weaknesses because it relies on building a possibly false image of one's achievements and attributes. This image may be hard to maintain.

People seem to differ in the extent to which they are subject to the self-serving bias. These differences have been encapsulated in the notion of locus of control (Lefcourt, 2014). Some have a stable sense that they determine their own destiny, actively deciding what happens to them and what they do about it – this is considered an internal locus of control. Those who feel they are subject to influences and circumstances beyond themselves have an external locus of control. Obviously, these are the two extremes of what is a continuum of attributional orientation: explaining what you do and what happens to you in terms of personal or contextual factors. Locus of control has been suggested as one of the core elements of personality.

In relation to the genesis of mistrust, the self-serving bias may be a motive initiating the questioning of the credibility or reliability of someone or something. The bias requires someone else, or something else, to be attributed with the responsibility, and probably blame, for some bad thing that has happened. Raising a question about the role others play in that event, and removing oneself from the blame frame, may be best achieved by arousing mistrust of them. The misdirection of mistrust in order to achieve personal advantage is quite common. Some of the techniques for doing this, such as rumourmongering, spreading gossip and disinformation, are presented in later chapters.

Risk Reactions

Individuals differ in their perception of risk and in how they characterise hazards (Slovic, 2000). Given the differences between people in their interpretation of risk information and their perception of hazard characteristics, it is hardly surprising if they were found to differ in their risk reactions. Socio-demographic factors were considered (age, gender, ethnicity, nationality and disadvantage) and studies, which were often subject to methodological critiques, yielded complex evidence of interactions between these factors in predictions of risk reactions (Breakwell, 2014b: 70–83). Personality was examined, particularly the 'Big Five' personality factors: impulsivity–sensation-seeking, neuroticism–anxiety, aggression–hostility, sociability–extraversion and activity (Zuckerman, 1991). Impulsivity and neuroticism regularly emerge as related to differences in risk perception and risk-taking, but any of the five can be significant under specific conditions (Barnett & Breakwell, 2001). In addition, some people are found habitually to have a greater tolerance of uncertainty and desire to control it than others (Shuper et al., 2004). This characteristic was labelled the 'uncertainty orientation', is associated with the personality trait 'openness to experience' and with authoritarianism (Hodson & Sorrentino, 1999). Individual differences in abiding 'cognitive styles' have also been examined. For instance, a pessimistic cognitive style has been found to be associated with unrealistic pessimism about personal vulnerability to health risk (van der Velde et al., 1992). It is not hard to see how these individual differences that drive the perception of risk and uncertainty will influence whether mistrust occurs. They also affect the targeting of mistrust and the expressions of mistrust. This is examined in later chapters. It is a particularly important issue when examining the way the personality of a leader affects attributions of mistrust (see Chapter 6) or adherence to conspiracy theories channel mistrust (see Chapter 9).

Current social psychological theory has begun to explore how variations in uncertainty and risk perceptions and reactions may be purposive, that is to say be motivated by some desired personal outcomes. It is in this context that identity processes have a strong bearing upon uncertainty reactions. For instance, variations in levels of self-efficacy are associated with seeking to reduce uncertainty about one's own health status by choosing to have genetic screening for disease (Hendy, Lyons & Breakwell, 2006). Perceptions of uncertainties in environmental harm estimates are biased by the significance of the specific environment to the identity elements of self-esteem and distinctiveness (Bonaiuto, Breakwell & Cano, 1996). Denial of anthropogenic climate change, which involves emphasising uncertainties in the scientific data, has also been shown to be linked to identity processes (Jaspal, Nerlich & Cinnirella, 2014; Pechar & Mayer, 2015).

While identity processes have been shown to be important, reactions to risk and uncertainty are rarely wholly individual or individualised. Responses can emerge at interpersonal, group, community, national or international levels. Shared representations of the uncertainty are constructed across time and place. An individual's reaction to uncertainty in contexts where the hazard is shared will be influenced by how others respond to it and particularly by how and what they communicate about it. However, it may be anticipated that the individual's engagement with the shared representation will be mediated by the desire to defend their identity and, inevitably, there will be disparities in the amount of influence different individuals have over the representations of uncertainty which come to be accepted or contested. Mistrust has a major role in this, which is considered later.

Rationality and Mistrust

There is a vast body of evidence that illustrates that individuals differ in their response to uncertainty and to many types of heuristics and biases that influence reactions to risk and uncertainty that are described in the psychological literature. The ones described here represent a small selection. They are the ones most relevant to understanding how mistrust evolves and operates. However, there is an underlying conclusion that can be drawn – people routinely do not make decisions driven by rationality or objective utility. When information is incomplete and individuals experience uncertainty, their judgements are a product of the interaction of social representations of the meaning of the bits of data they have and their motivation to protect their own identity. Identity and social representation processes, in situations of uncertainty, have the power to mobilise and shape the use of heuristics and biases.

Mistrust can be initiated, succoured or challenged by the use of heuristics and operation of biases that are, in turn, serving identity and social representation motives. Heuristics and biases are not the only shapers of mistrust but their significance signals that we should be careful about assuming that mistrust is an objectively rational approach to assessing a risk. Mistrust still can be subjectively rational in that it serves personal goals. In the context of uncertainty, mistrust may be an eminently 'subjectively rational' position to adopt. It acknowledges the objective irrationality of either trust or distrust when uncertainty is high. Given the current levels of societal uncertainty, mistrust may be the only rational option. Chapter 3 focuses further upon the role of societal uncertainty and the implications of shared mistrust.

CHAPTER 3
SHARED UNCERTAINTY

Uncertainty is an essential ingredient of mistrust. To mistrust is to be doubtful, unsure, undecided and quintessentially uncertain. Chapter 2 explored the strategies that individuals use when dealing with uncertainty, particularly the uncertainty associated with the possibility of harm (i.e. risk or threat). It emphasises that individuals do differ in the way they react to uncertainty, even though some commonly used strategies are evident. It is to be expected then that mistrust, which is so embedded in uncertainty, will be manifested in idiosyncratic ways. Individuals will differ in the way they think, feel and act when they mistrust. Yet shared uncertainties might be expected to lead to shared mistrust. Moreover, the very processes that ensure that uncertainties are shared will also encourage commonalities in the way mistrust emerges and the effects it has. Shared uncertainty is now, arguably, the 'new normal'. So shared mistrust is also probably the 'new normal'. The 'new normal' has many faces.

An Age of Uncertainty

Galbraith (1977) popularised the idea of 'the age of uncertainty' first in a TV series and later in a bestselling book. He depicted industrial societies in transition from the certainties of the 19th century philosophical and economic thought to the growing doubt and challenges of the 20th century. These realignments were said to be responses to changes in the means of production, control of wealth, geopolitical distribution of power and population mobility. Galbraith argued these changes created a state of societal uncertainty manifest in doubt about, or outright rejection of, previous aspirations, beliefs and values. Galbraith is describing what amounts to mistrust of previously held systems of thought and standards of behaviour. The notion that we live in an age of uncertainty has since become an integral part of different types of social science theorising (e.g. Giddens, 1991; Beck, 1992; Taleb, 2007) – all of which have added their own twist to the idea. However, it is notable that Galbraith was not just interested in how 'certainties' in beliefs and values mutate or become suspect. He was concerned with the societal consequences of such uncertainty.

Some argue that uncertainty has always been a characteristic of societies. They say the driving forces of societal uncertainty have always been there – changes in modes of production, technological innovation, bases of power and international conflicts have always occurred. So why should ours be labelled the age of uncertainty? It is a fair question when you compare historical periods. Uncertainty has always been more common than certainty. Yet there is something very different about the uncertainty of the 21st century.

Breakwell (2020a, 2020b) suggested that societal uncertainty now is different because of a series of fundamental societal changes that have happened since 1990 when the World Wide Web was opened to the public. What happened in 1990 was that historically unprecedented numbers and types of channels of communication and platforms for information exchange, dissent and the undermining of established authorities and belief systems began to be made available to a global public. Obviously, these changes post-date Galbraith's original bold (and often condemned) analysis. The difference that the digital era has made lies not only in the extent of information exchange available but also in the potential speed and geographical distribution of that exchange. These changes in the speed of information transmission and receipt have the power to accelerate changes in virtually all other aspects of social life. Just consider for a moment how connected you can be – if you choose – to any event, anywhere, now. Consider how you could access immediately, at your fingertips, the knowledge and thoughts of most of recorded history. Consider how you can tell or show thousands of people what you are doing, thinking or feeling instantaneously. While it is important to acknowledge that not everyone has this technology available, a very large number do.

The reason that these changes are a source of societal uncertainty is not simply that the rate of change has been accelerating year on year. It is because individuals and society as a whole are less confident about knowing what to do with this vast, inchoate data reservoir, or with the potential for it being used to bring about more change. These changes are without clear rationale or predictability. The digital matrix questions, erases or replaces the old narratives – ideological or religious – that held communities and hierarchies in place. It puts political systems into a state of flux, claiming that existing political structures are dysfunctional or irrelevant. It makes economic inequalities more visible, and may exacerbate them. Its disruptive technological innovations penetrate every aspect of daily life. It encourages the fragmentation of national allegiances and family structures. It challenges the consensual assurances of experts and elites. It makes all hazards, all risks, simultaneously knowable, everywhere across the world, and raises the looming doubt about what disaster may be next. Of course, the technology alone does none of this. The people who use it make this happen. The rate of change in digital technologies may intrinsically inspire uncertainty and suspicion but much of the societal uncertainty is a product of human motivations. We will return to the deliberate use of digital technologies in the creation of mistrust in a later chapter. Here it is worth noting that the fear of 'fake news' and disinformation (deliberately fabricated 'facts') is widespread (Lazer et al., 2018). Fact-checking websites are multiplying as people seek for information integrity. The irony of seeking truth through the medium that arouses mistrust in the first place is unmissable. Also, the internet age has added a new dimension to the age of uncertainty as originally conceived. Making distal risk more visible and proximate while simultaneously eroding the ostensible certainty that traditional authorities offered (such as scientists or health practitioners, Wellcome, 2018), it highlights uncertainty. If seen historically, we may live in a more certain and predictable world, but it just does not seem that way to a very large number of people.

No Uncertainty Lives Alone

No single element of uncertainty exists separately from the context created by the others. The meaning of each is dependent upon others. Changes in any one have a ripple effect across others. So, for instance, uncertainties about climate change and uncertainties about disease control, while technically distinct, affect each other in diverse ways in public narratives of societal risk. Societal uncertainty is a complex dynamic system. The system itself is the product of active continual interpretation of events through the agency of individuals, groups, communities and other social actors (e.g. the media, governments and professions). New or changed uncertainties thus become better understood by being reconceptualised, normalised or identified within the pre-existing system of societal uncertainty – often by reference to existing social representations of comparable events.

This may not automatically make them more trusted, acceptable or less frightening. On occasion, it can be quite the opposite. It all depends on how and where an uncertainty is embedded in the ambient societal uncertainty. For instance, explaining uncertainty about the occurrence of tsunamis by reference to uncertainty about the rate of climate change could elicit a range of responses depending upon where the audience was located in the societal debates about the existence and origins of climate change.

The linkages between uncertainties attached to different hazards change over time. Often as a result of deliberate manipulation by authorities that are most able to influence social representation processes. In relation to uncertainties concerning hazards, Barnett and Breakwell (2003) described how 'hazard sequences' and 'hazard templates' develop. They examined the history of oral contraceptive health scares (that linked the birth control pill to cancer) showing the way that the public is notified about a potential health risk by medical experts and by the mass media builds representations of the hazard over time. In the case of the link between oral contraceptives and cancer, this representation is complex because while some evidence linked taking the pill to a higher risk of cervical cancer, other evidence linked it to a lower risk of other cancers, for instance ovarian cancer. Sequential health campaigns add new layers to a template specifying what is known definitively about the potential hazard and what is still uncertain. Where the hazard changes or develops and its effects alter, the hazard sequence is identified. Commonalities and patterns across the different forms of the hazard are reported, as are the variations in effect (with emphasis on probability and severity). These hazard templates, mostly officially mandated, are part of the fabric of shared societal uncertainties. The template, though contributing to the social representation of the hazard, remains only one input to the negotiation that produces and evolves the representation. Hazard templates are interesting because they can provide both the anchoring and objectification ingredients that are predicted by SRT.

A contemporary example at the time of writing this in 2020 is the way the uncertainties surrounding the emergence of COVID-19 as a result of the SARS-CoV-2 virus (2019–2020) were explained by policy makers and reported in the media. This relied on understandings, or at least awareness, of other infectious fatal diseases (notably the 1918 influenza pandemic, H1N1 so-called Bird Flu, MERS-CoV, SARS, Ebola, measles and tuberculosis) – a rather broad range. The threat of the new coronavirus was anchored and objectified by reference to descriptions of health crises that shared some of its features. The object was to make the levels of uncertainty concerning the consequences of the new viral threat more intelligible to the general public by grounding the explanations in commonly (if not comprehensively) available understandings of what had happened before and so what might happen in the future.

In this case, the social representational processes deliberately served to lead the public to expect uncertainty to continue. Solutions (treatments, cures, vaccinations, containment etc.) it was said would be sought, but when they would be found was left uncertain. Little is known about the effects of acknowledging there will be persistent uncertainty about such a terrifying hazard that can harm so many people in so many different ways. History may well tell what impact these messages had in relation to COVID-19, it is not clear now.

It does mean, however, that it is worth emphasising:

- Acknowledging uncertainty in a high threat situation is a two-edged sword. It may inculcate trust (i.e. by appearing to be open and seeming willing to admit the limitations of what is known). However, it may just as easily suggest incompetence or, possibly worse, an unwillingness to reveal, for certain, what you actually know about the worst-case scenario (i.e. that you know disaster looms).
- The effects of acknowledging uncertainty will depend on what other uncertainties concern your audience. For instance, in the case of COVID-19, what people believe about the uncertain efficacy of vaccination or the uncertain significance of herd immunity. You may be concerned about the uncertainty of getting the vaccination but

others may be preoccupied about the uncertainty around the vaccine's safety. You may be sure herd immunity would not control the pandemic but others may believe many people might be resistant to the virus as a result of exposure to COVID-19 and that lockdown measures may have been unnecessary.

- The effects of acknowledging uncertainty depend on where you are in the lifecycle of the event - early in the crisis, uncertainty may be tolerated and even expected (anything else would be suspicious) but later more certainty might not just be expected but demanded. The temptation for anyone dealing with a crisis is to move away from acknowledging uncertainty as the situation develops; to shift to unrealistic claims of certainty. This may be manifested in shifting the choice of what is claimed with certainty. For instance, at the beginning of the epidemic it may have been uncertain when an effective vaccine for COVID-19 would be developed but it was possible to claim certainty about when a target number of tests for virus infection would be conducted and analysed. The object of certitude changes. The hope is that certainty in one domain will compensate for uncertainty in another. Sometimes it works - at least for a time. It becomes tricky when the substitute certainty turns out also to be uncertain - as sometimes happens. For instance, if the infection testing initially could not be delivered as promised.

- Irrespective of what acknowledgements of uncertainty are made, the ambient level of uncertainty will affect responses. Ambient uncertainty that is attached to the source of uncertainty messages is particularly important. If the credibility of the Minister of Health or Chief Scientist or Chief Medical Officer presenting some estimate of the likelihood of success in finding the vaccine is suspect, the uncertainty associated with the source becomes a contaminant for the message.

Responses to COVID-19 particularly illustrate the significance of the societal pervasiveness of uncertainty. The uncertainties posed by such a global pandemic encompass all aspects of human existence – including not just physical and psychological wellbeing but also economic and political security. It is barely possible to conceptualise the range and complexities of the social representation processes that would be needed to objectify and anchor these uncertainties. Such processes are inevitably iterative and often apparently chaotic. They are also inevitably open to contestation – conflicting representations will emerge (e.g. through conspiracy theories like the one suggesting that coronavirus did not occur naturally but was manufactured). Competition between alternative representations, often targeting different aspects of a complex hazard against a background of more general societal uncertainty, will be unlikely to result in a coherent, common understanding of a risk.

In our digital age, when the uncertainty linked to a new hazard arises it can be exposed to everyone, everywhere, without a pause, and so the complexity of the dynamic system of societal uncertainty is further enhanced. The implications of the potential for indiscriminate access to awareness of events, change and uncertainty through multiple communication channels are manifold. It offers the opportunity for great commonality of understanding and action. Equally, it offers the potential for great disparities and conflict in interpretation. There is little evidence, currently, that the communication opportunities now available are building harmony or common purpose, though some do argue that they serve to shrink individuality and autonomy (Byung-Chul, 2017). Indeed, they often work to heighten the perception of threat (Jodelet, Vala & Drozda-Senkowska, 2020). Danger is seen to abound and there is no way for those at risk to independently evaluate the threat posed to themselves, their friends and family, their community, their nation or the world. The broader societal uncertainty means that the structures that might have interpreted a specific uncertainty in the past (e.g. religions, politicians or scholars) have less automatic or privileged routes to creating a representation of the meaning of that uncertainty. Moreover, every facet of societal uncertainty may be seen to pose a further threat to the foundations of trust in those structures. Uncertainty erodes trust; erosion of trust enhances uncertainty.

Absolute Uncertainty

How uncertain is uncertainty? We do not actually find it an alien task to be asked to quantify our uncertainty. If we know that we are *not absolutely sure* about something, we will normally be willing to hazard a guess as to just how unsure we are. We rely on various frames of reference in doing this – all of those cognitive and motivational drivers, heuristics and biases, described in Chapter 2, that are products of experience and desire. Much of the psychology of risk perception relies upon people being willing to try to estimate how uncertain they feel. Somehow, someone's appreciation of an uncertainty is expected to be articulated through some interpretable, usually unidimensional, scale. It is understood that people may not be speaking a common language of uncertainty, but to some degree, any tongue is assumed to be amenable to measurement. This pursuit of the quantification of uncertainty has been fundamental to the development of modern behavioural science.

In a recent commentary on economic theory, Kay & King (2020) have raised the question of the role of complete and absolute uncertainty, what they call radical uncertainty, and others call irreducible or fundamental uncertainty. This is possibly what Keynes in his *General Theory of Employment* (1937) calls a situation of ignorance. When modelling economic behaviour, Keynes said that ignorance applies only to the very special case of long run calculations about the distant or very distant future. Kay and King argue that, in fact, we all live, all the time, with an unknowable future – one that may be unimaginable by us now. So we are deluding ourselves if we think we can make good predictions of what will happen based on probability calculations that are merely guesses. Quantification of uncertainty, translated into probabilities that are themselves based on incomplete knowledge, simply misleads us, giving us an unfounded sense of our own precision and control. Therefore, the tendency to deify optimisation of the probability of gain or loss in economic models of behaviour is seen as offering spurious certainty and misleading policy makers and practitioners alike. Individuals, businesses and governments should all be ready to make decisions with an awareness of their limitations in the face of an inherently unpredictable future. This is a world of uncertain futures and unpredictable consequences, about which there is necessary speculation and inevitable disagreements that will often never be resolved. This is the world that most of us will recognise as day-to-day life.

While they criticise the orthodox notion of the 'rational economic man', Kay and King are equally dissatisfied with behavioural economics. They would argue that the biases and heuristics described in Chapter 2 should not be thought about as flaws, or inadequacies, but as sensible strategies in the face of uncertainty. This conclusion is probably the same as the one arrived at by social psychologists some time ago. It seems that Kay and King also share the preoccupation of current social psychology with the way people and organisations make use of negotiation and collaborative processes, narrative framing and 'intuition' when coming to decisions in a radically uncertain world. Central to this is the recognition that understanding what is happening relies not only on economics and markets but also on other social, political and technological changes.

It is worth returning to the issue of 'intuition' as a basis for decision making later. Intuition as the stimulus for mistrust is particularly interesting. People often talk about their intuition or 'gut feeling' when explaining how they come to their risk estimates. They do the same when they talk about why they come to feel mistrust. The consideration of how intuition affects the interpretation of radical uncertainty suggests that it is necessary to think about the emotional and motivational factors at work.

Abandoning, or looking beyond, the simplistic models of risk assessment and decision making that are based on algorithms that assume uncertainty estimates are meaningful is not as easy as it might sound. Scepticism about these models may be only rational (not that rationality is so highly regarded nowadays). But what will be their substitute? The replacements are complex and rarely predictive. They are currently mostly explanations after the event. IPT and SRT can be used to interpret what has happened in risk reactions or conditions of uncertainty but their predictive power is inconsistent. They require many variables to be considered simultaneously. They do not choose to simplify the real complexities of the social world and do not encourage spurious assurance. These theories are actually attuned to interpreting the consequences of radical uncertainty for both individuals and society. It is not entirely clear, but Kay and King may believe that no models are needed to support decision making in radical uncertainty or that any would be doomed to be useless. However, there does not seem to be any reason to be so pessimistic. Taking to heart their own argument, since the future is unknowable, there is always the possibility that a process for creating a suitably adaptable theory will emerge.

Obviously, not all uncertainty is radical uncertainty. The same mathematical models that may offer spurious guidance in radical uncertainty may be very useful when uncertainties are capable of being delineated. Of course, even when this is so, there is no reason to adopt them uncritically.

Shared Mistrust

Shared uncertainties should often result in shared mistrust. The technologies and the social processes that entreat us to feel and then share uncertainties are also the ones that encourage us to feel and share mistrust.

Why should this be so?

Uncertainty exists if the future is unknown. Radical uncertainty exists if the future is unknowable. In either case, individuals or groups (or organisations – any label will do just at this point for the aggregation of individuals – greater granularity may be needed later) that share an uncertainty need to make sense of the situation for themselves. The uncertainty is always a threat because it might lead to loss rather than gain. It is always an opportunity because it might lead to a gain rather than a loss. Sharing the threat or opportunity associated with the uncertainty, once those involved recognise it is shared, initiates a series of reactions:

- Finding others are experiencing the same uncertainties provides the opportunity to join with them to try to understand what might happen. Building a shared interpretation of the hazard, exchanging information and consequently becoming more confident in what to think, feel and do about it. This is all part of the predictable processes of building a social representation.
- The process of building this common understanding of the uncertainty has corollary effects. Individuals seek to determine whether they share other things with those that face the same uncertainty – whether they are linked by some common characteristic (their background, their interests, their beliefs, their objectives etc.). The more similar to the others they deem themselves to be, the more likely they are to believe that they constitute an identifiable social category. At this point, it is what might be called a 'conceptual group'. A conceptual group (Breakwell, 1978, 1979) is a social category accepted to exist because circumstances identify commonalities across people or because it is arbitrarily imposed by others who assert the group exists. An example of an officially created conceptual group would be BAME. The acronym is now used to stand for Black, Asian and Minority Ethnic and does not relate to country origin or affiliation. Officially sanctioned labelling such as this often results in rejection. Conceptual groups that are self-made by people sharing a common experience have greater perceived legitimacy and can be very influential.
- The common sense of belonging to a conceptual group, occasioned by facing a shared uncertainty, will influence identity processes. Just as people seek to gain identity strength or resilience from other group memberships, conceptual groups will be expected to yield identity benefits (i.e. in terms of esteem, efficacy, distinctiveness or continuity). If they do not, the individual will try either to exit the conceptual group or to get the group to behave differently or be evaluated differently by others outside the group.
- Resolving the shared uncertainty becomes important to the conceptual group and the individual's identity. How this is to be done depends on the nature of the uncertainty. It often does not entail eradicating or lessening the uncertainty. In fact, radical uncertainty, by its very definition, could not be diminished. However, other forms of dealing with the uncertainty will be attempted, even when it cannot be objectively

lessened. The form and function of any acceptable resolution will centre upon protecting the identity of the individual and/or the group. For instance, it might diminish the significance of personal responsibility for any loss consequent upon the uncertainty but claim personal responsibility for any gain. Alternatively, the very existence of the uncertainty may be blamed upon something or someone outside the conceptual group. Another option would be to challenge the source or the accuracy of evidence that generates the uncertainty in the first place.

When you look at these steps in the development of shared uncertainty, and factor in the background societal uncertainty, it does not take a giant leap of faith to see that shared uncertainty will initiate new or magnify existing shared mistrust. Mistrust in others, especially people from other conceptual groups, is a by-product of trying to understand and minimise the personal threat of uncertainty. Mistrust of this sort is motivated and used as a weapon. Such mistrust is broadcast, made public to shame or undermine others in the interests of oneself.

Shared mistrust does not only arise from a shared uncertainty. The specific reasons for shared mistrust may vary. Friends may betray, employers lie, enemies attack. Sharing such experiences, when they occur, can stimulate shared mistrust because subsequent betrayal, lies or attacks are anticipated or feared. This is shared mistrust based on the possibility that history will be repeated. This type of shared mistrust, while it is linked to some uncertainty, may not be itself a motivated tactic to cope with this uncertainty. This sort of mistrust may not be publicised, indeed, it may remain the secret of those sharing it. This is shared, but private, mistrust.

Shared mistrust can also emerge from shared certainties. For example, some people believed with absolute certainty the claim that the MMR vaccine was implicated in the aetiology of autism (Deer, 2020) and this led to a considerable number of people who shared mistrust of the vaccine.

Whatever its origin, even when it has no empirical foundation, shared mistrust creates a conceptual group. Shared mistrust of some person, organisation, technology, or any other shared mistrust, unites people and can bind them in a sense of common purpose. It is a motive for common action and particularly a joint justification or excuse for aggression.

The thing about shared mistrust is that it can be self-affirming. It proves that you are not isolated in your suspicions and doubts. It fosters self-confidence – even in the midst of doubt and uncertainty. If others agree that mistrust is appropriate, you have confidence from numbers. Ironically, radical uncertainty may be the best breeding ground for shared mistrust. If nothing is sure, anything goes.

Shared mistrust differs from individual mistrust. It has more armaments to deploy. Shared mistrust can use joint action to target the object of mistrust. Later chapters delve in detail into the variety of weapons that are used. They also examine what defences can be mounted by the mistrusted against such attacks. To reiterate what was said in the first paragraph of this chapter, if shared uncertainty is now the 'new normal', shared mistrust is also probably the 'new normal'. The 'new normal' has many faces.

CHAPTER 4
IDENTITY, EMOTIONS AND MISTRUST

Expressions of Mistrust

Mistrust finds expression in many forms across a wide range of contexts. This chapter explores some of the psychological effects and symptoms of mistrust from both the perspective of the mistrustful and the mistrusted. These effects and symptoms are examined primarily in relation to identity processes. The focus is upon the emotional implications of mistrust and, in turn, upon their ramifications for identity resilience. The emphasis in this chapter is more on individual mistrust than on shared mistrust. The next chapter will return to shared mistrust manifestations. However, the line between individual and shared mistrust in practice is often blurred. Individuals sometimes come to be mistrusted because others share suspicions and doubts about them. Equally, individuals may come, through common experience, to a shared mistrust of some other individual or group. Even shared mistrust, in each case, resides with individuals and in their social actions. So, despite looking closely here at the psychological effects of mistrust on individuals, it is impossible to ignore or separate cultural and institutional mistrust influences upon these individual processes.

Mistrust and Emotion

Chapter 2 focused upon risk perceptions and reactions, examining the way cognitive processes through heuristics and biases are influential in shaping mistrust. However, being mistrustful has emotional as well as cognitive correlates. Typically, the specific form the emotional and cognitive reactions take depends upon the context or event that stimulates mistrust. However, normally being mistrustful arouses emotions on the negative spectrum. Regularly reported reactions include fear, anger, hatred, loath-ing, worry, depression, bitterness, hostility, embarrassment, rage, terror and anxiety.

The severity of the emotional reaction depends on many factors. These fall into three broad categories.

- The first concerns whether their mistrust is perceived as based on sufficient evidence (i.e. justifiable) by those who are mistrustful. Strong emotional reactions (whether aggressive such as anger, hatred and rage, or defensive such as fear) in mistrusting individuals emerge mostly when their mistrust is perceived subjectively as justified. This should not be taken to imply that they have shifted to distrust, they remain sus-picious that they have been wronged rather than sure, but they are assured that suspicion is appropriate. Where the justification for their mistrust is perceived as less robust, the emotional reaction reflects this; anxiety, worry and depression are com-mon in this situation.

- The second category concerns the perceived cost or damage to the mistrusting of the offence or offences that trigger suspicion. For emotional reactions to be strong, the cost or damage is normally perceived to be significant. For instance, a casual conversation with a tradesman who arrives to install high-speed broadband cable that leads you to believe that he is misrepresenting how many times he has tried to phone you before arriving late for his appointment may result in you mistrusting his veracity (especially if this is the second time he has done this). However, it is unlikely to precipitate a strong emotional reaction. In contrast, a casual conversation with a workmate that leads you to suspect your employer is intending to dismiss you, with-out warning or rationale, might lead you to mistrust your employer. This may well be associated with a strong emotional reaction. The personal cost of the offence in this scenario could be very great. It is noteworthy in both illustrations that the mistrust is not founded on absolute proof. They differ in severity of emotional impact because of the personal cost of the assumed trigger for mistrust.

- The third category concerns the feasibility of escape from the situation that engen-ders mistrust. The severity and longevity of emotional reactions depend on whether the individual has some route to resolve (i.e. eliminate, assuage, tolerate or substan-tiate) the mistrust. This will depend upon the resources they have available - both psychological and material. Mistrust sometimes can be resolved by direct measures. Typically, these involve seeking ways to remove doubt and uncertainty. That can mean accumulating evidence that either corroborates or discredits the suspicions. It can entail a direct challenge to the mistrusted. More often, it involves circumstantial evidence. This search for certitude undoubtedly will have emotional concomitants - especially anxiety and worry, and sometimes embarrassment. However, the search is directed at a utilitarian solution to mistrust. Once the solution is achieved, the emo-tional concomitants of mistrust can be sometimes dismissed or minimised. In contrast, there is also a 'resolution' to mistrust in which the emotional reaction becomes an end in itself. Where this happens, mistrust continues. However, the emotional response becomes habitual (normalised). This often involves depression, bitterness or help-lessness. This is clearly not an escape from mistrust; it is living with an emotionally debilitating mistrust.

The level of perceived justification for mistrust, the cost of its causes, and the opportunities for resolving it, all interact in determining the emotional consequences that it has.

In earlier chapters, the effects of mistrust on decision making were examined in the light of uncertainty and risk. It is worth noting that the emotions aroused by mistrust will also influence decision making. Emotion will mediate the impact of mistrust on decision making. So, for instance, medical mistrust by patients is associated with decisions to reject treatment (Cuevas, O'Brien & Saha, 2019) but this effect is often mediated by the fear that mistrustful patients feel (Davis et al., 2012).

The close link between mistrust and decision making has been found in many client–professional relationships. For instance, Redhead (2011) found mistrust of financial service professionals affects investment decision making in much the same way as risk does. Again, this effect can be mediated by emotion, notably anxiety. Anxiety also probably mediates the effect of pharmaceutical company mistrust on decisions to refuse influenza vaccinations (Harris et al., 2006). Emotions are the medium through which mistrust is translated into decision and action. Of course, the emotion will sometimes impair the quality of decisions and the efficacy of their implementation. Furthermore, mistrust may motivate several emotions simultaneously and they do not necessarily push intentions or actions in the same directions. Fear and anger may both be aroused at the same time by feeling mistrustful of your teenage daughter whom you suspect of using recreational drugs. In concert, they may result in ambivalence, self-doubt and inaction. Alternatively, they may result in ambivalence manifested in frantic, indiscriminate action or serial contradictory actions.

These interactions between mistrust, emotion and choice, intention or action sit in a complex system. The flows are not unidimensional or unidirectional. Emotions aroused will affect what is understood to be the status of mistrust, changing how justified it is seen to be, what costs it is thought to incur, and what routes to resolution are available. The theoretical model that eventually is developed to describe and explain these relationships will need to be concerned with dynamic processes. This is a system with only a very remote chance of ever achieving equilibrium. The model must also acknowledge that mistrust is not simply vested in the individual; it is always a social product. Social context is a paramount determiner of action.

Figure 4.1 depicts the elements of this model. It is a model that can be empirically tested in many contexts. It would be valuable to have simple but consensual operational definitions of the constructs that it includes in order, first, to allow the strength of the association between its components to be assessed, and then to allow valid comparisons across studies. The figure does not depict the cognitive processing of input from the social context (including effects of heuristics and biases described in Chapter 2) whose influence upon estimates of justification, cost

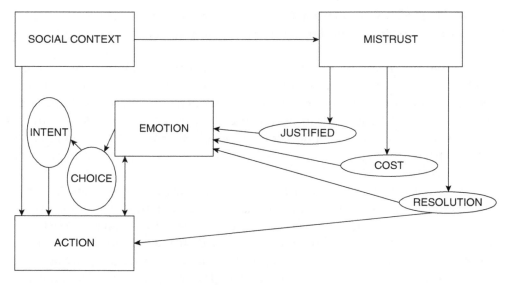

Figure 4.1   Mistrust, Emotion and Action

and resolution options are mediated and moderated by mistrust. These cognitive processes, nevertheless, are the prime mechanism for translating the social context into a psychological reality. Cognitive processes inevitably mediate between social context and individual experience. In fact, they are not included as a discrete box in the figure because the model is assuming that such cognitive processes are involved at every step in the model. For instance, emotion (affect) does not determine choice without cognitive accompaniment. Thus, this model, like many social psychological models, assumes the omnipresence of cognitive processes without articulating their specific roles.

The model, as it stands, concerns the flow from mistrust to emotion. It could also, and probably should, include an additional element that admits of the possibility that prior emotions initiate mistrust in the first place. A classic example of such a causal route would come from love associated with jealousy (the fear of losing someone) leading to mistrust which, in turn, can lead to a whole range of other emotions. However, the feedback loop from emotion to mistrust is not inevitable and therefore is not included in the figure.

It could also be argued that the model should allow for a direct route from mistrust to action without mediation. This is a logical possibility. Whether this happens or not in specific mistrust experiences is a matter for detailed empirical examination. Similarly, it is logical to assume that action may lead directly to changes in mistrust. The figure currently indicates this. However, it is likely that the association between action and mistrust will itself be mediated or moderated by other intervening variables – not least, perceived efficacy (i.e. whether the action is perceived to be effective in reducing the doubt at the centre of mistrust). The model also suggests a two-way influence between emotions and action. This is taken to reflect what may happen iteratively over relatively short timescales. This feedback loop, like that between action and intention, represents the dynamism of the system that is being described.

Being Mistrusted, Self-efficacy and Helplessness

Thus far, the discussion of the relationship between mistrust and emotion has focused upon the people who feel mistrustful. It appears to have omitted the mistrusted. Yet in some respects, the model outlined above works for the mistrusted too. The justification, costs and opportunities for resolution will mediate the effects of being mistrusted upon emotions and action. Being mistrusted arouses sometimes severe emotional reactions that have great significance for action and for psychological wellbeing.

There is, however, one big difference between the mistrustful and the mistrusted. The condition of the mistrustful is one of suspicion and doubt. They still live with uncertainty, even after they have declared they are mistrustful. The condition of the mistrusted has been determined – it is established that they *are* suspected or doubted. There is no uncertainty about the status of being mistrusted. Of course, there may be a period preceding this when the mistrusted suspect they are mistrusted but do not know for sure. Yet, once the mistrust is declared, they live with the certainty that they are mistrusted.

It should also be remembered that being mistrusted and being mistrustful often go hand in hand. Da Silva Rebelo, Fernández and Achotegui (2018) report a systematic review of studies that examined what effects the host societies' hostile attitudes and feelings of anger and mistrust towards them had upon refugees, asylum seekers and immigrants. Expressed in overt or more subtle ways, the mistrust and discrimination by host societies had harmful effects on the bio-psychological wellbeing of incomers, often instigating feelings of helplessness, anger, frustration and, most notably, general mistrust. This review reveals the circularity of the mistrust phenomenon – the mistrusted become mistrustful, probably only to become more mistrusted. The study also highlights the strong emotional correlates of being mistrusted. Most notable is the finding that mistrust, in this case supported by overt discrimination at a societal level, is associated with perceived helplessness.

Being mistrusted may be a catalyst for feelings of helplessness. In the case of asylum seekers or refugees, of course, this may be a realistic estimate of their situation. There is no reason to believe helplessness is inevitably associated with being mistrusted. Feeling helpless in the face of being mistrusted depends on the self-efficacy of the individual, or indeed the group, involved. Self-efficacy is usually defined as 'the belief in one's own competences to perform a behaviour in spite of barriers' (Bandura, 1977: 192). The significance of self-efficacy in identity processes was described earlier (Chapter 1). IPT emphasises how individuals will feel their identity threatened if their belief in their ability to achieve their goals and handle problems is challenged. People with high self-efficacy tend to believe they can overcome such challenges. Other things being equal, mistrusted people with high self-efficacy will not experience helplessness. However, people with lower self-efficacy may experience a sense of helplessness when facing criticism or obstacles (Zabelina, Tsiring & Chestyunina, 2018). For them, being mistrusted may be a nudge towards a helplessness response.

It is notable that much of the literature in this area focuses upon the link between 'learned helplessness' and 'self-efficacy' (Vergara et al., 2017; Sorrenti et al., 2018). There is a distinction between learned helplessness and, objectively assessed, actual helplessness. Learned helplessness develops when someone is subjected to aversive experiences (e.g. repeated abuse, harassment or accusations) which cannot be avoided or escaped. It embodies the strong belief that similar subsequent experiences will also not be controllable and, consequently, nothing the person can do will help, so they stop trying – even when they do have the ability to do something. They have learned to behave as if helpless in that sort of situation, even when they are not.

Being mistrusted on a regular basis over time can be a potent stimulant for learned helplessness. If you know that others mistrust your ability or willingness to achieve the goals set for you, then these evaluations that you receive about your actual or potential performance can encourage you to doubt your capacity. It simultaneously challenges your self-efficacy and creates the conditions in which you learn to be 'helpless'.

It may be useful at this point to turn again for a moment from the mistrusted to the mistrustful. People who manifest greater mistrust of others are also sometimes found to have lower levels of self-efficacy. For instance, lower self-efficacy in patients has been associated with greater mistrust of medical practitioners (Sutton et al., 2019). In fact, many studies (e.g. Molina et al., 2015; Patev et al., 2019) indicate self-efficacy mediates the effects of medical mistrust upon health care choices and attitudes. However, in some cases, higher self-efficacy is associated with being more mistrustful. For instance, some forms of political mistrust are associated with greater levels of perceived self-efficacy (Towler, Crawford & Bennett, 2020; Bostrom, Hayes & Crosman, 2019). The relationship between self-efficacy and being mistrustful seems to depend on the type of mistrust and the availability of opportunities for resolving it. Mistrust can either diminish or accentuate perceived self-efficacy – it all depends on the severity of, and arena for, mistrust and the prior level of self-efficacy. However, the direction of the causal effect varies. Changes in self-efficacy may modify levels of mistrust. Changes in mistrust may modify self-efficacy. Studies, such as those concerning medical mistrust, often are not designed to determine causation. They explore correlation. We need more longitudinal and experimental studies in this area that may start to unpick the complex causal relationships between mistrust, self-efficacy and helplessness.

Self-doubt and Mistrust

Wittgenstein (1963: 190), published posthumously, wrote 'One can mistrust one's own senses, but not one's own belief'. In so far as a belief that is doubted is no longer a belief, he was probably right. But then his assertion would be rather trivial, based merely on semantics. He may have been assuming that belief is always absolute – either you believe or you do not. Yet in practice, there is ample evidence that people do sometimes mistrust their own beliefs. They hold a belief but are suspicious that it may be wrong in some way or misleading them. It is a phenomenon that occurs when ideologies are brought under scrutiny or when religious principles are challenged. It happens in relationships when beliefs about the character of someone else begin to be doubted. In such contexts, one comes to mistrust what one believes. The growth of mistrust can initiate a tipping point. It may be the precursor to dropping the belief or to finding a way to erase the doubt. It may be reconciled quickly. Even if it is, it still has some lifespan. Moreover, sometimes it is not silenced easily or immediately. People can live with the nagging questions about their own beliefs for a long time. Mistrust of one's own beliefs is a fundamental source of self-doubt. This is because it challenges one's ability to come to the right understandings, values and conclusions.

Roush (2017) offers a discussion of the nature of epistemic self-doubt. This is defined as doubt about one's ability to achieve an epistemically favourable state. 'Epistemic' is an adjective that usually refers to knowledge and the degree to which it is validated. An epistemically favourable state, for example, might be attained if one were to feel no doubt that one's beliefs were true. Descartes (1641), in his *Meditations*, argued that if one doubts the soundness of one's own sensory perceptions, doubt is cast upon the source for all beliefs. Mistrust of one's own capacity to assimilate information accurately (which is dependent on the senses) makes it difficult to be sure of the veracity of one's beliefs. Mistrust of one's beliefs makes it difficult to be sure of the veracity of one's interpretation of information. This line of reasoning quickly ascends to consideration of the role of beliefs about beliefs (so-called second-order beliefs). Suppose that I believe that climate change is not the product of human activity (call this a first-order belief). I then may also believe that fake news and disinformation is targeted against anthropomorphic genesis of climate change (a second-order belief). The second belief challenges the basis for believing the first. Conflict between first and second order beliefs may be reconciled in various ways, including changing one or other belief partially or totally. Epistemic self-doubt resides in the interstices of the belief conflicts and their resolution. When thinking about mistrust, this form of self-doubt is clearly important. Mistrust often springs from beliefs being challenged or undermined by new beliefs.

Epistemic self-doubt is important, but self-doubt is more commonly defined as uncertainty about one's abilities, potential for success or competency. In this guise, the similarity of self-doubt with low self-efficacy is unmistakable. As self-doubt increases, self-esteem tends to decrease. Self-doubt is negatively related to variables such as achievement motivation and narcissism and positively related to self-handicapping, social anxiety and 'impostor' feelings in which success is perceived as undeserved. It includes thoughts and feelings that focus on the bad things that might occur, upon failure rather than success.

Mistrust of one's own beliefs is only one source of self-doubt but it is significant. Being mistrustful of other people is also related to self-doubt. For instance, Ross, Powell and Henriksen (2016) showed how cultural mistrust felt by Black students in the US was associated with loss of a sense of self-worth, self-doubt, psychological distress, and to their decision to opt out of post-secondary education. Cultural mistrust is an example of shared mistrust. Yet, like most shared mistrust, it is played out at the level of individual thought, feeling and action. It is important to ask whether level of acceptance of cultural mistrust is affected by identity processes of self-conceptualisation and evaluation. It is equally useful to ask how far the influences generating and perpetuating cultural mistrust simultaneously influence identity processes in individuals.

The finding that cultural mistrust co-exists in people alongside psychological distress, self-doubt and low self-efficacy needs careful examination. Recognition of the existence of cultural mistrust has certainly changed the way the interactions of people of colour with medical, educational and law enforcement practitioners are understood. 'Cultural mistrust' has come to have a very specific meaning in social science research over the last 20 years. Cultural mistrust has been commonly defined as an adaptive attitudinal stance in which a person of colour in the US is suspicious and guarded toward European Americans, particularly European American authority figures (Whaley, 2001). Such cultural mistrust was defined as adaptive because it was assumed to reflect an accurate appreciation of the systems of discrimination affecting people of colour and to be a basis for more effective self-protection. However, there is evidence that it is associated with decisions that are likely to cause self-harm. For instance, cultural mistrust is widely linked to rejection of health advice and treatment (David, 2010; Cort, 2004; Farquharson & Thornton, 2020).

Sadly, most studies do nothing to prove that cultural mistrust either insures against or exaggerates the appalling negative effects of ethnic disadvantage. Evidence that cultural mistrust is directly causative is missing. However, the intervention studies that have sought to ameliorate the link between cultural mistrust and hostility to medical treatment and practitioners have had some success. Brooks and Hopkins (2017) used a culturally responsive cognitive intervention to neutralise the effects of cultural mistrust on health care attitudes and utilisation. Their method entailed presenting research participants with video images of health care provision and providers that challenged their assumptions about the ethnicity of health workers and their approach to patients of colour. Their strategy was to disconnect generalised cultural mistrust from perceptions of the particular health contexts. They report a significant effect of their intervention. What works here is not exactly an erosion of general cultural mistrust. The experimental intervention serves to delimit the applicability of cultural mistrust. It tries to persuade people of colour that there are contexts where cultural mistrust is inappropriate. We will return to the issue of how shared mistrust becomes the target for manipulation.

Extreme Mistrustfulness

Against the baseline of what might be called 'common mistrust', it is valuable to juxtapose the manifestations of what is called 'extreme mistrustfulness'. Extreme mistrustfulness has a number of characteristics:

- It tends to be irrational, not based on any objective evidence and not responsive to refutation.
- It tends to be generalised – not specific to particular targets, shifting across targets and having multiple targets simultaneously.
- It lasts for long periods (but may involve periods of remission where mistrust abates).
- It has strong negative emotional concomitants.
- It tends to be associated with overt accusations made against others.

Extreme mistrustfulness is typically regarded as a trait (an abiding or persistent characteristic of the person). It is subjectively different from feeling in a state of mistrust that is a reaction to an identified, normally traumatic, experience (e.g. a physical assault or a betrayal). The extreme mistrust state, even though it may be very intense, is relatively transient and specific, linked to some temporally proximate experience. An example would be to become extremely mistrustful of a political leader when he questions the credibility of scientific evidence about the mode of transmission of a virus.

Extreme mistrustfulness as a trait is commonly often found in association with other traits: emotional detachment, loneliness, cynicism, irritability, inordinate anger, impulsivity and many others. While extreme mistrustfulness may exist as a trait without concomitant problems with psychological wellbeing, it is often linked to such problems. The severity of these problems varies. For instance, the literature on veterans shows post-traumatic stress disorder (PTSD) can engender mistrustfulness (Glover, 1984). Other studies suggest mistrustfulness can be characteristic of those who seek hazardous activities (e.g. anti-social and criminal offences but also extreme sports, Görner, Zieliński & Jurczak, 2013).

Extreme mistrustfulness is treated as symptomatic of various psychiatric conditions, including paranoia, and it is used as a diagnostic criterion (see APA, 2013, for discussion of such diagnostic classifications). Paranoia is thinking and feeling that you are being threatened in some way, even when there is no evidence that you are. As a clinical condition, paranoia involves intense anxiety and fear besides feelings of persecution and of being the target of conspiracies. Paranoia occurs in many mental disorders, but is more often present in psychotic disorders. Three main types of paranoia are commonly described: paranoid personality disorder, delusional disorder (formerly called paranoid disorder) and paranoid schizophrenia. Paranoia can also be a feature of depression and bipolar disorder. Extreme mistrustfulness is a diagnostic indicator of paranoia. In such cases, mistrustfulness may appear close to absolute distrust. Yet, extreme mistrustfulness is the label used clinically. This may be because in such cases there is no substantiation for the suspicion and doubt.

So, in the diagnostic classification of borderline personality disorders (which is a subtype of emotionally unstable personality disorders) extreme mistrustfulness is one of the indicators used. Borderline personality disorder (BPD) is characterised by a pervasive pattern of instability in affect regulation, impulse control, interpersonal relationships and self-image. Clinical signs of the disorder include emotional dysregulation (e.g. affective instability, including depression, irritability and anxiety), impulsive aggression, as well as repeated and chronic suicidal tendencies. The cognitive symptoms of BPD include transient stress-related paranoid ideation or severe dissociative symptoms. They also include identity disturbance reflected in persistent instability in the sense of self or self-image. BPD affects interpersonal relationships. Unstable and intense interpersonal relationships that alternate between being viewed as ideal or worthless characterise sufferers, who will also make frantic efforts to avoid real or imagined abandonment. It is clear from this that BPD comprises a heterogeneous constellation of problems. Paranoia and extreme mistrustfulness are fundamental to it (Bach & Lobbestael, 2018; Masland, Schnell & Shah, 2020; Fertuck, Fischer & Beeney, 2018). Causal factors are only partly known, but genetic factors and adverse events during childhood, such as physical and sexual abuse, which produce epistemic mistrust, are thought to contribute to the development of the disorder (Lieb et al., 2004; Winsper, 2018).

BPD centrally involves problems related to identity processes. BPD symptomatology and aetiology reflects problems with what in IPT would be called identity-coherence and identity-continuity, and in what is sometimes called identity diffusion. BPD sufferers are likely to have a history of attachment trauma. Such trauma are known to diminish the ability to build attachments; to be trustful; and to be open to benefiting from positive social experiences to construct a resilient self-image (Luyten, Campbell & Fonagy, 2020). The processes of assimilation, accommodation and evaluation that, according to IPT, maintain identity coherence and continuity are hampered by the limitation of these abilities. Epistemic self-doubt associated with mistrustfulness is particularly damaging. Not knowing whether to trust one's own beliefs, even beliefs about oneself, undermines identity processes. How do you know what should be assimilated? How do you know how to fit the components of identity together so that everything can be accommodated? How do you know what value to attach to any component of identity?

The effect of extreme mistrust on identity processes also comes from its effect upon social cognition and social communication. Both paranoia and BPD, in their various guises, illustrate how maladaptive extreme mistrustfulness can be. They also show that extreme mistrustfulness does not live alone – it is accompanied by a welter of cognitive, emotional and experiential phenomena. Some of these cause the mistrust. Some of these, it causes. It is their complex interactions over time that, at least in part, shape how identity evolves. BPD has been particularly associated with: impairments in the sense of agency or clarity of purpose; being closed to experience; and inflexibility, poor adaptability and lack of spontaneity. This may be because, perhaps in order to avoid more threat, extreme mistrustfulness erects barriers to social communication and this reduces the scope for assimilating the information needed for identity change or self-development. This causes what some call identity rigidity.

Identity Resilience and Mistrust

Everything which has been presented in this chapter, whether in relation to common mistrust or extreme mistrustfulness, has in some way involved identity, including self-efficacy, self-esteem, self-doubt, identity continuity, identity coherence and identity rigidity. All characteristics of identity are imbued with affective connotations and accompaniments. In practice, identity is awash with emotion. In the same sense, mistrust is not just a question of cognitions, it is always also a question of emotions. This leads us back to the earlier model of the relationship between mistrust and emotions.

Figure 4.1 presented a model of the relationships between mistrust and emotion in relation to action. Based on the subsequent examination of the role of identity, it is timely to extend that model by incorporating key identity features. It seems sensible to do this now because it is evident that the status of these key identity features mediates the relationships between mistrust and emotion. Furthermore, it is clear that identity itself is materially affected by mistrust and its sequelae. Figure 4.2 therefore adds the concept of identity resilience.

Many disciplines are now interested in the resilience of systems (e.g. in ecosystems, Cumming et al., 2005). A core concept that is now used in IPT is 'identity resilience'. Identity resilience refers to the extent to which an identity can cope with experiences that would damage its coherence (reflected in perceptions of stability and consistency), continuity and positivity (reflected in perceptions of self-esteem, self-efficacy and optimised distinctiveness). Any index of resilience is a measure of how far a system can retain continuity while permitting change. A resilient identity is one in which the identity processes of change assimilation and accommodation permit further development of coherence, continuity and positivity. This sort of resilience does not precipitate identity rigidity or stagnation. Recognising that change can be a prerequisite for continuity, it is focused on optimal adaptation to change – which will sometimes mean resistance. Two clusters of experience appear to facilitate the development of identity resilience: consistent access to self-confirmatory support

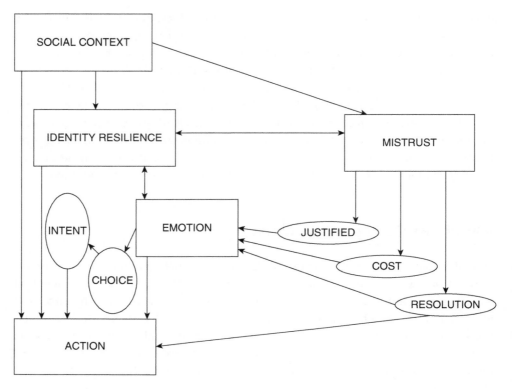

Figure 4.2 Identity Resilience, Mistrust and Emotion

structures (e.g. in one's family, community or place of work) and a track record of dealing successfully with threats (see i.e., Sleijpen et al., 2016; Shih et al., 2019; Libório & Ungar, 2010).

An identity already characterised by lower coherence, continuity or positivity is often less capable of adaptation to change and is less resilient to damage because it cannot implement those coping strategies that would mitigate potentially damaging experiences. Many studies have shown the relationship between identity positivity, coherence and continuity and ability to deal with a wide range of damaging experiences. These include work stress in the medical (Wald, 2015), military (White et al., 2020) and teaching (Day, 2018) professions. They also include discrimination regarding ethnicity (Lee, 2005) or sexual orientation (Meyer, 2010). In addition, the importance of identity resilience has been found in research on ageing and mental health (Manning & Bouchard, 2020) and reactions to trauma (Waterman, 2020). Common across domains is the discovery that identity resilience is associated with having available a repertoire of behaviours, beliefs and strategies that reduce risk exposure and protect against psychological damage.

The figure above now introduces identity resilience into the model previously presented that represents the relationship between mistrust, emotion and action.

The proposed model is informed by the studies that have been described earlier in this chapter that illustrate the relationships between mistrust and aspects of the identity (such as self-doubt, self-efficacy, self-esteem, identity continuity, identity coherence and identity rigidity). The model proposes a two-way influence between identity resilience and mistrust. The actual nature of these influences will possibly depend on three factors:

- The overall identity resilience.
- The resilience of specific elements of identity.
- The object and significance of mistrust.

Taking the effect of identity resilience upon mistrust first. Overall level of identity resilience will affect interpretation of the information upon which mistrust is based. The same information will be given different meaning and significance when identity resilience is high than when it is low. For instance, low identity resilience might exaggerate the import of some chance event and push towards mistrust, whereas high identity resilience might ignore such an event. In contrast, high identity resilience might precipitate mistrust if the information received serves to threaten the positivity or continuity of identity. So, the actual influence of identity resilience is not some simple equation (e.g. higher resilience = lower mistrust). The perceived basis and significance to identity of the mistrust would need to be incorporated into the equation. Also, since identity resilience is composed of a series of interacting processes, such as self-esteem and self-doubt, the specific significance that mistrust has for each of these processes will moderate how identity resilience levels affect mistrust.

The model does not indicate a direct route between identity resilience and mistrust justification, cost and resolution. It is assumed that there is an indirect route through mistrust. It merits empirical test whether there is a direct route to perceived justification, cost and resolution in specific types of mistrust situations. Logically, one is not required but, in practice, it may exist.

Mistrust is postulated to have a direct effect upon identity resilience. This is suggested particularly by the studies of extreme mistrust that have previously been described. However, it is also envisaged that mistrust will have an indirect influence upon identity resilience through its impact on emotion. Identity resilience, in turn, is acknowledged to affect emotion directly. Poor identity resilience would be expected to accentuate the extent of negative emotions across the spectrum.

Finally, action is seen to be directly influenced by social context, identity resilience, emotion and mistrust (via perceived resolution options). In addition to its direct effect, emotion will influence action indirectly through choice and then intention. In Figure 4.2, unlike Figure 4.1, the relationship between intent and action is not presented as recursive. In some situations, it will be the case that action feeds back upon intention. It is worth examining empirically when this happens in relation to mistrust. In general, the model here is not mapping the possible feedback trajectories from action. The exception is the direct impact of action on emotion. The capacity for action and its consequences to change emotion is significant. Identity resilience will also be a direct determiner of action particularly through the effects of self-efficacy. In addition, action will be affected to the extent to which identity is seeking to enhance coherence, continuity, distinctiveness or self-esteem. Each would presage modification of action, depending upon circumstances. Again, the research literature is littered with examples of the effects on behaviour of efforts to protect particular identity elements (e.g. Brewer, 2019, on distinctiveness; Saiphoo, Halevi & Vahedi, 2020, on self-esteem; and Baral & Arachchilage, 2019, on self-efficacy).

The model notes the independent influence of the social context upon both mistrust and identity resilience. In other chapters, the broader social circumstances that surround mistrust and the operation of identity processes are considered. Here it is worth re-emphasising the role of shared uncertainty, described in the preceding chapter, upon both mistrust and identity.

Figure 4.3 is identical to Figure 4.2 except that it deals with extreme mistrust and, consequently, indicates that there is a direct route between it and emotion. All of the literature on extreme mistrust, particularly from work on BPD and paranoia, suggests

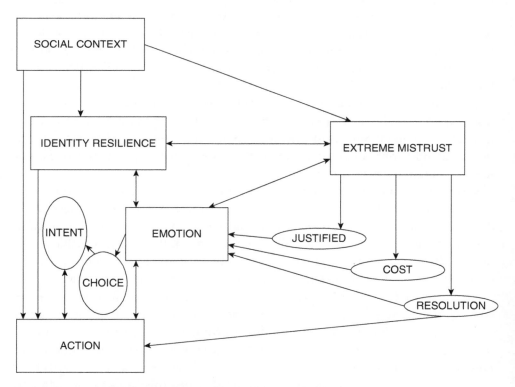

Figure 4.3   Identity Resilience, Extreme Mistrust and Emotion

that extreme mistrust will manifest in emotions, without mediation or moderation through assessments of justification, cost or opportunities for resolution. Extreme mistrust seems to be invested with inevitable emotionality. Emotions are an integral part of what define it as extreme.

Practical Relevance of Modelling Identity, Mistrust and Emotion Influences on Behaviour: An Example

This sort of modelling of the effects of identity resilience and mistrust on emotion and on behaviour has more than mere theoretical interest. In the context of the COVID-19 pandemic that was declared by the WHO in 2020, while treatments for the disease and vaccination against the coronavirus were developed, it became vital to control the rate of infection through behaviour change. The public were exhorted to adopt hygiene measures, social distancing, self-isolation and 'test and trace' protocols. In addition to imposed restrictions, the strategy for disease control depended upon voluntary compliance with these guidelines. In a series of studies, Breakwell, Jaspal and Fino (Breakwell & Jaspal, 2020; Jaspal & Breakwell, 2020; Jaspal, Fino & Breakwell, 2020) studied what factors were associated with the likelihood of people complying with guidance and regulation concerning COVID-19 preventive behaviours. Working within the IPT framework, they explored how identity resilience related to emotions concerning COVID-19 (particularly fear) and mistrust (particularly of science and scientists). They found that lower identity resilience was related to greater uncertainty about which preventive measures should be adopted, and with greater fear of COVID-19. Adoption of preventive behaviours was positively correlated with fear of COVID-19 and with low levels of mistrust of science and scientists. It was interesting that low levels of mistrust of science and scientists correlated positively with perceived personal risk of infection and this, in turn, correlated with fear of the disease. It seems that accepting what scientists had to say about the virus not only had a direct effect on the likelihood of taking preventive measures, it also had the effect of encouraging preventive behaviour indirectly through raising perceived risk, which in turn raised fear of COVID-19. This set of studies illustrates the practical value of modelling the interactive effects of identity resilience, emotion and mistrust. A key conclusion is that changing mistrust of prime targets is likely to change behaviour in such complex hazards.

Navigational Aids

Focusing on the association between mistrust and identity processes in both common and extreme circumstances emphasises the great complexity of their interactions.

This chapter has looked at the relative positions of the mistrustful and the mistrusted, and sought to understand the impact of mistrust on emotion. Self-efficacy and helplessness, self-doubt, and identity resilience were all considered in relation to mistrust, and in relation to its behavioural implications. There is quite a lot packed into this chapter. The models presented in the figures are meant to offer an initial navigational aid. However, they are also models that can be subjected to empirical test or, perhaps more accurately, elaboration. They are further elaborated in later chapters (see Chapters 7, 8 and 9) where the communication processes and channels within the social context are examined. The example here of the studies on COVID-19 preventive behaviours was meant to encourage further empirical work. It is only by examining manifestations of mistrust in specific circumstances that we will be able to determine the nature and extent of the causal influences at work.

CHAPTER 5
IMAGES OF THE MISTRUSTED

It is time to look at the characteristics attributed to people that are mistrusted. There are prototypes, stereotypes and caricatures of 'the mistrusted'. The mistrusted are not homogeneous. In fact, they come in all sorts of shapes and sizes. Indeed, the concept encompasses things as well as people (e.g. machines). 'The mistrusted' is a conceptual group like those described in Chapter 3. A conceptual group is a social categorisation accepted to exist because circumstances identify commonalities across people, or because it is arbitrarily imposed by others with power who assert the group exists. The mistrusted is, in practice, a superordinate conceptual group encompassing within itself many different exemplars. Many images of the mistrusted prevail in modern societies. Each captures its own multi-faceted aspect of the conceptual group. The form of each will depend on the purpose it evolved to serve.

Prototypes, Stereotypes and Caricatures

Prototypes

In considering the variety of images it is worth distinguishing between prototypes, stereotypes and caricatures because they serve different purposes. A prototype in psychology refers to what is believed to be a complete cognitive representation of something in a certain category, with all its expected qualities and characteristics present. It can be used to as a template against which to judge new people or things, facilitating identification, categorisation and information storage besides indicating appropriate behavioural responses. A prototype is an amalgam of characteristics representing the ideal (or more often the central) type within a category. It does not have to be embodied in a single actual member of the category, past or present.

However, real individuals sometimes are used to represent the prototype. For instance, who would you say quintessentially represented the category of monarchs of England, or Presidents of the US, or practical engineers, or professional tennis players, or pioneering scientists or fast automobiles? Would it be Queen Elizabeth I, Abraham Lincoln, Isambard Kingdom Brunel, Martina Navratilova (or Roger Federer), Marie Curie and Bugatti? There is much room for debate. You might have chosen other figures. The examples given probably reflect positive prototypes of their category; you might have chosen negative ones. The categories are broad. In such categories, the prototype morphs over eras and for different generations of people. Navratilova may give way to the Williams sisters, Lincoln to Obama.

Nevertheless, such prototypes are usually a common currency for social representations of the category. In fact, they can only emerge and be useful as prototypes if there is some social consensus about their value in typifying the category. This does not have to be total consensus. Actually, quite often there are contending figures that are put forward as prototypes and people choose which better fits their own idea of the category or which suits their own purposes. For instance, advocacy for a prototype can be political or cultural positioning or an act of aggression. Prototypes are one of the many tools for disseminating the social representation of a category.

When it comes to the mistrusted, the range of prototypes reflects the wide variety of bases for mistrust. Who do you think is a prototype for mistrusted physicians? Or for likely-to-cheat spouses? Or for dubious politicians? Or for possible sexual harassers? Or unreliable airlines? Or suspect healthy diet regimes? While it is difficult to guess who or what you will have chosen, it is a fair bet that you will have chosen different prototypes in each class of the mistrusted. It is an even better bet that the ones you have chosen would also be chosen by people you know or respect. You might want to check that out. If you concur, it suggests that you agree with these others about the characteristics of people or things that deserve mistrust.

It is likely that the nature of the questions will have pushed you to nominate publicly available exemplars. For instance, you might have said Dr Harold Shipman, who was an English medical doctor convicted killer of over 200 of his own patients, for the prototype of the mistrusted physician. To the extent that they are publicly identified, some prototypes of the mistrusted tend to have been proven worthy of distrust in retrospect. Others remain genuinely exemplars of mistrust in that the jury is still out about them, and the questions and doubt persist. Prototype figures for the class of mistrusted who sit on the periphery of societally unacceptable behaviour or criminality (e.g. collaborators with or beneficiaries of crime) may be long-lived because suspicions are neither confirmed nor dispelled completely. For instance, frauds in the financial sector, sexual abuse in religious contexts or dirty tricks in politics, all produce exemplars of 'the peripheral mistrusted' over whom doubt hangs.

The status of these exemplars as prototypes sometimes long-outlives the individuals or organisations concerned. The Crédit Mobilier scandal of 1872–73 (Foner & Garraty, 1991) in the US illustrates this. Crédit Mobilier, created by major stockholders of the Union Pacific Railroad, was a company that was given contracts to build the railroad. Shares in the construction company were given or sold to influential congressmen, who subsequently approved federal subsidies allowing the railroad builders, and indirectly themselves, to make inordinate profits. A newspaper revealed the story on the eve of the 1872 presidential election. A congressional committee was convened and it censured two House members who were involved in the scandal. However, the affair also tarnished the careers of the outgoing vice president, Schuyler Colfax, and incoming vice president, Henry Wilson. The scandal is used now as an illustration of how corruption tainted 'Gilded Age' politics in the US. The individuals associated with it could be said to be long-lived prototypes of the peripheral mistrusted at the interface of politics and business.

Stereotypes

A stereotype is a set of expectations and beliefs about people who are members of a particular category of people. 'Red-haired people are quick to anger' is a simple stereotype. Like other stereotypes, it represents an erroneous overgeneralisation. Like others, it is used as a justification for ill-founded prejudices or ignorance, for failing to rethink one's attitudes and behaviour, and for excluding or demeaning people. An example of a stereotype of the mistrusted can be derived from a detective agency advertisement. It said watch for the signs of a cheating spouse: changes in intimate behaviour; suspicious phone habits; changes in appearance; suspicious internet use; changes in work routine; and changes in bathing habits. The stereotype of cheating spouses emerging is clear – even though it does not mention unexplained absences or clothes redolent with an unfamiliar eau de cologne.

Stereotypes of the mistrusted are interesting because they populate the imagination with things to be suspicious about or fearful of. Also, they may seriously mislead. By failing to conform to the stereotype, someone that should be mistrusted may evade mistrust. Equally, by conforming to the stereotype, someone may be mistrusted that should not be mistrusted. Stereotypes are dangerous bases for making good decisions, though they can be made excellent bases for rationalising bad ones.

Stereotypes do often reference mistrust even when they are not focused on the mistrusted per se. Being 'mistrusted' appears in such stereotypes alongside other descriptors of a category (e.g. paparazzi photographers have been stereotyped as being aggressive and intrusive, lacking respect and without a sense of guilt and as people always to be mistrusted). This pattern of using 'mistrusted' as a part of a group's stereotype is widespread. Incorporated into the group stereotype, it immediately challenges the worthiness and value of the group and its members. It is more useful as a basis for discriminating against a group than saying it is distrusted because an accusation of mistrust does not have to be substantiated with so much evidence. Merely by pinning suspicion to the group, the damage can be done.

In intercultural and intergroup relations, the use of mistrust in stereotypes is commonplace (Chambers & Melnyk, 2006). Gibson et al. (2017) emphasised that even in cultures where there are strong norms against explicitly expressing negative outgroup attitudes or stereotypes, children are still taught to mistrust other groups. Mistrust comes to the fore particularly in the stereotypes of specific groups. Gypsies, Roma and Travellers have faced daily prejudice for generations based on negative stereotyping, and the associated racism and myth-building (Powell, 2008). While there have been serious attempts to challenge and erase these stereotypes, through work in the arts and media, academia and education, and in political and human rights organisations, the stereotypes persist. They are shown time and again to be ill-founded and to result in grave mistreatment but they survive, supported partly through media representations (Council of Europe, 2011). The element of the stereotypes that is most resilient to change is that which paints these people as liars, thieves, swindlers, outside the law and so on, to be mistrusted.

That mistrust is such a common characteristic in intergroup negative stereotypes suggests the power that it has both as a means of cementing the ingroup together and as a way of undermining credibility and opportunities for gaining support for the outgroup. Mistrust can be seen as a foundation stone of intergroup relations. Later chapters will come back to the use of manipulating mistrust as a weapon.

Caricatures

Caricatures offer a picture, description or imitation of a person or thing in which striking characteristics are exaggerated in order to create a grotesque or comic effect – but usually to make a point, to highlight a weakness or lay bare inconsistency. Caricatures are often used to unveil aspects of an individual or object that should be mistrusted, or to be scornful of the mistrusted.

When one thinks of caricatures, the cartoons in daily newspapers that lampoon politicians, the rich and the famous immediately spring to mind. These often present their targets in ways that show they should be mistrusted. For instance, during the debate preceding the decision of the UK to leave the EU, subtle and not-so-subtle mistrust images were common. One entitled 'Brexit Suicide' showed a man wearing a Union Jack, looking uncomprehending, and walking off a cliff into the sea. Another, published in the US, depicted the incumbent Prime Minister of the UK saying 'I've decided to step down …' as he walked the plank off a pirate ship with a cutlass at his back (on which was pinned a note 'Brexit Vote').

Caricatures can say things about the mistrusted that various social mores would not permit elsewhere. For instance, the British satirical television puppet show Spitting Image, started in 1984–1996 and revived in 2020, cast a withering (and often hilarious) eye on politics, sport and culture in the broadest sense. The puppets are caricatures of the leading figures in the era of the show including Prime

Ministers, Presidents, Royalty, footballers, cricketers and celebrities of all sorts. The show set out to satirise and parody and if there were kernels of truth they were not allowed to get in the way of the role allotted each caricature in the cast. But not infrequently, the shows reflected public surmise and suspicions about the characters portrayed – suspected drug or alcohol abuse, purely selfish motivations for political decisions, excessive cosmetic surgery, sexual-obsessions, cloak-and-dagger cover ups and malicious in-fighting. Mostly scurrilous, and if presented in almost any other way unacceptable, it allowed mistrust to surface, especially interpersonal mistrust between the puppets.

While cartoonists and puppeteers may go beyond the pale and might be given latitude others do not have, they serve a vital role in representing subterranean mistrust. They have unique channels to say things about leading figures and raise issues of mistrust. The images of the mistrusted that they portray may be comic and sometimes difficult to decode, but are they are all the more interesting for that.

Objectification and Anchoring through Prototypes, Stereotypes and Caricatures

Prototypes, stereotypes and caricatures are all routes into understanding the images that we hold of the mistrusted. They all act as conduits for social representations of the mistrusted. They also are the subject of social representation processes. Two social representation processes, anchoring and objectification, were described in Chapter 1. Prototypes and caricatures most obviously objectify the characteristics of types of people, one through identifying a core exemplar of the type and the other by making the characteristics visible through exaggeration and use of commonly understood symbols. Stereotypes particularly offer anchoring – individual candidates for mistrust are attributed with an array of characteristics that are part of a well-understood image of the mistrusted.

Ranking Untrustworthiness

Another way to understand the features of the mistrusted conceptual group is by perusing the many rankings of individuals, professions and groups in terms of their level of untrustworthiness. Basically, these describe which groups most people mistrust. They are not exclusively about the mistrusted as a single conceptual group. Instead, they indicate which types of groups feature most regularly as mistrusted by most people.

Surveys asking samples to rate categories of people and things on the dimension of trustworthy–untrustworthy are done regularly, but with varying degrees of methodological rigour. These surveys also differ in the actual questions they pose.

For instance, some are concerned with which categories are believed to tell the truth and some are concerned with who will be able to deliver on promises. Furthermore, they vary in the specificity of the questions they pose. For instance, some are explicit about the timeframe for the assessments (e.g. what do you think today?); others are more open-ended (not even saying in which country the target groups reside). Sensible comparisons across findings from different surveys are consequently hard to make.

Some polling organisations have done surveys using the same method over several years and they do allow interesting comparisons over time. In the UK, Ipsos MORI is one such company. In May 2020, Ipsos MORI (2020a), in the midst of the COVID-19 pandemic, surveyed 1000 people over the age of 15 in the UK, and asked them to say if they generally trusted each of 27 sorts of people to tell them the truth (they call this a Veracity Index). Their findings included: 97% of those sampled believed nurses could be generally trusted to tell the truth (up 2% from December 2018), 95% trusted doctors (up 3%), 89% teachers, 87% scientists (up 2%), 83% weather forecasters, 82% police (up 9%), 58% EU leaders (up 15%), 54% ordinary person in the street (down 7%), 47% government ministers (up 20%), 45% charity chief executives, 43% business leaders (up 5%), 42% journalists (down 4%), 33% bankers (up 6%), 32% politicians (up 10%), 30% estate agents, 17% advertising executives and 8% social media influencers (down 2%).

Such lists are interesting – the jump in the number perceiving EU leaders as truthful after the outcome of the Brexit vote, and the improvement in the position of government ministers after a radical change in the Cabinet and of politicians generally after changes in Party leaderships, for instance. The decline in numbers trusting the truthfulness of the ordinary person in the street in the context of the pandemic is worth consideration. Such lists do not say anything about how much a category is trusted or mistrusted with regard to specific issues or tasks. There is no insight into whether, for instance, nurses are believed to tell the truth about everything or just about health issues. Do the majority think estate agents can be trusted to tell the truth about nothing? Do the majority think weather forecasters tell the truth but that their forecasts are not to be trusted? This line of argument leads to a fundamental question. Is trusting a person to tell the truth the same as believing them to be trustworthy? Perhaps that depends on what they are telling the truth about. The weather forecaster may tell you what she honestly believes will happen and you may trust her truthfulness. But do you trust her ability to provide an accurate prediction? Truthfulness is only one aspect of trustworthiness.

Nevertheless, the approach in the Veracity Index is useful because it does allow the tracking perceptions of truthfulness in a single group over longer periods and for that trajectory to be mapped against significant events. Ipsos MORI is able to track changes for some groups since 1983. There are ups and downs in public trust in their truthfulness over the 1983–2019 period but in the main their relative positions do not change and there is remarkable stability in the percentage trusting them.

There are two marked exceptions to this. Perceived truthfulness of the clergy and priests declined by 21% in contrast to an increase of 40% for civil servants.

The method also allows trust in these groups to be cross-tabulated with characteristics of the sample. For instance, differences between Conservative and Labour party supporters were examined in the 2019 survey (Ipsos MORI, 2019). Labour supporters were more likely to trust doctors, teachers, scientists, judges, civil servants, trades unionists, local councillors and journalists to tell the truth. Conservative supporters were more likely to trust the police, armed forces and bankers. Educational attainment also differentiates trust levels. With regard to most of the different categories of people, degree holders are more likely to trust than are those with no formal qualifications. However, degree holders were more likely to mistrust bankers, estate agents, advertising executives and politicians to tell the truth. Who is mistrusted is dependent upon the broader belief systems and upon the personal experiences of those surveyed.

While these polls reveal individual variations in trust given to different professional groups, they also present a sort of temperature reading for the level of prevalent mistrust of each of the groups. The stability in relative mistrust levels over three or more decades is worth noting. They may be reflecting the vitality of the stereotypes of each of the groups. They probably indicate that, with minor variations, they are not responding to evidence that would contradict them or that the evidence available just reinforces them. However, they are not immune to change. The decline in numbers trusting the clergy or priests shows that significant shifts do occur. This is particularly noteworthy in a profession that had been trusted by a high percentage of people previously. Various types of scandal, not limited to one form of religion, may have brought about this change. Evidently, trust is not immutable, neither is mistrust (illustrated by the improved position of civil servants).

It is against this backdrop of long-term public trust or mistrust that the behaviour of groups and their membership in any contemporary situation is interpreted. Over a 37-year period to 2019, British government ministers were not trusted to tell the truth by between 89% and 75% of those sampled. During that time, there were 14 Governments under seven different Prime Ministers. The majority's mistrust of government ministers is consistent over time and irrespective of personnel. This is mistrust of the ministerial category rather than the individual (though prototypes of the mistrusted minister have undoubtedly occasionally emerged).

This has enormous importance when a Government is faced with a crisis and ministers are required to develop and implement unpopular strategies – for instance, when dealing with a global pandemic. They start with a trust deficit. Perceived to be untruthful by the majority, ministers have to find a way to 'sell' their strategy to the public – especially if it requires public compliance, which is the case in many crises. The role of intermediaries (e.g. the mass and social media, social influencers and trusted professionals) in this is vital. For instance, in 2020, the UK government sought to bolster public trust in their response to COVID-19 by reference to the scientific and medical expertise they were marshalling to develop their plans to control the spread of the virus. At this point, it is important to acknowledge that mistrust of the truthfulness of ministers in this sort of situation will bleed into doubts about their competence and suspicion of their motives. After all, the argument goes in pubs across the country, if they cannot be trusted to tell the truth, what can they be trusted to do? This question really is rhetorical; no one wants to hear an answer. The answer might mean having to change the stereotypical mistrusted image of politicians in general and ministers in particular.

The Mistrusted in Popular Culture

So far this chapter has been concerned with some of the major vehicles for encapsulating images of the mistrusted (like prototypes, stereotypes and caricatures) and the sort of evidence (such as polling data) revealing what categories of people are most mistrusted. It is worth considering now how these images are propagated and sustained through the work of popular culture. Popular culture is the set of practices, beliefs and objects that embody the most broadly shared meanings of a social system. It is the medium within which the archive of social representations lives. It includes the products of the mass and social media (music, print, televisual and digital), as well as fashion, art, leisure, advertising and majors sports events among other things.

Images of the mistrusted pervade popular culture. For instance, popular songs are a great source of images of people who cheat in a relationship. What's more, it is possible to trace how these images shift, or actually barely change, over the decades since the 1950s. You might take a wander from 'Your Cheatin' Heart' by Hank Williams Snr in 1953, through 'Careless Whisper' by George Michael in 1984, via 'Love the Way You Lie' by Eminem in 2010, to 'Sorry' by Beyoncé in 2016. Songs like these are products of their time and place (and the artist who wrote them of course). Songs like these capture contemporary memes. The commonalities over several decades in the image of cheaters in such songs are evident – they lie, they are plausible, they are calculating, they are incorrigible but suspected of being redeemable, and, of course, they *do* betray you. It is interesting that the songs often carry messages of both heartbreak and forgiveness. Simple castigation of the cheater is rare. The songs reflect the complexities of retaining real relationships. In doing so, they tell us something about the image of this sort of mistrusted character. It is one most people will come across and one which many people will find applied to themselves at some point. The songs also have a part to play in telling us what to expect in relationships and how to react in them. They talk about the process of being cheated as one of doubt, suspicion and ultimate discovery but, often, with continuing uncertainty about what it means. This is a mistrust process. Of course, the generalisations based on popular music from the post-industrialised West of the mid-20th century would be misleading if applied in some other cultures or other times. The real point here is that such societal 'ephemera' are a window into images of the mistrusted. Also, because of their form, they are powerfully memorable (even if only in fragments and phrases).

Other forms of popular culture tackle different categories of mistrusted. Soap operas portray possible fraudsters and scoundrels. The story lines unravel the complex fabric of truth and lies woven around these characters. The medium allows a depiction evolving over many episodes; allowing suspense and suspicion to flourish, building the reality and relevance of the characters. Embody the character in a well-known actor and the image of the mistrusted becomes iconic – prototypical. Also, this cultural form can be eloquent in showing how mistrust can be misplaced. It can illustrate how people can be mistrusted unjustly. It can present the complex multi-layered structure of the social representations of mistrust. Gloriously, from the point of view of the social psychological analysis, it can do this without the audience generally recognising that their images of the mistrusted are being influenced.

It would be possible to go on listing examples of the ways popular art forms capture images of the mistrusted. One that immediately surfaces is the way film and television dramas present terrorism and link it predominantly to particular categories of people (defined by ethnicity, or political beliefs, or religion and so on). The association, even if only in fiction, between the social category and the tragedies of terrorism may justify mistrust of its members. This may both initiate and enhance a stereotype of that social category.

Rather than continuing with examples, it may be as profitable to divert into a consideration of how far popular cultural forms manufacture mistrust and how far they merely mirror what is already out there in society. It is obvious that they can do both. However, that is too simple a description of what happens in practice. In the main, they do not merely copy what is already evident and common knowledge, nor do they invent a full-blown novel image of the mistrusted. They absorb, from diverse sources, images that are nascent. They elaborate them, ensuring that they chime with dominant social representations but without losing their ability to entertain and capture followers. Among many other forms, they do this through comedy, horror or, indeed, sports coverage. Who can forget the repeat broadcasts of the Maradona 'Hand of God' goal in the 1986 World Cup football quarter finals match between Argentina and England against the backdrop of the jingoistic international mistrust following the Falklands War of 1982?

The public are immersed in these various forms of popular culture. They are, for many people, the prime sources of their images of the mistrusted. As we go on to examine deliberate manufacture and manipulation of mistrust in other chapters, this foundation role of popular cultural forms will be seen in the broader context.

One vital aspect of popular culture has not been discussed here. The role of social media platforms has deliberately been left until later. It deserves to be considered separately, even though it is dependent on other popular culture outlets. Indeed, social media channels provide material for those outlets. They also recycle and re-evaluate the products of those outlets.

Images and Social Representations

The important thing to remember about social representations is that they are nego-tiated through social communication. Images of the mistrusted (whether presented as prototypes, stereotypes or caricatures or in some other format) are constructed through social interactions that are complex and iterative over time. These are con-strained and mediated through the available channels of communication. Popular culture (in its various guises) is one element in the system that shapes communica-tion opportunities. Popular culture is the prime medium for social representation processes.

The image attached to any one category of the mistrusted is normally initially a product of reported personal experiences and second-hand narratives shared and often censored or elaborated and moulded through conflict and compromise. However, this initial formulation of the image is then subject to other processes which act to develop it but also to proselytise for it. A plethora of social psychologi-cal theories, including models of social influence, cognition and prejudice, has been used to explain the processes involved. Each of them offers insight into why the images of some mistrusted groups are stable over time and resistant to evidence that should change them. Some of these models have been introduced earlier in rela-tion to the effects of mistrust on identity processes. Social cognition models used alongside SRT are helpful in explaining the stability of images of the mistrusted. The role of popular culture in preserving the stability of an image through the rehearsal and valorisation of pre-existent social representations is important. SRT would also suggest that popular culture could mobilise social interaction in such a way that, when faced with a novel target for mistrust, a new image will be manufactured. In fact, this has been seen to occur. Many of the health scares that have been swathed in mistrust (and demonising of those mistrusted as a result) have relied on the plat-forms of popular culture in order to take root and grow. For instance, news reports online and in the press over more than a decade have suggested that Chinese manu-facturers of products such as children's toys are flaunting safety standards adopted in other countries and as a consequence are threatening children's health. This has continued despite recent repeated scientific refutations (Igweze, Ekhator & Orisakwe, 2020). These claims may be resilient because they chime with anti-Chinese feeling and rhetoric.

Images of People, not Institutions

The images considered above largely refer to types or categories of people. They are not targeted at institutions. Of course, capturing the distinction between an insti-tution and the people who populate it is in practice a difficult task. How do you distinguish the Government from its Ministers? It becomes easier if you define an institution in terms of its purposes and practices rather than its personnel. So, for instance, once you think of government as the generic institution whereby political direction and control is exercised rather than as any specific Government, the separation of the institution from its current employees may be simpler. You can think in the same way about the distinctions between religion and clerics, science and scientists, law and lawyers, or education and teachers. Institutions outlive their members. Institutions typically have codes of practice and rules targeted at the behaviour of their members but impinging more widely.

Institutions are magnets for mistrust. Ward et al. (2016) described the predictors and extent of institutional trust in government, banks, the media and religious organisations. Images of mistrusted institutions tend to be characterised in terms of their failure to deliver on their professed purposes and their failure to live up to their own declared codes of practice and rules. This may happen because, among other things, individuals within the institution break its rules or because circumstances change and the institution fails to adapt. Whatever the reason, the failures change the level of trust in the institution as a whole.

The intriguing thing is that the perception of the trustworthiness of an institution is massively affected by the personal circumstances of the perceiver. The OECD (2019) research has found that lower levels of education and income are linked with lower levels of trust in other people in general and in government. Hudson (2006) reanalysed data from the Eurobarometer surveys covering the 15 countries of the EU prior to its expansion in 2004 to examine the relationships between trust/mistrust in various institutions and psychosocial characteristics of the respondents. He found trust in some institutions is associated positively with people's psychological well-being. Trust in the national government, the European Central Bank, the law and the United Nations is correlated positively with greater happiness. Personal experience of the workings of the institutions was also related to trust. Divorce was linked to greater mistrust in the law, and unemployment to greater mistrust of institutions responsible for economic policy. He also found trust varies over a life cycle. For some institutions, the age–trust relationship is non-linear, with mistrust reaching a peak between the ages of 44–56 years. Furthermore, trust in different institutions differed substantially within and between countries. Hudson took this to support the contention that trust is partly endogenous, reflecting the attributes and performance of the institution, even though it is also partly a product of the socio-cognitive status of the person rating trustworthiness. So it does seem that over and above personal viewpoints, institutional failures change trust levels in institutions.

Changes in trust levels in institutions are important for a number of reasons. Perhaps most interesting is the effect that they may have on social trust. Social trust is a slippery concept but there is some consensus that it is a belief in the honesty, integrity and reliability of other people in general. A link between institutional trust and broader social trust levels is regularly found. Sønderskov & Dinesen (2016) found that trust in state institutions is actually a prominent explanation of social trust.

Previously, mainly cross-sectional analyses had provided correlational evidence regarding this relationship. In contrast, their study utilised two Danish panel surveys containing measures of both types of trust for the same individuals surveyed at multiple points in time over a long timespan (up to 18 years). This allowed them to address the question of direction of causality and to determine whether any common confounding factors (e.g. dispositions underlying both types of trust) were actually accounting for the correlation usually found. Using individual fixed effects and cross-lagged panel statistical modelling, they presented strong evidence of trust in state institutions exercising a causal impact on social trust. This is important, if only because it suggests a ripple effect in mistrust from institutional failure to wider social life and communication processes.

When these institutional failures occur, social representation processes operate to describe and explain them. Since institutional failures most often represent a major threat, public awareness becomes a matter of great significance. Managing the resultant mistrust may be the prime objective not only for the miscreant institution but also for any others associated with it in any way. In respect to images of the mistrusted, it is important here to say that institutions wholesale can be reclassified as 'mistrusted'. The financial crisis of 2007–2008 illustrates the point. Excessive risk-taking by banks combined with the bursting of the US housing bubble caused the values of securities tied to US real estate to plummet, damaging financial institutions globally, culminating with the bankruptcy of Lehman Brothers, a financial services firm, on 15 September 2008, and an international banking crisis. This sparked a recession that at the time was the most severe global recession since the Great Depression of 1929. Mistrust of the whole financial sector but particularly of banks was rampant. This mistrust, in various manifestations, has persisted. In 2020, as economic recession followed global pandemic, suspicion and doubt about the banking sector again was quick to come to the fore. Once reclassified into 'the mistrusted', it is hard for an institution to escape. There is an old German proverb to the effect that 'mistrust carries one so much further than trust'. It certainly reverberates around an institution for longer.

Institutional trust is closely linked to broader cultural belief systems in historical and contemporary context. Yang and Tang (2010) point to the finding that China displays a very high level of trust in institutions. Using survey data, they showed that institutional trust in China is more than a product of traditional values. It primarily stems from an individual rational choice based heavily on the evaluations of the institutional performance, though it is also a result of government-controlled politicisation. Trust in administrative institutions, in particular, mainly came from perception of satisfactory institutional performance. Again, the significance of perceived 'failure' to deliver on its professed purposes and standards seems to be basic to institutional mistrust. The differences between China and some other countries in trust levels could therefore originate in several sources: Chinese institutions actually fail less; Chinese people are less likely to identify that failures have occurred; or

Chinese people are less likely to respond to surveys in a manner that reveals their mistrust. However, it seems highly likely that levels of institutional mistrust are a product of both the actual institutional performance (and its evaluation by the public) and the historical and contemporary cultural context that shapes what is thought to constitute poor performance and justify mistrust.

Methodological Limitations

Much of the empirical research on images of the mistrusted relies on survey methods. The findings must be used carefully so as not to go beyond what can be justified by the data (Breakwell, Wright & Barnett, 2020). In order to be safer when using data on trust/mistrust there are certain things to take into account:

- What was the precise question asked?
  - Were respondents asked how much they trusted people to tell the truth? Or were they asked how much they trusted people to do what they said they would do? Or were they asked how much they trusted people to be able to do what they said? Or were they asked how much they trust people to be motivated to do what they said? Essentially, the question might be about trust in the person's or institution's talk, action, competence or motivation. The reason it matters is that levels of trust in the same person may differ markedly across these four domains. For instance, UK politicians did not do very well when the question concerned trust in them telling the truth; circa 20% of people in samples taken across several decades trusted them. But if asked whether they could be trusted to do what is right, circa 40% of people trusted them.
- Who or what is it that is being asked about?
  - Were respondents asked about a specific person or people in a general category? Were they asked about someone they know or about hypothetical characters? Were they asked about a discrete entity (e.g. a particular school) or about a broad construct with many interpretations (e.g. education)? Again, estimates of trust will vary with familiarity and specificity of the target for evaluation.
- What is the scale that is used to index trust?
  - Every type of scaling instrument under the sun has been used at one time or another to index trust. There is the straightforward: do you or don't you trust X? There is the comparative approach: rank V, W, X, Y & Z in order of how much you trust them. There is the 'how much do you trust X?' approach. This usually entails rating trust in X on a 5pt, 7pt or 9pt Likert-type scale, where the points on the scale are often given labels ranging between not at all to completely. Sometimes this approach is converted into a pseudo-ratio measure by having the rating done on a continuous scale (like a ruler). Essentially, there are big differences in the levels of measurement used to index trust. Relative levels of trust in different targets are found to vary across levels of measurement (OECD, 2017). Not surprisingly,

if given greater latitude to distinguish between targets by using more differentiating scales people will discriminate more. Targets that would have fallen into the mistrusted category if only a binary measure is used will often be placed on the mid-point or higher on a more graduated scale. This matters a lot if you are using scaled data to guide your conclusions and perhaps as a foundation for action or policy.

- Are the statistical analyses used appropriate for the level of measurement of the data?
  - o Sometimes, researchers use complex statistics to model relationships between variables in their data sets. This can be enormously valuable. However, it is essential that the data used is compliant with the basic assumptions of the statistics employed. When accessing reports of studies of trust/mistrust it is always safest to check that you understand how the data have been used.

- What population was sampled? What is the socio-demographic structure of the sample questioned?
  - o This follows on from the previous point. Any sample can be interesting and potentially valuable but you need to know what it comprises before using it. Attached to this is the issue of how data were collected. This may have had an impact upon the sample and upon what the sample were willing to say. Online surveying is increasingly used and certainly quicker than other questionnaire-data collection methods. However, since it relies on digital access and competence, it can skew samples towards the more affluent, younger and better educated. For some research topics, this may not matter, for work on trust it probably is significant. Good researchers will examine their data to identify evidence of effects of the medium of data collection on either sampling or on responses. They will alert their readers to these issues.

- Is it only self-report?
  - o Most surveys involve questionnaires and people simply give the researcher a direct answer to a question. They report on themselves, their thoughts and their own actions and feelings. The problem is that the researcher has no idea whether they are accurate reports or biased by lack of self-awareness, by error, or by intent. Questionnaire designers try to get over this by asking questions several times, in different ways or by including deliberate lie detector tests. None of this is certain to ensure data validity or reliability. Interestingly, Murtin et al. (2018) report that the OECD tried using alternative experimental techniques and observation to measure trust in government in samples of circa 1000 people in six countries. They found a positive correlation between levels of trust revealed in self-report and those exhibited in experimental conditions. So you could argue that self-report is a reasonable source of information about mistrust (even though we may be wise to seriously think about how much we trust it).

- Does it conflate correlation and causation?
  - o Most studies of trust/mistrust will not be experimental or longitudinal, and certainly not cohort-sequential longitudinal (Breakwell & Fife-Schaw, 1994). In itself,

this is not a problem. It becomes one when data that only allows correlational relationships to be detected is interpreted as proving causal relationships. It is important to be alert to this slippage of interpretation when using research findings.

It seems appropriate to end a chapter on images of the mistrusted with a section on some of the characteristics of research on trust that might make us wary, but not naively, mistrustful of it. As long as we are alert to the methodological limitations of the research, it may still be very valuable. Nevertheless, it is somewhat irritating to anyone interested specifically in mistrust that so many researchers tend to focus on measuring only trust. There is a tendency to ask 'How much do you trust ...?' There are then the assumptions that if trust is low mistrust exists, and if trust is absent then distrust exists. This is actually psychologically a leap of faith. Respondents are not being asked explicitly about whether they mistrust or distrust. If trust, mistrust and distrust do not reside neatly in unidimensional space, anchoring the 'measurement' of the other two on responses to questions about trust is problematic. It relies on their measurement being inferred and makes it difficult to be sure whether to infer distrust or mistrust. Since mistrust is distinguished from distrust both logically and psychologically, it does seem sensible to measure them independently. Moreover, it would be more valid and reliable to seek a direct measure of mistrust. Some researchers have been doing this. It would be good to see methods of assessing mistrust per se further evolved.

CHAPTER 6
LEADERSHIP AND MISTRUST

It seems logical to examine leadership and mistrust after discussing how 'the mistrusted' are identified, treated and characterised. Leaders are often the focus of mistrust. They have a unique position that allows them to arouse people to mistrust others. Their unique position also makes them a prime target for mistrust. In exploring the leader's role in mistrust manufacture and mitigation also takes us further into understanding the way groups and organisations manifest and manage mistrust. A leader can set the tone for mistrust within an organisation and between it and other organisations. Where its leader is mistrusted, an organisation may find itself mistrusted by outsiders, or riddled with internal schisms fostering mistrust.

The dynamics of mistrust around leadership are complex. In examining them, it is necessary to consider what forms of leadership are involved. A leader is defined typically and simply as the person who leads a number of people. The vagueness of the definition is a clue to how varied the role of a leader can be. 'Leaders' do not form a homogeneous category. The entities they lead vary widely, from the transient, informal gathering of a very small number of people to the long-term, formally structured organisation with millions of participants. Leaders may lead by consent or through constraint, and through any combination in between. They can have situation-specific mandates, for instance to tackle an immediate task of short duration. Alternatively, they can be asked to lead in a very broad brief across a lifetime. When thinking about leadership and mistrust it is wise to remember how very different the roles of leaders can be. The concept 'leader' is like Rorschach's inkblot – open to motivated interpretation.

Researchers of leadership have a similar problem. To the extent that it is about the process of leading, the leadership concept can encompass what any type of leader is or should be doing. In fact, much leadership research is about what leaders should be doing rather than what they actually do. It is also often overly influenced by assumptions about what constitutes 'good' leadership in the view of the researcher. This matters greatly when it comes to interpreting what is written about the relationship between leadership and mistrust. Normative assumptions about inadequate leadership, based on prior preconceptions or theoretical frameworks, may skew assessments of mistrust and the bases for it.

Of course, it is vital to distinguish leadership roles from the leaders that are their specific incumbents at any one time. Also, leadership may not rest with a single person. As a process, leadership is often the sum of the contributions from a number of people in different leadership roles. So, it helps to examine how different leadership hierarchies or structures in varying types of organisation generate and respond to mistrust. Over and above all of these elements, it is useful to acknowledge that there may be broader cultural influences, such as religion or political ideology, which shape the emergence and life cycle impact of mistrust upon leadership. In reality, given the mountain of research concerning them (for a meta-analysis see Dirks & Ferrin, 2002), these topics deserve a whole book in their own right. However, this chapter presents a distillation of some of the main findings and conclusions. These should be interpreted against the backdrop of the discussions of emotion, risk, uncertainty, identity and images of the mistrusted in earlier chapters. They should also be considered with due regard to how multi-faceted the constructs of leader and leadership are.

The One Thing that Changes Everything

Covey and Merrill (2006) argue that trust is at the heart of organisational success. Greater trust brings success faster. Trust reduces transaction costs. Transaction costs include those associated with gaining good information; making decisions effectively and bargaining successfully; and the policing and enforcement of the implementation of strategy. Mistrust inflates these costs. Mistrust saps energy, introduces a climate of suspicion and second-guessing, lowers morale and diminishes performance standards. Mistrust hampers change (Phong, Hui & Son, 2018). If all this is so, it seems reasonable that leaders should seek to minimise mistrust. Or, more pragmatically, it makes sense that they should seek to channel and direct mistrust where it will best serve the purposes of the organisation and, possibly, their own.

Types of Leadership

The capacity of the leader, or the leadership, of an organisation to influence or optimise mistrust is dependent on a broad array of factors. A key factor is the type of leadership that is in place. As indicated earlier, leadership is a construct defined in many subtly different ways according to the theoretical and practical concerns of the researcher. Montaudon-Tomas et al. (2020) define it as the art of motivating people towards accomplishing a goal. It includes guidance, direction, management and control. Mileham (2008), writing in the context of a discussion of officership in the British Army, was clear that leadership is about the 'art of motivation of self and others'. He goes on to say, 'to lead effectively is to generate realistic expectations, inspire mutual trust and ensure full and successful realisation of … intent'.

It is worth emphasising again when thinking about leadership as an abstract construct that in most organisations there will be many different leaders, each with different authority and purposes. The overarching leadership of the organisation is a product of the interaction within this leader network. Trust in the more senior leaders in organisations has been found to be affected by trust of employees or members in their direct leaders (Fulmer & Ostroff, 2017). In addition, there are often 'informal leaders' operating in the organisation. These individuals are not appointed as leaders. They achieve authority through their personal qualities and informal networks within the organisation. Personal influence can be achieved through many routes. For instance, it can be acquired by being a long-term worker in the organisation or by having recognised, valued skills or by having supported other workers when they were in difficulty. These informal leaders are crucial lynchpins in the systems that can propagate mistrust. So when thinking about types of leadership, it is useful to acknowledge that any one leader resides within an ecosystem of other formal and informal leaders (what can be called the leader ecosystem).

Over the last century, social and organisational psychologists have categorised different styles of leadership. A 'style' is the leader's method of providing direction, implementing plans and motivating the 'followers'. 'Followers' is used as a catch-all for employees, group members, subordinates, co-workers and so on. Descriptions of these styles usually do not explain how different leader ecosystems influence the way the style works. This might be very important where varying styles are being used by leaders at different levels in an organisation. Interactions between these different leadership styles could be very significant in shaping organisational performance. They could also fundamentally affect trust in the leader network. The categorisation of leadership styles focuses upon what any one leader might be doing, although they assume there will be some impacts upon subordinate leaders. Styles that have been described include:

- *Autocratic leadership* - in which one person controls all decisions and takes little input from followers.
- *Transactional leadership* - which sets clear objectives and goals for the followers and uses either punishments or rewards to encourage compliance.
- *Democratic leadership* - which shares the decision making with followers according to their skills and abilities but within an equalitarian deliberative framework determined by the leader.

- *Laissez-faire leadership* – which allocates all the power to make decisions to the followers, while offering support and advice if requested.
- *Transformational leadership* – which seeks to change the followers' needs and redirect their thinking, giving them purpose and stimulating excitement. This style, if it is a leadership style rather than a particular type of leadership objective, relies on the leaders communicating a vision of what they aspire to be.
- *Paternalistic leadership* – which supplies complete concern for followers and expects complete loyalty and trust in return.
- *Servant leadership* – involves the characteristics of empathy, listening, stewardship and commitment to the personal growth of followers.

Other styles have been 'identified', however, all the styles appear to fall roughly into two clusters: the participative (interpersonal orientation) and the directive (task orientation). Several other forms of leadership have also been identified as the cultural expectations of leaders have changed. These may be less a matter of style and more concerned with values that are espoused (that then may shape style). For instance, the concept of authentic leadership has been variously described (Gardner et al., 2011) and assessed (Walumbwa et al., 2008). It seems to envelope several earlier descriptions of leadership approaches, including the notion of servant leadership. It appears to have four elements. First, self-awareness arising from understanding one's own values, emotions, goals, knowledge and weaknesses. Second, a personal moral code regulating action. Third, relational transparency achieved through openness and self-disclosure. Fourth, making decisions objectively but after accessing all relevant information and considering input from others.

It is not hard to see that these different leadership styles (or philosophies) rely upon trust to varying degrees. Trust of the followers in the leader and vice versa. The styles also lend themselves to different types of organisations and hierarchical structures. In fact, some styles would simply not be permitted in some types of organisation. For instance, autocratic leadership might have a hard time in an Oxbridge College, just as laissez-faire leadership might not last long in a military unit. Leadership style is constrained by the purposes, norms and history of its host organisation.

Within, and around, an organisation, powerful social representations develop of the role of the leader and the appropriate leadership styles. These social representations typically allocate a core position to the degree of trustworthiness allotted the leader role (and, at any one time, the incumbent). The Social Identity Theory of Leadership (Barreto & Hogg, 2017) emphasises that a group's evaluation of and support for its leader is significantly influenced by the extent to which the group perceives the leader to be a typical group member who closely matches their prototype of their group. All things being equal, people are more prepared to trust, endorse and follow leaders who they believe are 'one of us' – especially if the group is important to their feelings about the certainty of their own identity. Of course, sometimes, in fact quite often, not all things are equal. For instance, in crises followers may look to support a leader who is different from the earlier prototype they held and not similar to the stereotypical group member. They may actually want or need what Fernandez and Shaw (2020) call an allostatic leader, who has the adaptive capacity to learn and change in the crisis.

Individuals undoubtedly have some latitude in interpreting the leadership role and style, and in some organisations this latitude is greater than in others. Typically, smaller and younger organisations offer greater opportunities for personalisation of the role by individual incumbents. It is notable that as organisations change, the demands on leadership changes. For instance, there is some evidence that the style and skills of revolutionary leaders are not acceptable post-revolution (Suedfeld & Rank, 1976) and, if they do not change, particularly the cognitive complexity of their style, they are deposed. Similarly, the style of the entrepreneurs who establish start-up companies is often not suited to the task of growing them (Holmberg-Wright & Hribar, 2016). However, the broader cultural and ideological context around the organisation also exerts an influence (Higgins, 2020; Yu & Miller, 2005). For instance, national cultures that have traditionally relied on strict demarcation of societal hierarchies and roles are more likely to support autocratic or certain forms of transactional leadership (Lonati, 2020; Arun & Kahraman Gedik, 2020). Indeed, Montaudon et al. (2020), in a study across Japan, France and Mexico, showed how autocratic, transactional and servant leadership styles vary in relation to culture across region.

Leadership Style, Trust and Efficacy

All this points to the power of context in shaping leadership processes and leadership efficacy. Fiedler (1967) showed how the situational specificity of leadership could be systematically examined. His Contingency Model of Leadership has four basic components:

- leadership style (varying between interpersonal and task orientation)
- leader-member relations (reflecting how much the leader is liked, respected and trusted by followers)
- task structure (if goal clarity, solution specificity and decision verifiability are all high, the task is highly structured and much activity relating to it is predetermined)
- position power of the leader (position power refers to the authority invested in the leader. This is a function of the nature of the organisation. Great position power gives the leader great personal control over decisions and their implementation.)

The contingency model of leadership is regarded by many as having the status of a classic theory in social psychology. It has been the subject of many empirical verifications and meta-analyses (Ayman, Chemers & Fiedler, 1995; Strube & Garcia, 1981). It has the great advantage of highlighting the complexity and variability of the leadership process, and challenging any naïve assumptions about the significance of purely individual characteristics of leaders.

The significance of the position power of the leader role in the model is notable. Leaders with great position power notionally have the authority to lead without follower consent. Use of their power is not formally reliant upon follower trust. However, for any one incumbent to retain such a position of power may be reliant on follower trust. Yet, even if the incumbent is removed, the power of the leadership position itself may remain intact. Actually, once an incumbent of such a leadership role is removed for reasons of mistrust, it is unlikely that the power invested in the position will remain totally secure. Indeed, the definition of the position itself may be changed with associated modifications of the power assigned to it. This all serves to emphasise the importance of the interactions between the four components in the contingency model.

Fiedler was most interested in leader effectiveness and he argues that it is optimised when the characteristics of the leader were matched to the demands of the leadership context. He called this 'leadermatch'. Leaders capable of adapting their style to their context were more likely to be successful. Fiedler's model does not give primacy to any one style of leadership. The mantra 'horses for courses' springs to mind. Yet the model does emphasise the interaction of leadership style with leader–member relations. Efficacy of an appropriate leadership style for a situation can be enhanced by getting the right dynamic with followers. Mistrust can be a major obstacle to getting the dynamic right.

Some leadership approaches seek to minimise mistrust. Authentic leadership appears to focus upon fostering trust through explicit internalisation of moral standards, openness, self-disclosure and participative decision making. It aims to enable both leaders and their followers to stay true to their values, identity, emotions, motives and goals. While authentic leadership is typically differentiated from its sister approach transformational leadership, there is considerable overlap. Transformational leaders are characterised by inspirational motivation through setting clear and reasonable goals; idealised influence through being a strong role; intellectual stimulation by encouraging creativity and innovation; and individualised consideration by supporting and mentoring followers. The difference between authentic and transformational leadership appears to lie in the somewhat greater emphasis placed upon mutual openness and honesty in the former.

There is some indication that seeking to minimise mistrust can enhance leadership efficacy. For instance, there is evidence that authentic leadership is positively associated with job satisfaction of followers, follower satisfaction with the leader, group or organisational performance, task performance, organisational commitment and leader effectiveness (Banks et al., 2016; Wang & Hsieh, 2013). However, there is also evidence that what might be labelled 'trust-oriented' or 'relationship-oriented' leaders are actually most effective in conditions that are already moderately favourable, that is when their position power is neither very great nor very poor, where the task structure is neither completely clear nor totally undefined. Task-oriented leaders are most effective in very favourable or very unfavourable circumstances. So, it seems that the value of leaders focusing on building trust pays dividends, but less at the two extremes. This may be because at the one extreme a record of trustworthiness is irrelevant to task success – where the leader already has great position power and clarity of task definition. At the other extreme, previous mutual trust is irrelevant because the leader has no position power and the task is incoherent – trust alone will not assure efficacy. Trust seems to be most meaningful in situations where the outcomes of effort are uncertain.

What do You do to be Less Mistrusted?

We have seen that some leadership approaches are linked to trying to build trust between leader and followers. The obvious question then is: what do leaders need to do in order to be trusted? Echoing the material on leadership style effectiveness, the popularist advice to budding leaders who want to be trusted would include:

- emphasise what you have in common with your followers – encourage them to believe their self-interest is aligned with yours; show you share important beliefs and group identifications
- show you trust your followers – do this by keeping them informed
- admit your mistakes and accept responsibility for them
- do not pretend to know things that you do not know
- do not criticise or gossip about people behind their backs – if you do, followers will assume you may do it about them too.

In fact, the consensus across organisation researchers (e.g. Sanders et al., 2006) is that to gain trust leaders need to be characterised by:

- ability – demonstrating competence at doing their job
- benevolence – evidencing a concern for others beyond their own needs and having benign motives
- integrity – adhering to a set of principles acceptable to others encompassing honesty and fairness
- predictability – behaving as expected, regularly over time

The last three are just the same as the things we look for when deciding whether to trust anyone (Dietz, 2011). Most leaders would know that they need to have these features (plus competence) if they are to be seen as trustworthy. The problem lies in establishing what they can actually do to be perceived as having these character-istics. It is problematic because it is dependent on the specifics of their situation. It will depend on the followers' predisposition to trust (which, in turn, will have its roots in their experience of leaders – and not necessarily of this one) as well as their own abiding character traits. It will depend on the nature of the established leader–follower relationship. It is affected by the leader's actual role (i.e. freedom of action, seniority, organisational function etc). It is also influenced by the existing reputation of the leader.

Of course, to produce their impact, all of these factors interact with the leader's actual character, motives, objectives and abilities. There is an interesting illustration of this interaction from a military context. Sweeney (2010) examined soldiers' re-evaluation of their trust in their direct leaders prior to following them into battle in northern Iraq. The majority of soldiers did reconsider their trust in their leaders prior to combat operations, assessing whether they had the competence and character to meet the greater demands of leading in combat. The findings also suggested that the trust leaders developed during peacetime training transferred to the combat environment and that leaders' abilities emerged as the most influential factor in the development of trust in the high-vulnerability context of combat.

Leaders wishing to minimise mistrust never start with a clean slate. Even if they are new to an organisation, they live in the penumbra of predecessors and their works (Rowe et al., 2005). This argument is founded upon the assumption that few leaders start with a certain fund of trust at their disposal. They probably start with a trust deficit that they have to minimise, and eliminate if they can. The deficit comes from what happened in the organisation in the past. It may also come from the reputation, earned elsewhere, that the leader brings into the organisation. It may just be a concatenation of rumour, fact and malign intent. The point is that the struggle for trust is an uphill battle.

If mistrust is to be minimised, it takes time, courage and determination on the part of a new leader. Part of the process will be some form of conciliation. What Mitchell (2000: 35) called a credible gesture that initiates 'an accommodative sequence of mutually reinforcing benign behaviour'. It might be simpler to call it a token of good faith that starts re-evaluation and reconciliation. The process takes more than single disjointed acts – no matter how positive. It takes a clarity of vision too. A strategy must be designed to fit the specifics of the situation and the resources available to the leader. Its purpose will be to align trust in the leader, trust in the organisation, trust among followers, and trust in external relationships. Inculcating trust in the leader separately from this holistic system of trust is fraught because there are feedback loops between these different forms of trust in an organisation. The trustworthiness of the leader does not stand alone – or at least, not for very long. So the strategy will involve the leader evincing personal ability, benevolence, integrity and predictability. But there will be a need to do more than that. These behaviours and watchwords must be inculcated throughout the organisation.

Watchwords are important in this process of repairing the trust deficit. Communication is of great importance. Groysberg and Slind (2012) described how trusted leaders use conversation to power their organisations. Having decided on the strategy to grow trust is just the first step. Then, others need to understand it. To achieve this, it has to be communicated simply, clearly, repeatedly and with energy. The audience needs to be engaged, to like the message and to see its personal relevance and, if possible, advantages. The problem lies in growing trust where mistrust is already flourishing. Leaders have found often, and at great cost, that merely giving people the truth, presenting facts, providing evidence, offering information will not supplant virulent misconceptions tied to wider belief systems and invested with emotions both positive and negative. The communications that transmit the strategy have to address the audience's beliefs and feelings. Moreover, communication has to be genuinely a two-way (possibly multi-way) process to be effective in this situation. One-way, leader to followers, communication often serves only to reinforce mistrust. This may be why the leadership styles that rely on whole organisation cultural change, modelled through the behaviour and values of the leader, are in certain situations effective. It is an interesting paradox that leadership styles that are avowedly not self-serving may be the best to engender self-serving trust for the leader.

Too often, when talking about leadership efforts to minimise mistrust it is assumed that there is no concerted, deliberate push back within the organisation. In fact, there frequently will be. We will look at this later.

Leader Personality and Mistrust

Whatever is said about the personality of leaders must be heavily caveated. So we may as well start with some questions.

- There are many sorts of leader roles, associated with variations in training, power and security of tenure, so should we expect the leaders in all, or even most, of them to share similar personality traits?
- Leaders stay in role for varying lengths of time, so should we expect leaders at the start of their tenure to manifest the same traits as later in their period in office?
- Different leaders have different objectives and face different challenges, so should we expect them to evince the same traits irrespective of their varied circumstances?

The answer to each of these questions is almost certainly no. Any generalisations about leaders and personality consequently must be treated cautiously. Care is also needed because the research data usually presented is correlational. It is hard to know whether the personality trait said to characterise leaders predates their experience as leaders. We do not know whether the indicators of the trait were already there on appointment and, if they were, whether they were then intensified by the experience of leadership. Much analyses of the personalities of leaders is done either retrospectively (e.g. historically via records of actions, speeches, decisions, or the publicly available information on how other people responded to them) or contemporaneously through long-distance observation (e.g. by media commentators). In depth, empirical analysis of the personality structures of actual leaders, especially those in very senior positions, is very rare. Having flagged all these disclaimers, it is worth looking at some of the more robust findings in the field.

The Big Five

Since both context and leadership style affect level of mistrust aroused by a leader, we should now consider whether the leader's personality has been found to relate to mistrust. There is a lot of research on how leadership personality traits affect upward trust. The so-called 'Big Five' personality traits (extraversion, neuroticism, agreeableness, conscientiousness and openness to experience) have been assessed in leaders. Extraversion seems linked to acquiring a leadership position, while openness and conscientiousness is associated with subsequent success as a leader. There is some suggestion that extraversion and agreeableness in leaders are linked to greater trust but there are also established cultural differences. For instance, Ping et al. (2012) examined the relationship between leaders' ratings on the Big Five personality traits and upward trust in a Chinese sample. They report that extraversion and neuroticism have a negative influence on upward trust, agreeableness' impact is insignificant, conscientiousness has a positive influence and openness to experience has a negative impact. Their results suggest that the degree to which the leaders' Big Five personality traits affect upward trust differs from that of the West. This should come as no surprise since general prototypes of personality trustworthiness differ across cultures.

The Dark Triad

Three offensive, yet non-pathological, personalities are particularly prominent in Western literature: narcissism, subclinical psychopathy and Machiavellianism. These are known as the 'dark triad'. Until Paulhus and Williams (2002) examined their relationship empirically, the three were considered, at least in non-clinical samples, to be essentially the same thing. Paulhus and Williams argued that, even though the three constructs were moderately intercorrelated, they were distinct. For instance, they showed that they were differentiated in terms of their relationship to the Big Five. The only one of the Big Five that they all correlated with was disagreeableness, after which they part company. Subclinical psychopaths displayed low neuroticism. Machiavellians and psychopaths were low in conscientiousness. Intriguingly, narcissism was positively associated with cognitive ability.

The dark triad is still used as an umbrella term for the co-presence of these three personality features. People scoring highly on these traits are more likely to commit crimes, cause social distress and create severe problems for any organisation of which they are a part – especially if they are in a leadership role. They are more likely to be antagonistic, manipulative, exploitative, callous and lacking in empathy. From what we have seen about what makes someone trustworthy, leaders rated high on the dark triad would not score highly on trust. In fact, honesty has been found to be strongly and negatively correlated with the dark triad traits (Aghababaei, Mohammadtabar & Saffarinia, 2014). Furnham, Richards and Paulhus (2013) in a 10-year retrospective review of research on the dark triad describe how they appear in images of 'toxic leadership', 'bad bosses' and, charmingly, 'snakes in suits'. Such leaders typically may not thrive but there are contexts in which they do – at least initially. Furnham (2010) described cases where high levels of dark triad traits, when combined with other factors (such as intelligence and physical attractiveness), helped individuals acquire leadership positions.

Research that, even indirectly, explores empirically the relationship between leader mistrust and the dark triad as a syndrome is extremely limited. Intuitively and initially, one might expect dark triad leaders to be mistrusted. The dark triad, on the surface, seem like the polar opposites of what Norman, Avolio and Luthans (2010) lauded as the required characteristics for trust: positivity and transparency. Being overtly selfish, impulsive, exploitative and antagonistic might instead be expected to trigger mistrust. However, it will depend on the way the triad traits manifest. Dark triad leaders have been found to be operationally successful (Furtner, Maran & Rauthmann, 2017) and followers adapt to them and use them strategically for their own goals (Schyns, Wisse & Sanders, 2019). So the simple equation that dark triad = mistrust is misleading. One reason is probably that the dark triad traits focus on manipulation and exploitation. Leaders who feel contempt for their followers because of their own narcissism, psychopathy or Machiavellianism need not necessarily behave contemptuously. Emulating trustworthy behaviour for ulterior motives would not seem to be an unlikely ploy. The only question would be how long this would work. How long can the mask be maintained? Furnham (2010) pointed out that dark triad leaders could thrive by manipulating trust but only for limited periods. Once they reach that point, they may no longer rely on trust or minimising mistrust to maintain their position. Other, less acceptable, tools such as abandonment of democratic or consultation processes may be brought into play.

Does Leader Personality Matter in Determining Mistrust?

This section on leader personality started with a word of warning about the limitations of the empirical material available. The very strong conclusion that can be drawn from all the work is that personality alone is not determining mistrust. There is a formidably complex interaction between the leader's personal characteristics, including personality traits, and situational factors, including the nature of the organisation and followers and the challenges they face, which shapes levels of mistrust about the leader. So, leader personality does matter but it is only one of many determinants of mistrust. That mistrust does not stem from one cause cannot be reiterated too often.

This discussion has focused on how followers may develop mistrust of leaders in part because of their personalities. The other possibility is that some personality types will be more likely to mistrust their followers. Scoring high on one or more of the dark triad or on neuroticism might be expected to precipitate mistrust about your followers. Studies of leader mistrust of followers have shown that it results in over-scrutiny of their work, extreme enforcement of rules and reducing their latitude for making decisions. Those leadership styles that rely on building mutual trust would find it hard to co-exist with these tendencies.

Leadership Experience may Change Personality: The Hubris Syndrome

So far we have not considered whether the experience of leading may actually change the leader's personality – or, at least, the expression of that personality. There is work suggesting that it may. The best-documented personality 'change' is often labelled hubris. Over-confidence in one's abilities is what the Greeks called hubris: pride that offended the gods, and invited punishment in the form of humbling. Illustrated by Daedalus falling from the sky. Bertrand Russell (2004) talked of leaders that became 'intoxicated with power'. The proposition is that 'power corrupts', fosters egotism and recklessness, arrogance and contempt for others. Owen and Davidson (2009) described the hubris syndrome, based on an analysis of the behaviour of US Presidents and UK Prime Ministers over 100 years. They said if someone in a position of power has three or more of 14 symptoms they were suffering from the hubris syndrome. These symptoms are:

- seeking self-glorification
- acting to enhance personal standing
- excessively conscious of their own self-image
- displaying messianic tendencies
- believing they 'are the organisation'
- using the royal 'we'
- excessively confident in their own judgements and contemptuous of others' opinions
- displaying exaggerated self-belief
- feeling accountable only to history
- believing unshakably that they will be vindicated
- being isolated – and deprived of critical feedback
- behaving recklessly, restlessly, impulsively – lower self-control
- being impractical and overlooking detail and potential pitfalls facing a course of action
- implementing plans incompetently because excessively self-confident

It is telling that they referred to 'symptoms' and not indicators. The use of 'symptoms' is a signal that the syndrome is seen as an ailment or an acquired personality disorder. This is a syndrome on the dark side of personality. Through the list, the significance of 'self' is evident. But this is centred on deluded self-perception. The symptoms echo those of the narcissistic personality. These symptoms may develop in leaders during their tenure. The power they wield as leaders is thought to act as the catalyst for their change. They become more 'self' oriented because power precludes the need to pay heed to others. It was noted earlier that narcissism often coexists with charisma and charm, at least initially. Freud even suggested that we have a proclivity to admire people who admire themselves.

Success does seem to be the necessary precursor of these sorts of changes in the way leaders behave and, more importantly, think about themselves. So great success, especially achieved early and apparently effortlessly through personal agency, might be even more likely to foreshadow hubris appearing (Lovric & Chamorro-Premuzi, 2018). Such changes will shift leadership style – certainly not exhibiting, if they ever did, the sort that engender greater follower trust. Furnham (2018) indicates the hubris syndrome drives the leader to mistrust others (echoing the effects of the dark triad) and other research has shown that leaders who mistrust are mistrusted in turn. Perhaps this downward spiral of mistrust is situationally dependent. The mistrust stimulated by the syndrome may be moderated if the leader's success continues. In fact, Sundermeier et al. (2020) showed that even though the majority of hubristic founders of start-up ventures are likely to fail, they also excel in establishing a vision for their company, steering employees through critical situations and extracting commitments from third parties. This can be vital in creating initial success. It seems likely that mistrust starts to matter more when failures emerge, perhaps accentuating the significance of leader error and triggering blaming. These processes can turn a leader error into a disaster (Owen & Davidson, 2009).

There is some debate about whether hubris represents a long-term change to personality or is context specific. If it were context specific, it would be expected to diminish or even disappear if the leader's situation changed. In fact, once established, the hubris syndrome seems difficult to eradicate. Failure may abate it. But resurgence follows. The case of serial resurrection of failing entrepreneurs, or indeed politicians, illustrates the point. This resilience of the syndrome raises the question of whether its foundations are laid in the personality of some people long before they go on to be leaders. There could be a 'sleeper effect' – the nascent syndrome is there, waiting to be triggered by context. In which case, hubris would be a product of the interaction between extant personality traits and new events and experiences. This would certainly explain why not all successful leaders are marked by hubris. However, another possibility cannot be ruled out. Hubris may not be a discrete syndrome of personality traits. Hubris may simply be a pattern of behaviour and self-expression adopted by some particularly successful leaders. As such, it could be just one way of enacting the role of leader – actually another leadership style. This would suggest it is chosen by the leader, not something beyond control. The empirical evidence as to which of these options is correct is not, thus far, conclusive but research is ongoing (Sadler-Smith et al., 2017; Asad & Sadler-Smith, 2020). In either case, hubris is important in the processes of initiating and enhancing leader mistrust of followers and followers' mistrust of leaders.

Gender, Leadership and Mistrust

The generalisations about personality and leadership styles as determinants of mistrust are fine as far as they go. But they ignore a very large elephant in the room. The gender of the leader matters, and moderates the effects of other factors. There are two main reasons why this should be so: stereotyping and style.

Stereotyping Women Leaders

Stereotypes of women leaders have changed over time and they vary significantly now across cultures. Irrespective of what image they portray of women leaders at one time or place, they have power in two ways. First, they will influence the behaviour of women leaders themselves – and not necessarily in the direction of conforming to them. Second, they will influence the way a woman leader is perceived, evaluated and treated.

These stereotypes are a product of social representational processes and they are heavily influenced by power differentials between men and women that are persistent. Eagly and Sczesny (2009) argued that there are three stereotypes at work of what are seen as separate groups: men, women and leaders. The dominant stereotypes of leaders and men overlap but the stereotype of women is dissimilar from that of leaders. So they are not seen as so eligible for leader group membership. The access routes to leadership are consequently less available, and may be less attractive to women. However, depictions in stereotypes of women as a group do vary. The values attributed to the traits they assign to women also vary. For instance, Barnes, Beaulieu and Saxton (2018) refer to the gender stereotype of women as being more ethical and honest, more risk averse, and as political outsiders. They used this to explain their findings that women leaders in the police force are perceived to reduce public concerns about corruption in the police.

Leadership Styles and Gender

On average, the leadership styles of men and women do differ. Eagly, Johannesen-Schmidt and Van Engen (2003) report a meta-analysis of transformational, transactional and laissez-faire leadership styles. Female leaders were more transformational than male leaders. They also engaged in more of the contingent reward behaviours that are a component of transactional leadership. Male leaders were generally more likely to manifest the other aspects of transactional leadership (active and passive management by exception) and laissez-faire leadership. This is interesting because other research has established that all of the aspects of leadership style on which women exceeded men relate positively to leaders' effectiveness whereas all of the aspects on which men exceeded women have negative or null relations to effectiveness. The direction of the disparities also suggest that women leaders would be less mistrusted by followers. The leadership style preferences of women may have positive effects for their organisations but it is less clear that they work for the women themselves. Vinkenburg et al. (2011) investigated stereotypical beliefs about the importance of leadership styles for promotion of men and women to different levels in organisations. Inspirational motivation was perceived as more important for men than women and especially important for promotion to the Chief Executive Officer (CEO) role. In contrast, individualised consideration was perceived as more important for women than men and especially important for promotion to senior management. Zheng, Surgevil and Kark (2018) encapsulated one key problem: women leaders need to be perceived as both agentic and communal, and then to balance the incongruities between communal gender-role expectations and agentic leader-role expectations. Failure to conform simultaneously to both the gender and the leader stereotypes will put trust at risk. As Carli & Eagly (2016) claim, women face a labyrinth in their road to leadership success.

Intersecting Identities

Any deviation from the expected leader persona triggers mistrust that must be managed. Even after generations of feminism, it is still incongruous to see a woman in certain leadership roles. It is even more extraordinary if she breaches stereotype or stylistic expectations of a woman in such a role. People find it hard to know how to explain her and how to react to her. They are ambivalent about the leader persona she embodies. It brings to mind what François Mitterrand, President of France, said of Margaret Thatcher, first woman Prime Minister of the UK. He said she had 'the eyes of Caligula but the mouth of Marilyn Monroe'.

In many leadership roles, women will have to face this ambivalence and the mistrust that accompanies it. However, gender also interacts with other marginalised or stigmatised identity characteristics (ethnicity particularly) in shaping mistrust. Jaspal and Bayley (2020) use the notion of 'intersecting identities' to crystallise how several different group or social category identifications co-exist in an individual's total identity configuration. These intersecting identities matter greatly in leadership processes. Taken at its simplest, if leaders are more trusted if they are seen as 'one of us' by followers (as the social identity theory of leadership would suggest), a leader who is different from the majority of followers on two group identifications (gender and ethnicity) will be more mistrusted. This is actually a double jeopardy risk for a women from an ethnic minority: she can be different on either or both of the group identifications.

How this works in practice will depend on the stereotype of the ethnic identification. Sales, Galloway Burke and Cannonier (2020) studied African American leadership across contexts. They report that women from diverse ethnic backgrounds have different experiences in the workplace. African American (Black) women leaders were found to feel overlooked, marginalised, undervalued and unappreciated as leaders in their professions due to their dual minority status. At a time when the Black Lives Matter movement was asking for active engagement with being anti-racist, it became even more important to consider how Black women leaders actively tackle mistrust that arises based on their identifications. Dickens, Womack and Dimes (2019) found that Black women who are tokenised in their workplace and experience race and gender-based discrimination might try to mitigate its effects by identity shifting. Identity shifting is the conscious or unconscious process of altering one's language or self-presentation. It is a process of identity negotiation. This may reduce feelings of negative distinctiveness or visibility. Thus, it may limit some of the negative consequences of stereotyping and discrimination. The strategy may have some advantages professionally but switching is likely to be stressful and psychologically costly (e.g. increased anxiety). It can feel fake to the woman herself and look inauthentic to co-workers. As a tactic in a context that is already disposed to mistrust, identity shifting is potentially going to heighten suspicion and doubt. It is a Catch-22 situation: you identity shift = you are a fake; you do not shift = you are an outsider to be mistrusted. In reality, to bring about change, the formal societal empowerment of people with intersecting stigmatised identity characteristics has to happen alongside the efforts of individuals. Trustworthiness then becomes less a matter of category membership with its appended stereotypes.

Besides gender and ethnicity, other socio-demographic characteristics interact with each other and with personality to determine leader behaviour and perception. These would include age, socio-economic background and variations in physical ability. Each may affect perceived trustworthiness of leaders. However, for each, the same arguments can be made as for gender. They have their impact on perceived trustworthiness through the two routes: stereotypes and styles.

Life Cycles of Mistrust in Leaders

Mistrust of leaders typically varies across their time in role. The life cycle of such fluctuations in mistrust is not particularly generalisable across leaders. Some have a low rating of trust at the start, peak and then decline again. Others start high and gradually or suddenly drop. What matters is that there will be variations. They probably typically depend less on changes in the leader and more on the changes in the issues the leader is addressing and the way any competitors for the leadership role are performing. This is particularly evident in relation to political leaders in democratic systems. Therefore changes in trust can happen quickly as conditions change.

Ipsos MORI (2020b) based on a survey of representative samples of British adults aged 18–75 at two data points, reported that between October 2019 and June 2020 the percentage trusting the British Prime Minister (Boris Johnson) to tell the truth most of the time increased from 22% to 31%. The number saying he would never or very often not tell the truth reduced from 48% to 39%. The timeframe for this reasonably significant shift is important. Many things happened between these months. They included a General Election, the removal of the leader of the main opposition party, the ratification of the UK withdrawal from the EU, the emergence of the COVID-19 global pandemic (with the PM being infected and hospitalised), and the national lockdown consequent upon it, which was eased as infection rates initially reduced by June 2020. It is against this backdrop that the change in trust levels must be understood. Harold Macmillan, British Prime Minister (1957–63), is reported to have said, when he was asked what would determine his government's course, 'events, dear boy, events'. They probably also have a seriously large part to play in determining trust in leaders. The events during the course of the COVID-19 pandemic and the way Prime Minister Johnson responded to them will reverberate through his trust ratings. In fact, surveys were done in May and June 2020 of public perceptions of the competence in handling of COVID-19 of the political leaders at the time in the UK, the US, Italy and Australia (Ipsos MORI, 2020b). These showed that leaders that are most likely to have been seen to use expert advice, been open and transparent and have been capable of working with others are generally seen to have also handled the outbreak most effectively. Perceptions of the threat of the virus and of leader competence in the handling of COVID-19 and trustworthiness tended to correspond to how the crisis unfolded in each country.

The impact of specific events on leader trust has to be considered in the context of broader trends concerning trust within society. The Pew Research Center (2019) reported on a series of polls of Americans' trust in the US government taken between 1958 and 2019, spanning 12 Presidencies (starting with Eisenhower and ending with Trump), presenting the moving average across surveys at any one time of the percentage of respondents reporting trust in Government. In 1958, about three-quarters of Americans trusted the Federal Government to do the right thing always or most of the time. Trust in government began eroding during the Johnson Presidency in the 1960s, dropped precipitously during the Nixon years and continued to fall during periods in office of Ford and Carter. By the time Reagan took office in 1981, around one-third of Americans trusted the Government to do the right thing. Reagan saw the numbers trusting rise again over his eight years as President, following the attempted assassination at the start of his term, but they never topped 50% of those polled. Bush Snr saw trust first fall, then rise, and then fall dramatically in his four-year term during which the first Gulf War was waged. When Clinton took over, trust was at around 20% and rose to over 45% by the end of his term (with fluctuations within the period that included his impeachment acquittal). In 2001, when G. W. Bush became President, roughly 50% again trusted the Government, but the figure slipped inexorably down over his eight-year tenure to around 25%. Obama inherited that trust level and, despite some fluctuations across his Presidency, did not see trust rise above that figure. Elected in 2017, Trump by 2019 had seen trust in the Government shift down again. The overall picture is that trust in the Federal Government to do what is right declined over these 60 years from about 75% to about 20–25%. It echoes the arguments that faith in all kinds of institutions has been falling for decades.

Trust in the US President is clearly not the same as trust in the Federal Government. However, the level of trust in Government is the context in which Presidents must operate and seek to be trusted. There is a further complexity to consider. People tend to trust the Government more if it is led by the party they support. Republican voters are more likely to trust the government to do the right thing when there is a Republican President; Democrats show the same pattern but with less extreme variation swings in trust against the government when there is a Republican President (Morisi, Jost & Singh, 2019). The finding emphasises how trust in institutions is founded upon how far they resonate with one's own beliefs and group identifications. We noted earlier that the same is true of trust in leaders. In the case of political leaders, they fundamentally rely on being able to hold the trust of supporters of their political party. It is interesting that the more they are trusted by their own party's supporters, the less likely they are to be supported by the opponent parties' supporters. This sort of polarisation of trust–mistrust in a leader is unusual in other organisational contexts.

Even against the backdrop of overall declining trust in Government over the 60 years of the Pew review, it is notable how towards the end of a Presidency, except in the notable case of Clinton, trust in Government falls. The transition between presidencies is typically signalled by a decline in trust in Government. Perhaps this is because it is a time of uncertainty about who will next have power. Perhaps it is that the exiting President is seen already to have less power to ensure a Government does 'do the right thing'.

This phenomenon happens outside of politics. The transition trust deficit is certainly characteristic of what happens when leaders in other spheres are due to leave their job. Followers recognise that change is imminent. The growth of mistrust in this situation may have nothing to do with what the leader is doing or failing to do. It may be a pragmatic assessment of the odds that the leader will be able to deliver on promises. This 'lame-duck' stage of a leader's tenure varies greatly across organisations. In big commercial operations, it tends to be very short in order to minimise any impact on organisational performance. In American politics, the Presidential lame-duck period is lengthy (roughly from the midterm elections to the House of Representatives and the Senate, which take place two years into a president's four-year term) (Potter, 2016). This is a rather long time to be managing as a lame duck, especially if in the second term in office.

The lame-duck leader typically incurs mistrust of a special variety. It is often a no-blame mistrust. They may not be able to do what they said they would, but followers will often recognise that they probably do not have the power to do so. Consequently, they cannot legitimately be blamed.

Lame-duck mistrust is inevitably part of the cycle of leadership mistrust in some organisational contexts because the organisation's governance structure determines that there is a long lead-time into the leader's exit. As defined here, such mistrust is closer to scepticism about capacity to deliver than it is to suspicion about motives or intentions. This may not actually appear to be mistrust. The leader may just be treated as irrelevant or sidelined. Especially if the leader has previously been regarded to have integrity and competence, a form of benign mistrust may emerge. The scepticism and doubt about delivering on stated goals is present but not accompanied by animosity or confrontation.

It is notable that very successful leaders, particularly in business, will manage their exit to avoid becoming lame ducks. They will often create a well-ordered succession and clear, preferably short and predictable, timelines for the transference of power. Sometimes, this will be accompanied by publicly explaining the reasons for leaving (if not at the end of a fixed term appointment) and showing what their next activity will be. This is a process of consolidating the positive identity already achieved as leader and readying an account of the new elements of identity to be assumed. Doing this successfully in any large or complex organisation is enormously difficult. It may only be possible if certain conditions are satisfied:

- The leader controls the departure schedule or, at least, indicates acceptance of it.
- The leader is not already under attack from forces internal or external to the organisation.
- The leader has established effective channels of communication with followers.
- The leader has high identity resilience (i.e. strong self-efficacy, self-esteem, positive distinctiveness and sense of continuity). Doubt about any of these prime facets of identity will make managing the transition harder.

It is, of course, also useful to have been considered trustworthy up to this point, though not essential. A managed departure may enhance trust in and reputation of a leader. An example of the high-profile, well-managed departure hails from the story of Bill Gates. Gates co-founded Microsoft in 1975 and led the company as Chairman and CEO until stepping down as CEO in 2000, but then remained Chairman and became chief software architect. In 2006, he announced he would move into a part-time role at Microsoft and work full-time at the private charitable foundation he had established with his wife in 2000. He gradually transferred his Microsoft duties to Ray Ozzie and Craig Mundie, finished as Chairman in 2014, and in 2020 left all his board positions at Microsoft.

This 20-year transition process was coterminous with the expansion of his philanthropic works concerning climate change, global health and education. During this period, he received at least seven honorary doctorates, and some of the highest international honours. These included in the US, the Presidential Medal of Freedom;

in France, Commander of the Legion of Honour (both with his wife Melinda for their philanthropic endeavours); and appointment as an Honorary Knight Commander of the Order of the British Empire by Queen Elizabeth II. Over this time, Gates appears to have used in his charitable work the same extraordinary intellectual ability and task-focus that made Microsoft thrive. Interestingly, Microsoft remained resilient, despite the bursting of the dot.com bubble. That may be, in part, because Gates managed his transition out of the leadership so well.

In the context of his philanthropic second career, Gates has gained enormously in prestige and respect. Yet it is clear that this does not translate simply into him being universally trusted. Quite the opposite. During the coronavirus pandemic, he became one of the top targets (together with Fauci, an expert on infectious diseases) for baseless anti-vaxxer conspiracy theories that suggest the pandemic is a cover for a plan to implant trackable microchips during mandatory vaccinations against the virus. Perhaps this should not surprise us. The attack comes initially from people opposed to all vaccination. Gates is a champion for improved global health and that is dependent in large measure upon vaccination programmes. He is the obvious target and coronavirus offers the opportunistic vehicle for the attack. In addition, Gates is highly visible and explicit about his moral stance on the need to reduce inequalities, and has enormous influence, particularly given his great wealth. Any attack on him is bound to attract media and public attention. The attack message may not be perceived as credible but it will be aired and heard. It makes the anti-vaxxers visible again and that is, in itself, a sort of victory for them. Even leaders who make an extraordinarily successful transition out of their role cannot assume that they can avoid mistrust later. Significant ex-leaders are magnets for those who would manipulate mistrust.

Identity Processes, Social Representations and Leader Mistrust

Most leaders, not just billionaires, are magnets for mistrust. Mistrust can come from within the organisation they lead and from outside. It can reside in friends as well as enemies. It can be manifest or hidden. Its genesis may lie in what the leader does and how they do it. It may be targeted at the leader because of her or his group or category identifications. It may be that the personality of the leader and the way it is expressed through actions and attitudes attracts mistrust. Circumstances within or beyond the leader's control may precipitate it. In most leadership roles, all of these influences will be working on arousing or dampening mistrust continually.

In large measure, leadership is based on managing mistrust. We have seen that if the leader is mistrusted organisational performance declines. This is one reason why a leader will seek to manage mistrust. Another priority reason is that mistrust is a threat to the leader's own identity. Mistrust threatens one or more of the key principles of identity: self-esteem, self-efficacy, positive distinctiveness and continuity of identity. Leaders facing mistrust will try to minimise the impact on their identity. Typical coping strategies used when dealing with a threat to identity can be mobilised. In this case, there are four types of strategy:

- denial - refuse to acknowledge it is there; ignore or minimise in one's own mind the significance of the mistrust
- attack - evict or remove those who mistrust
- delegitimise - show that mistrust is unjustified; based on fake information or false interpretation or on ulterior motives
- redirection - show that someone else should be mistrusted instead

Essentially, the coping involves changing the meaning of mistrust, controlling its sources or refocusing its target. Managing mistrust more broadly is discussed in later chapters. The prime point here is that leaders experiencing mistrust will be driven by their own desire to protect their own identity, just as they are motivated to protect their organisation and the role they have within it.

The identity processes that direct coping with threat to identity are always at work in every choice a leader makes – not just those regarding mistrust. However, it is evident from what has been said earlier about stereotyping and prototyping that leaders will sometimes encounter mistrust simply because of who and what they are. They will be mistrusted on occasion because of the dominant social representations of their ethnicity, or gender, or age, or nationality, and of any group identification that you might imagine. Mistrust is not uniquely a product of discrimination, but it is one manifestation of it. In this case, their identity is the reason for the mistrust. It is doubly threatened: by being mistrusted and by being the reason for mistrust. While the significance of identity processes in responses to mistrust may be more pronounced in leaders, they are similar to those evident in anyone managing mistrust. It is reminiscent of the images of the mistrusted considered in an earlier chapter. Being labelled a 'mistrusted leader' becomes a part of the accused's identity configuration. Labelled as mistrusted, a new set of stereotypes can be applied to the leader and these have the power to trigger responses and judgements about the leader in the future. It is not hard to see why mistrust might be mobilised as a weapon against a leader in any conflict. Equally, it is not surprising that leaders try so hard to manage mistrust.

CHAPTER 7
COMMUNICATION CHANNELS FOR INCITING MISTRUST

In the last chapter, the emphasis was upon the need of leaders and organisations to acknowledge the importance of mistrust and to attempt to assuage it. It needs to be said that some people, some organisations and some leaders will want to do precisely the opposite. Their object is to inflame mistrust. The discussion of stereotyping the mistrusted in an earlier chapter illustrated how arousing mistrust could be a tool for control. Mistrust can be a weapon wielded to threaten and undermine competitors and enemies, or people who are just different.

This chapter explores some ways in which mistrust is deliberately incited. The role of gossip and rumour is described. Traditional routes and reasons for creating and spreading gossip and rumour are examined, including gossip columns and poison pen letters. The contemporary uses of social media that can also incite mistrust are presented. Gossip, rumour and social media channels can each be powerful instruments for building or threatening identity resilience. They all contribute to the genesis and transmission of social representations. They can each be used to incite mistrust. However, also, each of these channels bear the stamp 'beware – we are mistrusted'.

Just as organisations and those who lead them are a fundamental part of the social context in which mistrust resides, so too are the communication processes through which mistrust is incited. The three figures in Chapter 4 included a box representing the social context. That box includes the leadership and organisational processes considered in Chapter 6 and the communication channels for inciting mistrust discussed in this chapter. It also includes the phenomena described in Chapters 8 and 9. When thinking about the communication channels that are used for inciting mistrust it is worth remembering that they operate within this broad social context where many influence processes are at work at the same time.

Gossip

Gossip: What is it and Who Does it?

Gossip is typically defined as casual or unconstrained conversation or reports about other people, mostly involving details that are not confirmed to be true and normally not in the presence or with the knowledge of the person or people who are talked about. Gossip will usually include explicit evaluative information. However, gossip may be subtly crafted, having nothing explicit but having evaluation insinuated into its substance. Anyone or anything can be the topic for gossip. Gossipers do not need to know the person targeted, they just need to know of them.

Who gossips? Almost everyone. What do they gossip about? Almost anything. Wilson et al. (2000) suggested that people 'gossip with an appetite that rivals their interest in food and sex' (p. 347). There is no actual evidence, but it is a fair bet that the human race has been gossiping since they learned how to speak. We certainly have evidence that children gossip practically from when they start to talk and begin to recognise other people (Fine, 1977). They learn about other people and their reputation through gossip and, at an early age, their gossip is not usually focused on criticism of others (Engelmann, Herrmann & Tomasello, 2016). In fact, children learn quickly to evaluate the credibility of gossip and the things that bias it (Liberman and Shaw, 2020). By mid-childhood, they will use gossip to victimise their peers. Interestingly, Shinohara et al. (2020) found that 7–8 year olds shunned negative gossipers, even though they recognised that the information they offered could be a useful guide to their own behaviour. Adult gossiping tends towards more negativity and an accompanying deferment of disbelief in the gossip offered by others. Some commentators suggest that two-thirds of conversation is taken up with gossip (Emler, 1994). Much of it is trivia but two-thirds of gossip by adults that is evaluative is negative.

Gossiping occurs in all cultures (Dunbar, 2004). No differences in participation in gossiping have been found across socio-economic or educational groups within cultures, though the topic of gossip does vary. Of course, women stereotypically are said to gossip more. There is some evidence that they gossip in different venues and about different things than men, but not that overall they gossip more. This is, obviously, a difficult assertion to justify because what constitutes gossip depends on who is doing the labelling. Women's talk is more likely to be labelled gossip than is men's talk. The stereotype of gossip is that it is something women do, so whatever it is that men are doing when they pass on information it is less likely to be regarded as gossip. Stereotyping has a virulent way of self-fulfilment.

What Does Gossip Achieve?

If so many people do it, it begs the question what are the functions of gossip. It is quintessentially an exchange and it has functions simultaneously for the gossiper, the recipient, the community to which they belong and for the wider society.

At one level, for the gossiper, the purpose may be simply to change the way the targets of the gossip are seen or treated. However, additional to these direct effects, the gossiper may have other motivations; for instance to achieve acceptance, social influence, enhanced status, self-justification or vindication. From an IPT perspective, therefore, gossip can be a route through which self-esteem, self-efficacy, positive distinctiveness and continuity may be supported. For example, I tell you some intimate detail that you did not know about a person important to you but which intuitively appears to be accurate. In doing so, I make myself look more associated with the important person, I raise myself in your estimation, I illustrate my ability to get valuable information, I show myself to be different from you, and if I do this regularly I emphasise my own reliability and consistency. Yet not all gossip is motivated by self-interest. It is often perceived as the 'moral' thing to do, passing on necessary information and is justified as such. Of course, doing the moral thing can also be self-interested!

Identity processes may also motivate involvement in gossip for its recipient. The value of any gossip depends upon the response it elicits. That response will depend upon how it resonates with the psychological, social and material needs of its audience. People pay attention to gossip that supports their prior attitudes and beliefs or that provides information that they regard as useful in terms of their own objectives. Martinescu, Janssen and Nijstad (2019) treat gossip as a resource when used in relationships within hierarchies where there are power differentials. They found that people gossip with others at the same level of power to seek information and social support. They gossip with those at a higher level of power to exert informal influence. In this sense, gossip is a form of social exchange. This exchange when in informal contexts is not always utilitarian in any simple or direct way. A lot of gossip between peers is laced with humour (often at the expense of the target of the gossip) and, as such, is part of relationship maintenance – effectively, just being friendly or seeking to bond.

This notion of gossip as a form of social exchange indicates that it has a function not just for individuals but also for organisations and communities. Gossip is a process that can bring them together or tear them apart. Gossip can be the medium for transmitting cultural norms and behavioural expectations, through praising and shaming. It can model what should be believed and what cannot be tolerated. Pascua (2019) illustrates this vividly by showing how gossip was used to reveal 'heretics' to the Spanish Inquisition. Beersma & Van Kleef (2011) suggest that gossip keeps people 'in line', enhancing group bonding by 'outing' deviants and the non-compliant.

This suggests that isolated individuals do not create their own narrative for their gossip. They use schema or memes that are commonplace in their circle of contacts. These touchstones make what they say understandable, credible and relevant. The individual customises the message to fit the recipient but stays within the recognisable framework. For instance, if I want to gossip with you about our mutual boss, I have a limited range of issues that will be most likely, for example favouritism, competence, meanness.

Gossip: A Process of Social Representation

In this sense, gossiping can be seen as part of the social representational processes that have been discussed throughout this book. Gossip is shaped by social representations. Yet also, through the customisation available to individuals, gossip can contribute to the social representation's evolution and development. This can be seen most clearly when gossip acts to promote a particular social representation. In the occupied Palestinian territory, Albarghouthi and Klempe (2019) examined the complex social representations of cancer that existed. They showed the significance of religious discourses in these social representations: cancer as predestined by the will of God; cancer as a punishment or trial; and, as a spiritual journey of healing. In telling the story of local cancer sufferers, gossipers have these discourses pre-eminently available. Their use in gossip about particular cases has implications not only for future health behaviours but also further perpetuates them and offers them colour through exemplars.

Beside sex, illness is high on the list of gossip favourites. Illness arouses curiosity and fear, probably in equal measure, so gossip about disease and medicines is commonplace. Community understandings, social representations of new diseases and their treatments often rely a lot on gossip. Gossip translates and promulgates digests of the formal information available. The translation is not necessarily either accurate or unbiased. This often means people accumulate false understandings and may make poor decisions on self-protection from the disease. It may also mean that people are led to mistrust authorised or well-founded statements about the illness. It can induce further uncertainty. Then a vicious circle develops. More uncertainty about their risks motivates people to search out and pay attention to more gossip about them. Uncertainty also drives people to look for more than one source for their gossip. Like a bee, they sample and collect sustenance from many sources. Commonality and agreement across sources is not inevitable, so gossiping may exaggerate uncertainty. The disparities between samples of gossip actually can be a source of mistrust about a disease or its treatments. During the COVID-19 pandemic declared in 2020, elderly people in England were reported to be tapping into their established gossip networks for information and reassurance. They used the gossip to test whether they were understanding what the government was broadcasting and to come to conclusions about what could be believed and what they should do. This is a nice example of how gossip can both assuage and encourage mistrust dependent on its precise content and purpose.

Gossiping is not a one-shot affair with a single narrator. Gossip is passed on. It is shared. Through sharing, it is elaborated. The process of transmission results in its mutation. As we pass on gossip, we add something or fail to include something that we were told. This is not just because our memory is fallible. What we transmit is shaped by our motivation and predilections and they are likely to be somewhat different from those of the original narrator. Elaboration and embellishment, especially of salacious details, is both permissible and rather expected.

Anthropologists talk about different types of gossip and debate whether it is defined in terms of its collective function as a group-binding, boundary-maintaining mechanism, (Gluckman, 1963) or whether it is simply 'informal communication' by individuals (Paine, 1967). The description offered for the purposes here of examining mistrust assumes that gossip can serve group purposes but that it can also serve personal purposes that are not founded in group dynamics. Gilmore (1978) argues that there are numerous forms of gossip and they occur in different types of venues (e.g. in the street, barbershop, the market) and have many sorts of subjects (typically including local personalities, the dead and sometimes the long-dead, motor cars or neighbourhood events). In his study of a rural Spanish village, Gilmore found 11 different words for gossip, each describing a perceptible variation in style or nuance. They included (using a loose English translation of the Spanish labels): the critical, the cutting (malicious), unrelenting abuse (tonguelashing), collective whispering, collective scandalous murmuring, niggling, idle talk, speaking 'sotto voce' (typically about someone with power) and 'telling' (betraying a confidence). Gilmore's analysis showed that gossip varies; in purposefulness, in the extent of community involvement, and in how far it is seen to be acceptable or legitimate. Once the diversity of types of gossip are recognised, it is evident that it has both individual and collective functions. Equally, it is clear that it can be a dyadic or a community production. Either way, it works to mould social representations – those accepted and used by the individual, and those in circulation societally.

Gossip Columns

In this context, it is interesting to note that the newspaper or magazine gossip column became one mass media incarnation of this sort of activity (without the immediacy of interaction) long before the arrival of social media. The gossip column was that part of a newspaper in which stories about the social and private lives of famous people used to appear. Columns mixed substantiated facts (such as marriages, divorces, arrests, event attendances) with speculation or innuendo (e.g. about affairs, mental health or financial problems). They were 'infotainment' at its most obvious and titillating. Wilkes (2003) identified the first informal chatty newspaper column as that in *The Review*, founded in Britain in 1704 by Daniel Defoe, who was twice put in the pillory for libel and who later wrote the book *Robinson Crusoe.*

Gossip columnists are said to have had a symbiotic relationship with their subject matter. They needed the stars; the stars needed them. Celebrity is based on public awareness and gossip columnists were given privileged information by publicity agents that would 'spin' awareness in a positive direction. Columnists would inevitably adjust the spin to keep their readers interested and customers. Indeed, columns sometimes skirted the edges of libel (defamation).

The role and prevalence of gossip columns in their traditional format has changed massively with the advent of social media. The big difference is evident: originally, with limited print sources and the dominance of a few long-lived gossip columnists, gossip columns had great power to stimulate particular social representations of individuals or of organisations. The gossip column was the voice of the newspaper proprietor, editor or writer. It could initiate a social representation and it could elaborate or reiterate it. Unlike the gossip in a small Spanish village, the gossip column was not part of an immediate feedback loop with its readers. Social media, given its interactive nature, is more similar to the Spanish village. However, the gossip column clearly has a common root with face-to-face small community gossip. It was also predicated upon the proclivity of the initial reader of the column to then act as a transmitter. The column becomes the basis for subsequent gossip in dyads and small groups. We will return to the way social media represent a platform and channel for gossip later in this chapter.

In some contexts, for instance in relation to the film industry, gossip columnists became celebrities in their own right (not infrequently subject to gossip pedalled by others). They were gossip 'stars'. However, the role of gossip 'stars' is not limited to columnists. In ordinary communities, gossiping occurs within a sociometric network. The network describes patterns of contact between people. Sociometric status refers to how much a person is liked and noticed by peers and reflects peer acceptance. Someone can gain high status in a network by being the most influential gossipmonger (i.e. pedlar or trafficker of gossip). It is interesting that the label 'gossipmonger' is used, paralleling the term fishmonger. 'Monger' has two meanings. It can describe someone who is selling or dealing. It can also be used to describe someone who encourages particular thoughts or behaviours, especially in a way that causes trouble. Both definitions seem apposite when applied to gossip. Gossip is a sort of commodity. It has value in social exchanges. Gossip is also eminently capable of causing trouble – especially when it is targeted at arousing mistrust. Ask yourself, in your own circle of contacts, at work or in the family, who is the person who most will go to for a gossip update. How does that person use their status? Gossip star is an influential position, if not necessarily admirable.

Poison Pen Letters and Hate Mail/Speech

A poison pen letter is a figurative rather than literal description of a written message containing unpleasant, abusive or malicious statements or accusations about the recipient or a third party. It is usually sent anonymously or with a pseudonym. It can be sent to multiple recipients simultaneously, and can be widely public if digital dissemination is employed. Hate mail (now often appearing as hate speech) is a distant relative of the poison pen letter and dating from a more recent era and usually extreme. Hate mail or speech tends more toward harassment, intimidation and threat. The recipient is mostly chosen because of social category membership, life style or beliefs, though it can be simply because they are highly visible in the mass media (e.g. sportspeople or victims of crime). Hate mail or speech currently usually gravitates towards social media platforms or other electronic conduits (Fan, Yu & Yin, 2020).

Poison pen letters and hate mail or speech are very different from negative gossip. Typically, they are more extreme. When produced in a series over time, they tend to become even more vitriolic. Their originator typically strives, at least initially, for anonymity. Originators of hate mail often suffer with some psychiatric illness. While gossiping can yield social reinforcement for the gossiper, poison pen and hate mail or speech producers usually get social opprobrium. The reward for them seems to lie in the damage they inflict on others.

Mistrust as Collateral or Intended Damage

Mistrust of an individual or an organisation can be incited by gossip, as we saw in relation to disease and medicine. The gossiper(s) may set out to do this by deliberately choosing to disseminate information designed to build an image of someone as a cheat, liar, thief, scoundrel, bigot or other things that indicate that this person must be mistrusted. This intended incitement of mistrust has been seen often in gossip in workplaces, where employees gossip about the motives or competence of their managers to undermine their authority or to influence their decisions (Michelson & Mouly, 2000, 2002).

However, spontaneous gossip in most contexts would be unlikely to be that explicit or direct. The gossip might provide clues to merit mistrust and these might need to be pieced together, perhaps over several elaborations and retellings, with the recipients feeling that they had come to their own conclusions. Whether the mistrust produced was intended by the gossiper is a moot point. Imagine the scene in the barbershop as two customers talk, overheard by those waiting. One man says to the other: 'I was really surprised to see Joe leaving your house the other day in the middle of the afternoon. You and the wife having some decorating done? I hear the ladies like his work.' One of those overhearing this sniggers – just enough to be noticed. Whether there was actually any intended sexual innuendo is unclear. The way the remark is interpreted will depend on many factors: the husband's relationship with the gossiper; his faith in his wife; his relationship with Joe, the state of any decorating, and the import of the snigger.

The example points to the fact that the capacity for casual gossip to incite mistrust rather depends on whether the seeds of mistrust are already present and whether the source is deemed reliable. A rather different example illustrates the same point. Mistrust in a finance house can be inflamed by small pieces of 'juicy gossip' about the depression suffered by the chief executive that are taken out of context and over-generalised, but this would usually only occur when some question about the probity or underlying strength of the firm has been raised before. What both examples suggest is that different pieces of gossip over time, not necessarily from the same source, may precipitate mistrust but the effects depend on context. The initial instances lay the foundation for the effect of those occurring later and can manufacture a context amenable to mistrust.

Collateral mistrust occurs when the target of the gossip is one person but the attack on that person causes another to be mistrusted in addition. So for instance, the gossip in the barber's shop may have been targeted at Joe and was deliberately intended to arouse mistrust about him. If it worked to do that, it probably also raised mistrust of the wife. Inciting mistrust through gossip can be a rather indiscriminate instrument. It is hard to be certain who will actually be mistrusted. In fact, collateral mistrust does sometimes veer back on the gossiper. In the barbershop, did the husband mistrust Joe or the customer who raised the question?

It could be argued that most techniques for inciting mistrust have drawbacks. Initiating mistrust may be relatively easy but then controlling its direction and implications is very difficult in most circumstances. Although they differ in many respects, gossip, poison pen letters, hate mail and hate speech are all channels through which individuals can be stigmatised, normally without redress. They each provide a way to incite mistrust, irresponsibly and with limited chance of reprisal. As they each migrate to social media, their capacity to do this is magnified. They can also become more potent when used as tools in planned attacks. Disinformation campaigns and conspiracy theories can mobilise gossip and hate speech, in particular, to suit their own ends. We look at disinformation and conspiratorial tactics in later chapters.

Rumour

Rumour and gossip are closely allied. A rumour is a story or report of uncertain or doubtful truth that is currently in circulation. Gossiping can transmit rumours. Rumour can be based on gossip, but not necessarily. In terms of inciting mistrust, rumour is a sharper and more sophisticated tool than gossip. However, fundamentally, both are good methods for developing and changing social representations. The people who engage with them also tend to be seeking to satisfy similar needs.

Types of Rumour

Social psychologists became interested in rumour in the 1940s. Knapp (1944: 22) defined rumour as 'a proposition for belief of topical reference disseminated without official verification'. He noted that they are topical, informative and/or express or gratify the emotional needs of the community where they circulate. He went on to analyse rumours circulating in Boston, US, during winter 1942 as the Second World War raged. It is interesting that he got his data by having the Massachusetts Committee on Public Safety, for whom he worked, ask the *Reader's Digest* magazine to appeal to its readers to send in rumours they had heard. His report does not consider the implications of such a method for the conclusions he draws, though he does suggest the study should be done again using a national sample. In any case, he came up with a tripartite classification of rumours: the pipe-dream or wish rumour (reflecting hopes and desires); the bogey rumour (reflecting fears and anxieties); and the wedge-driving or aggressive rumour (reflecting hatred and aimed at dividing loyalties).

Knapp's study is enlightening because it shows how rumours provide an insight into the structure of a community, its divisions and its innermost concerns. Typically, he argued, rumours are confined to clearly delineated sub-groups or factions. Since he believed that the type of rumours that prevail in a group reveal the morale of its members, monitoring 'rumour symptoms' constituted a way to assess differences between groups. He also suggested that the amount of rumour being circulated was inversely related to the extent to which official information is viewed as trustworthy. Illustrating this, he described how the vacuum created by the absence of information after the Japanese attack on Pearl Harbour in December 1941 was coterminous with a high incidence of rumours, exaggerating the havoc it caused.

Knapp acknowledged the role of rumour as an instrument of propaganda. Given the time at which he was writing, the propaganda of the Axis alliance (Germany, Italy and Japan) was uppermost in his thinking as was their use of short-wave broadcasts to seed rumours designed to disrupt enemy morale. Wedge-driving type of rumour is a typical tool in propaganda (we will return to this in discussing disinformation in the next chapter). Rumours can also be used as 'smokescreens' for actual intentions. If believed by officials and reproduced by them, then at some strategic moment when the enemy discloses them as 'mere' rumour, they can discredit the officials that had been duped. One of Knapp's key messages was that rumour needs to be monitored and analysed, then it can be counteracted.

Knapp's research is worth considering in a little more detail because it highlights so many of the ways in which rumour is still important today. The technological channels through which it is transmitted have certainly changed and, consequently, rumours are less contained within group or sub-group boundaries. The numbers that can be influenced simultaneously have grown exponentially. The sheer range and complexity of competing rumours now outstrips anything seen before. Yet the fundamental uses of rumour have hardly changed at all. That is why it is valuable to consider what Knapp thought makes a 'good' rumour. What are the key elements that make a rumour work well?

A Good Rumour

Knapp recognised that rumours change as they are retold and can be substantially distorted before achieving their ultimate form. He used the classic work of Bartlett (1932) on reconstructive memory to inform his thinking about the transformations that rumours go through as they pass from one person to another. Bartlett had shown, using experiments such as that involving the 'War of the Ghosts' story, that people altered the stories they were asked to remember when they subsequently recounted them. They not only omitted details but they inserted new material. Moreover, the way remembering transmutes the original material is influenced by our prior knowledge and experience of similar material. Bartlett proposed that people use schemata (systematised cognitive representations of previous memories) to help them store and retrieve memories. The schemata were said to distort new memories to fit into their existing structure. While there have been many critiques of the Bartlett schema theory, like so many of the early models in psychology, it has a fascinating way of recurring in other guises. The idea of abiding 'schema' organising the way we think and feel is common across many recent models. It can be seen as one of the roots of SRT. While Bartlett was primarily concerned with individual schema, Moscovici was primarily concerned with social schema.

Both individual and social schema are likely to be at work in shaping the transmission of rumours. Knapp observed that the further the rumour gets from confirmed evidence, the more distorted it gets when passed on. Distortion is greatest when the rumour relies solely on person-to-person transmission and, at the time he was writing, if the rumour was reported in the mass media, distortion was less. Presumably this is because the media report, at that time, was regarded as evidence in its own right or because more people received the same version of the rumour simultaneously. Nowadays, that is not how the mass media operate and we will examine their current role later. In his day, Knapp found that the circumstance most likely to give rise to distortion of the rumour is when it is relevant to ongoing unrest or acute needs for information. Certain details are more subject to revision (e.g. names and detailed numbers). Also, in transmission, the identity of the originator of a rumour may morph into someone of greater authority (by association giving the rumour higher credibility).

A successful rumour is one that is transmitted sequentially, with minimum distortion, by lots of people. So Knapp argued that to be successful a rumour must be short, simple and salient. It must constitute a 'good' story – having the elements that make it appealing but easy to remember. For instance, it should have a simple plot with a humorous twist, presented in striking detail, including exaggeration, and omitting qualifying clauses or syntactic complexities that imply uncertainty or ambiguity. Effectively, the successful rumour is modelled on the characteristics of the great memorable stories present in all societies. It will incorporate the preoccupations and prejudices of the group within which it circulates and, as these change, it will alter. There is an echo here of the characteristics of persistent gossip. These features of a 'good' rumour are also characteristics that social psychologists in the 1940–50s were finding in other forms of messages that proved influential and persuasive. Aristotle taught that persuasion is founded upon three appeals: logos (facts), pathos (emotion) and ethos (values). A good rumour will have these appeals offered in a package resilient to distortion (Allport and Postman, 1947).

Motivations for Making and Spreading Rumours

Why make rumours? Spontaneous rumour (as opposed to propaganda-driven rumour) appears to exist to satisfy the human desire to make sense of the world and thereby reduce uncertainty, with its attendant anxiety. The need to impose 'meaning' on an event will often result in rumourmongers synthesising a story from quite different events, at different times or places and with different characters. Brought together they make a story that has its own internal logic. Rumourmongers (note the use of 'monger' again) act as unintentional (what Bartlett called unconscious) scavengers of data that will substantiate the chosen meaning of an event. It is noteworthy that rumours are most prevalent in groups that are inactive or bored or locked down in a monotonous, unchanging environment. In such cases, rumour is not simply used to give meaning to events, it is used to all intents and purposes to fabricate events to satisfy the need for novelty and interest.

Rumour can also serve other motivations by providing interpretations of events that make the rumourmongers and their audience feel safer, stronger, more loved, more part of the community and so on. This might explain the pipe-dream rumours. It will not explain the bogie rumour. That seems to portray a story meant to raise anxiety and fear. Perhaps it is simply cathartic to give voice to a fear that is already present. That seems unlikely, since bogie rumours are often precursors to panic and irrational behaviour. Of course, it may just be that the rumourmongers are representing the threat that they see and thereby justifying their fear. Knapp came to that conclusion.

Aggressive, wedge-driving rumours are also prevalent when people are afraid. These rumours are not directed at the manifest, external source of the fear. Instead, they tend to focus on drawing intra-group boundaries and attacking those on the 'wrong' side of the border. Such rumours find scapegoats for failure and fear. Knapp points out that another feature of rumourmongering is projection (in the Freudian sense, imputing one's own motives to others). This might be thought to be most obvious in rumours where someone's sexual exploits are recounted. However, as always, it is hard to prove when that sort of projection is at work.

Why spread rumours? This is about the motives that propel individuals to spread rumours. Knapp describes some patterns. The selfish reasons include expressing hostility against the target of the rumour, achieving status by apparently having information others lack, or manipulating others. The less selfish reasons include using the rumour to provide others information that might protect them or might reassure and provide them with emotional support. The overlap with explanations of gossiping are obvious.

The Meta-function of Rumour in Inciting Mistrust

Specific rumours may be targeted at inciting mistrust of particular people or things, just as gossip may be. However, rumour has a meta-function in inciting mistrust. Rumour production (in rumour mills – the social processes described above) is anti-thetical to assurance in the usual media of communication, undermines confidence in leaders, and creates unrealistic demands for access to information. By doing this, if done at scale, it engenders broad-ranging mistrust. This is generalised mistrust, akin to that described in earlier chapters. Wozniak (2003) described an example of how largescale and fast-moving rumours in a time of crisis can vie with the control governments have over information and challenge their authority. She summarised how the Severe Acute Respiratory Syndrome (SARS) epidemic initiated mass movement of rumours over the Short Message Service (SMS) and the Internet in Hong Kong and Mainland China. Governments can restrict or block these electronic channels of rumour migration. However, because this will inevitably be discovered, doing it can be a further stimulus for mistrust. Members of the public are not the only participants in the rumour mill. Rumour may also be used by those within the political system to incite mistrust. Mlambo & Zimunya (2016) report on the malicious use of rumour by politicians to sway public opinion against their political enemies in Zimbabwe during a period of economic and political turmoil in 2008. These rumours carried by word of mouth and by social media platforms, included character assassination and incitement to harm opponents. The study illustrated that such rumourmongering affected the boundaries and norms of political interaction. Such rumours can shift the terrain of mistrust like a tornado can transform a landscape.

Social Media

While it seems appropriate here to consider contemporary social media, it has to be acknowledged that a book is a poor medium for describing social media – too static, not interactive, unilinear and unidimensional. Bearing that in mind, they have been mentioned repeatedly earlier and they will come up again in later chapters, so some elaboration here is appropriate. Their use resonates with the way gossip and rumour operates. In fact, social media have created a completely new way to gossip and spread rumours. However, they take these processes to a very different level.

Trying to describe social media is a complicated business. This is partly because social media evolve rapidly; by the time this book is published they will have changed and make some of what is here simply of historical interest. It is also complicated because people, even now, have such varied experience of and access to social media (digital natives probably do not need to read the rest of this paragraph, Generation Z and Alpha certainly do not). Here, we focus on the basic skeleton of the phenomenon. Social media are interactive computer-mediated internet technologies that allow people to create, edit and share information in many forms (text, audio, photographs and video), often in virtual communities or networks. Social media rely on web-based applications that run on desktop, laptop and mobile devices, and that constitute the platforms for this interaction. Social media differ from traditional print and broadcast media (increasingly called 'legacy media') in many ways. They rely on users making the content. Content formats have become increasingly diverse, allowing various visual effects. For instance, some encourage users to interact with augmented reality objects or to present 'stories' about themselves through pictorial representations sequenced chronologically. Vast quantities of new material are shared daily across billions of active users.

Connections between users are typically immediate. Transmission occurs between many sources and many recipients simultaneously. Some popular social media websites (including Facebook, Twitter, Instagram, Weibo, LinkedIn and Qzone) each have over 100 million registered users. Material appearing on a site can be permanent but can also be restricted to grouped network members and password protected. However, some platforms (e.g. currently Snapchat) do make pictures and messages available to recipients for only a short time. Some social media services have adapted to offer organisations the facility to communicate virtually in real time across numerous sites and involving multiple personnel (e.g. currently Microsoft Teams or Zoom). Some include advertising from commercial organisations.

Social Media Use

Of course, not everyone uses social media. Perrin (2015) reporting data from a large number of surveys showed that 65% of American adults in 2015 used social networking sites, up from 7% in 2005. Usage among those 65 and over was 35%, compared with 2% in 2005. The groups with the most rapid increase was 30–49 year olds (8% to 77%) and 18–29 year olds jumped from 12% to 90% users. Women and men used social media at similar rates and no notable differences were evident by race or ethnic group. Usage was positively correlated with household income and with level of educational attainment. Usage across the board is probably greater now. In some ways, social media is the ultimate social leveller, even though the richer and more highly educated do still appear to use it more. If they have technical access, people, irrespective of age, have equality of presence on social media. They face very limited censorship. There is virtually no quality control. Typically, frequency and amount of contributions is not rationed.

Differences between people in their prior experience of social media cannot be ignored. Variations in exposure result in people thinking about social media in different ways. If you grew up with social media used in your home, school and university or college, and now are surrounded by it in your workplace you will have developed a certain type of relationship with it. Taking for granted, and becoming reliant on, the omnipresent, omniscient, interconnecting Web becomes inescapable. It is like oxygen, just there. It is only when it is not there that it becomes noticeable. If you did not have the benefits of early exposure, you may not take it for granted. You may feel strange depending on it and inept in using it, but it is still inescapable. Your children, your health service, your bank, probably your employer and even your neighbourhood watch, all expect you to use it. There is a pressure to participate, to network, to share and to utilise. The data available suggest that over a very short time, differentials in understanding use and acceptance of social media will fade away – echoing what has happened when other technological innovations have transformed social interaction in the past.

As this happens, the use of social media for practical purposes will grow, but so will their use for psychological purposes. The relative mix of the two purposes will differ across individuals. For habitual, natural users, the psychological motive may be greater. This positions them differently in relation to their tendency to use social media to express their identity or to establish their social position, beliefs and values or to mobilise others to do so.

Social Media and Identity Processes

The existence of social media has significant consequences for both identity processes and for social representations. There is a perceptible shift in the location of the private and public boundary of the identity representation. More of identity is now expected to be public property, or, at least, at risk of being publicly accessed. This makes the task of maintaining identity resilience harder. Self-esteem, self-efficacy, positive distinctiveness and, particularly, continuity have to be managed in this virtual world, as well as in the material world. IPT would predict that people use their social media presence to maintain or enhance these identity principles. One example of enhancement would be attempts to improve the virtual physical image of oneself (e.g. through 'selfie' editing using digital filters, Tiggemann, Anderberg & Brown, 2020). An example of self-protection would be the 'emergency detagging' of posted photos before job interviews to defend reputation.

Identity maintenance on social media is not easy. The examples above entail content that individuals place about themselves. 'Identity signalling' on social media in one form or another is common. People do it explicitly, by revealing who they like, what they believe, where they go and so on. They also do it implicitly, for instance by their responses to others' posts. Identity signalling is complex (Grewal, Stephen & Coleman, 2019) and often backfires, not achieving the results expected. Additionally, individuals are not in control of most of the material posted about them. Dealing with it can become a time-consuming and emotionally draining obsession or compulsion.

However, social networking sites that are prominent on social media platforms can reinforce an element of identity that is shared by bringing together individuals that have that element in common so that they can affirm its value. Kaakinen et al. (2020) describe how 'identity bubbles' such as this form on social media, especially around identity characteristics that may be under attack (e.g. sexual orientation). Identity protection through social media participation in a virtual group is an option. Similarly, identity reconstruction can be achieved through a concerted presence on social media of individuals who share some traumatic past experiences or heritage. Goldschmidt-Gjerløw and Remkes (2019) offer an example of how the children of political activists who were 'disappeared' during the Argentinian military regime of 1976–83 have used social media narratives of their life stories to create a recognisable group identity and a place for themselves in history.

This is a good illustration of how choosing how you present yourself is an expression of agency. The online identity is a creation that has purpose. It can influence how others perceive you. It may be a way of achieving social acceptance and status and thereby enhance identity resilience. It can also venture into places that the offline identity cannot go. Online it is possible to replace one's social categorisations (age, gender, social class, ethnicity and so on) with ones that appeal more. Life stories can be rewritten. The extent of the disparity between online and offline identity can be very great. The question that then arises is how far is this online creation an alternative identity rather than a figment that supports the offline identity? To the extent that it deviates markedly from the offline identity, can it become a threat in itself? The dynamics of the relationship of online and offline identities have only recently been examined. Some studies have focused on cyber-identity theft and the fears it creates for offline identities (e.g. Roberts, Indermaur & Spiranovic, 2013). Others are concerned with the influence that online identities can have over actual behaviour. For instance, Evans (2018) pointed out that online identities that acquire social acceptance by reporting or representing engaging in risky behaviour may motivate risk-taking offline. The merging or dissociation of offline and online identity requires further investigation.

Given the pervasiveness of social media interactions, the role of online identity in models of both individual and group identities will inevitably become more significant. While the individual will strive to manage online identity, it will also be affected by what others choose to present about the individual. The importance and prevalence of attacks against individual and group identities on social media cannot be ignored.

Super-efficient Gossip and Rumourmongering

That leads to the essential question: can social media be used to incite mistrust? It is certainly possible and there is evidence that they do.

People have the opportunity to incite mistrust because of the openness of access and limited policing of content. It can be used as the stage for a sort of super-efficient gossip and rumour. It really is great for gossip and rumourmongering. As an initiator, you can remain anonymous or create a false persona, so you can limit reprisal risks. You can get your message across to a very large number of people at one shot. That means the message has less chance of being corrupted by others in transmission – though the speed with which content can be shared may militate against retaining the 'purity' of the initial rumour. Yet, even as the rumour morphs with onward transmission, typically the original message will remain accessible for anyone motivated to search.

On social media, you are actually expected to produce messages that have the characteristics of good rumours (simplicity, brevity, humour, memorability) and you have the added advantage that you can use not just words but images (tending to make it more memorable). Unlike in offline gossip and rumour, online the target normally has the option and mechanism for responding quickly and at scale. Gossip and rumour may work almost the same online as off, but the scope for random message distortion is probably somewhat diminished and the opportunity for rebuttal probably increased. Both of these factors would need to be weighed against both the sheer scale of the social media audience and the speed with which new elements can be added to the story that is circulating.

Offline gossip or rumour can range from the trivial and benign to the accredited and devastating, so can online gossip and rumour. The latter has particular potency because it can have the weight of numbers. Finding that a million people are publicly accepting that you are a bad person (especially when you are accused without cause or proof) can be very upsetting, probably more so than having three people at the local shop gossiping about you being bad.

It was inevitable that social media would become havens for celebrity gossip (like the gossip columns of yore but turbocharged). Celebrity bloggers are numerous. Blogs, frequently updated online journals, by celebrities and about them, are big business. A typical blog combines text, digital images and links to other web materials. Video blogs (vlogs) are also increasingly popular but seem to serve the same function. Followers of these blogs can leave comments and interact with other commenters. Bloggers are paid through ad networks for the number of people who view the blog. The bloggers' motives include self-promotion and income generation, and both these rely on attracting and maintaining a large pool of followers. So the task is to make the blog addictive. Is it surprising what attracts followers. Apparently, for non-celebrity bloggers, knitting, fitness and parenting do well. For celebrity blogs, the more personal the better, possibly because it opens a door to a life most readers find inaccessible and virtually unbelievable.

Celebrities of all sorts blog. Blogs are currently increasingly mainstream methods of outreach and opinion forming. Politicians, academics, sports people, artists, musicians, as well as media personalities, blog. Such use of social media can satisfy the motive for power and recognition, and secure employment. It offers much greater, visible influence than the gossip or rumourmongering of the past. For the followers, it satisfies the urge to be in the 'know'. Everyone can get in on the act. The followers have the opportunity to be judge and jury. Bloggers who can rouse high levels of support have a significant tool for applying public pressure for change. In many ways, they are not fettered by the gatekeeping that constrains content in traditional media, though content is sometimes moderated or filtered to remove hate speech and other offensive content.

Organisations now use corporate blogging. They tend to use them differently than television celebrities. For instance, the charity Oxfam, an international NGO delivering aid and development work to overcome poverty and suffering, has a blog as the hub for its news, analysis and debate. In May 2020, as the coronavirus pandemic raged, Oxfam used the blog to illustrate the role of trust in the world's most vulnerable communities (van Koot, 2020). While the use is different, the purpose is similar and is to bring influence to bear.

'Social media influencer' (SMI) is now a recognised role. SMIs act as third-party endorsers who shape audience attitudes through vlogs, blogs, tweets and other routes. Freberg et al. (2011) examined the perceived personality of SMIs. They were thought to be verbal, smart, ambitious, productive and poised but not submissive, fearful or anxious. SMIs are typically 'self-branding', creating a distinctive public image for commercial gain or cultural capital. Just like commercially branded products, they benefit from having a unique selling point. The more the SMI is seen as attractive, prestigious, expert, informative and interactive, with taste, and an opinion former, the greater the power of the endorsement through initiating the audience's desire to mimic the SMI (Ki Kim, 2019). SMIs have power as long as they can maintain the trust of their audience. To do this their endorsements need to be seen as authentic and not driven by a commercial link with the commodities endorsed (Audrezet et al., 2020).

Exclusion via Social Media: Cancel Culture

For those individuals who use their social media presence to build and maintain their identity, exclusion from the networks they inhabit can be a great threat. Interactions on social media sites afford users virtual friendships, audiences and group affiliations. Being expelled from, or criticised on, these online social circles can be enormously traumatic. Yet deliberate exclusions are increasingly common. These processes are given some memorable labels: 'silencing', 'blanking', 'ghosting' and, most prominent, 'cancelling'.

Cancel culture (or call-out culture) refers to the processes of ostracising someone from social or professional groupings online. It is usually associated with 'calling people out' for alleged wrongdoing or wrong thinking. People who experience this are labelled 'cancelled'. This indicates they are blacklisted. This is a highly emotional process of accusation, often involving vitriolic angry statements. The attack acts as a magnet for large numbers of people to 'pile in' and add their weight to the rejection, disdain, derision and dismissal. The 'cancellation' accumulates momentum and grows in its capacity to damage reputation and perceived trustworthiness. Such attacks may be spontaneous snowball phenomena but they can also be organised campaigns deliberately arranged to undermine the target. Targets for cancellation are usually celebrities or influencers; they are more likely to attract the snowball involvement of attackers. However, the simpler, more individualised, process of unfriending (removing someone from a list of contacts on a social networking site) that tends to occur with less illuminous individuals is also used to express disappointment, disagreement or dislike.

One high-profile target for cancellation in 2020 was J. K. Rowling, the author, among many other works, of the Harry Potter books. She attracted the attack after she posted a tweet that was seen as transphobic and offended some transgender people. Rowling fought back, defending the views that she had expressed. She also joined with 152 other notable signatories (e.g. Chomsky, Rushdie, Kasparov) to publish an open letter in *Harper's* magazine (Shead, 2020) denouncing 'cancel culture' and the online shaming of individuals who have done or said something that angry social media users consider objectionable or offensive. The letter warned of the development of a climate intolerance of free speech or open debate and 'a vogue for public shaming and ostracism, and the tendency to dissolve complex policy issues in a blinding moral certainty'.

It is hard to say whether or how cancelling hurts the target. There is an absence of closely relevant research. However, there is every reason to believe that it should affect psychological wellbeing. Loss of approval and removal of supporter networks have been repeatedly shown to be associated with anxiety and depression. To the extent that online cancellation parallels offline abandonment or chastisement, it would be expected to have ill effects on mental health. The related processes of cyberbullying and cyberharassment (which involve sending messages of an intimidating or threatening nature) certainly have serious consequences for some of those attacked. Lowered self-esteem, fear and withdrawal, especially in younger victims, are common. Cancellation and cyberbullying are both likely to result in victims finding it difficult to feel safe. They may feel vulnerable and powerless. In the case of cancellation victims, the sheer volume of opprobrium they experience, often from faceless masses, may make them feel there is no escape.

There have been suggestions in the popular media that, because many of the targets of cancel culture are people with power and celebrity, they are immune from such reactions. Some even go so far as to imply that these particular types of target are fair game. The problem with this line of argument is that the content of the accusations made is usually designed to challenge the victims' motives, morality or beliefs. The threats are not trivial because they are focused against the foundations of the individuals' identities. Moreover, in many instances, the attacks are part of a broader sequence of cyber-manipulations that aim to pressure the victims to conform to socio-politically correct precepts or some new anti status quo canon. Faced with this sort of onslaught, even the rich and powerful might be expected to experience the threat and react. If they did not, what would be the point of attacking them?

This leads to the question: why do people get involved in the online cancel culture? It seems that online disinhibition and deindividuation effects may account in part for individual participation (Lowry et al., 2016). This is not the whole story. Cancel culture operates within a synchronising rhetoric. There are themes that cut across specific cancellations; for instance, abuse, climate change, racism and sexism. These reflect societal uncertainty, the omnipresence of risk and the meme of mistrust. People get involved in the cancel culture because it allows them to embody and personalise the supposed sources of their uncertainty, risk and mistrust. Even better, it allows those sources to be punished.

Cancel culture is a vehicle for speaking explicitly about mistrust. It serves to translate generalised mistrust into some particular thing that some identified person has done. If that person is powerful, it becomes a way of speaking mistrust to power (an echo of speaking truth to power). It is more than a symbolic act. The object is to effect change. Knowing they are mistrusted and publicly shamed, they are implicitly, if not overtly, asked to recant and conform. This mixture of overt mistrust and public shaming is a powerful tool.

Trolling

Social media trolling is different from cancelling. Trolling is defined as creating discord on the Internet by starting quarrels or upsetting people by posting inflammatory or random unsolicited messages in an online community (Bradshaw & Howard, 2017). A social media troll is someone who purposely says something controversial in order to get an emotional reaction out of other unsuspecting users. Trolling is typically malicious deception. To be considered successful, the troll must not be recognised as a troll. Once detected, the game is lost.

Trolling is usually a one-on-one game. However, there are frequent reports of orchestrated trolling. Instances on Twitter of people accusing each other of being a paid troll or a bot (botnets are covered in the next chapter) crop up with remarkable regularity. They seem especially popular during political elections (where the troll master is normally seen to be a foreign power or opposition candidate (McCombie, Uhlmann & Morrison, 2020). Marital disputes between celebrities receive media coverage routinely, but when one half of a couple claims the other is paying for a smear campaign by creating, controlling or manipulating social media accounts this tends to go viral (see Brown's, 2020, coverage of Johnny Depp and Amber Heard dispute).

Trolling undoubtedly can be, and is, used to incite mistrust. However, the existence of trolling acts also to undermine the trustworthiness of social media itself. Often, the troll relies on being anonymous or employs a fake identity. Once discovered, this arouses generalised mistrust. Additionally, an accusation that a social media user is a fake will tend to get many clicks – the awareness of the possibility of fakes is thus disseminated further. It is also known that verifying attribution (i.e. the identity of the user) on social media is very difficult. Brooking and Singer (2016) showed that the behaviour of older Facebook users is 'essentially identical' to 'online sock puppets' steered from abroad. 'Sock puppets', in this context, are multiple accounts associated with fictional identities controlled by the same user. They are typically used for creating false majority opinions or vote stacking and for vandalising genuine sites of information. Sock puppets can network with each other, to support each other (Kumar et al., 2017). The complexity of these systems and the speed with which they can be deployed and then, once acknowledged, adapt to attempts to restrain them has become a major concern. Mistrust of social media is itself a growing issue.

Mistrust of Social Media

This link between influence and trust is fundamental to the power of any social media activity. The credibility of the material and of those who provide it will shape its reception and use. This is not peculiar to social media. What is different is the extent to which social media material is inchoate. It is internally inconsistent and conflicting, fragmented and from multiple embattled sources. This should be a recipe for mistrust of social media. Indeed, it does appear to have grown.

Manifest mistrust of social media has been most evident in relation to the circulation of 'fake news'. Fake news essentially reports false stories, sometimes based on prior gossip or rumour and, sometimes, concocted de novo with malicious intent. Fake news is not the preserve of social media; such reports can appear in any of the mass media. Typically, fake news arising in one outlet is then picked up and passed on in others. It could be argued that fake news is simply another form of gossip or rumour, but dressed up clearly as fact. The fake news that social media carries concerns everything from the trivial minutiae in the lives of domestic animals to internationally momentous politico-economic affairs. No subject is too small or too great for fakery.

The problem that users face is separating the truth from the lies. The fact that there are many contending versions of the 'news' usually available accentuates the problem. A surprisingly large percentage of those receiving fake news say they believe it. In a study of public responses to fake news on social media in the 2016 US Presidential election race between Hilary Clinton and Donald Trump, Allcott and Gentzkow (2017) found that around 50% of those recalling the fake news believed it. Flew et al. (2020) in a study of Australians also found roughly half of their respondents mistrusted social media and the numbers were increasing. People are more likely to believe social media reporting if it supported their own views. This echoes the usual proclivity to both remember and believe things that agree with what you already think. Thorbjørnsrud and Figenschou (2020), in a study of perceptions of immigration patterns, noted a recognisable pattern of behaviour in those sensitised to accept fake news. They identified what they called the 'alarmed citizen' who is characterised by alertness, fear and low institutional trust, who actively shifts between alternative media and established news media, and constructs personal news repertoires and supportive networks. It was notable that the strategies adopted were still tending to support the individual's justification of their existing beliefs and attitudes.

Mistrust of social media seems to be moderated by the contents of the fakes on offer. It also seems that the public is now a discerning customer for social media, and, indeed, for other media. They shop around. They discount what is unpalatable. Any mature market where many providers are available has these characteristics. It may mean that overall social media carry the warning 'treat with caution'. It does not mean this doubt or suspicion eliminates their influence. Even where fake news is recognised and dismissed, it will have had an effect – if only to highlight what someone, somewhere, wants you to think or feel. Also, generalised mistrust of social media is sometimes accompanied by a deep trust of one aspect of it. Open access allows individuals to colonise social media space. They can create a place to proselytise for their own version of the news. This slice of social media for that individual or group is vested with complete trustworthiness. Hopp, Ferrucci & Vargo (2020) report how some individuals present their arguments against mainstream news media in Twitter and Facebook. They found that sharing this 'countermedia content' was associated with ideological extremism. It is interesting that 'owning' the use of some fragment of the social media will ensure a residual belief that at some level social media can be trusted; not everything about it has to be mistrusted.

Nevertheless, there is a strong social representation that social media should be mistrusted. Mechanisms to fact-check online content are now widespread. Despite this, sharing fake news is the norm (Talwar et al., 2020). Sometimes it is shared because it is fake or suspected of being fake. The controversy around it makes it newsworthy in its own right, passing from social media to mainstream news media, and sometimes back. All of this happens very rapidly. The chances of a post 'going viral' enhance considerably with the controversy.

Three Platforms for Inciting Mistrust and Being Mistrusted: Gossip, Rumour and Social Media

People are social beings and they rely on the transmission of information to maintain their social structures. Gossip and rumour are essential ingredients in the processes of developing and sharing understandings of what is happening and what should happen. They are typically unauthorised narratives and open to challenge and mistrust but they are also valuable conduits for doing social business – such as encouraging moral behaviour, shaming the miscreant, warning of danger, and signalling who or what is to be mistrusted. Gossip and rumourmongering historically were relatively small-scale, unorchestrated and uncommercialised activities. But they were always platforms for inciting mistrust. Now gossip and rumour have an additional platform: social media. It is a much more efficient platform than its predecessors are, yet it serves the same ends and co-exists with what went before.

Gossip and rumour were always open to being mistrusted. Living with mistrust of social media is now also a necessity. Social media are part of the fabric of social relationships and everyone, except perhaps the very young, is sensitised to the possibility that they will be misused. Yet there is little evidence that this mistrust of social media reduces its overall power to incite mistrust about others. Social media play a key role in building the prototypes and stereotypes of 'the mistrusted' that were described earlier. They are vital in ensuring the efficient spread of unfounded insinuations and claims about people and organisations. In fact, like gossip and rumour, social media have a meta-function of undermining established authority and sowing doubt. Ironically, they retain their power probably for the same reasons that gossip and rumour continue to shape behaviour. They offer roads to influence that people would not have otherwise. Anyone can gossip, rumourmonger and post. Anyone and anything can be their target. People will discount their own mistrust of the platforms, if the messages transmitted are amenable to or serve their self-interest.

CHAPTER 8
WEAPONISING MISTRUST: DISINFORMATION AND PROPAGANDA

Harking back to the model of identity, mistrust and emotion influences on action described in Chapter 4, disinformation and propaganda are part of the social context that forms and houses mistrust. This chapter explores the use of disinformation and propaganda as tools in manipulating the thoughts, feelings and behaviour of individuals and groups. Disinformation and propaganda are used in many ways. One important use is to turn mistrust into a weapon in political and commercial conflicts and competitions. Fake news, trolling and cancelling were introduced in Chapter 7. They all involve forms of disinformation or propaganda. In fact, disinformation and propaganda are intrinsic to many of the ways mistrust is incited, including in gossip and rumour. However, it is worth examining them as concepts and methods in a broader context.

The Concepts of Disinformation and Propaganda

Disinformation is distinct from misinformation, though it can be regarded as a subset of it. Disinformation involves the deliberate and purposive presentation of information, knowing that it is untrue, as if it were true. It is not done in error. It is done with intent. It is meant to deceive and mislead. Some might argue that disinformation is just another word for propaganda (Cunningham, 2002). Propaganda entails spreading selected information, ideas, opinions or images, often only giving part of an argument or one way of looking at the facts, with the intention of influencing people's opinions or actions.

In contemporary usage, there are negative overtones to labelling anything disinformation or propaganda. However, it is questionable whether their use is universally morally repugnant or intrinsically evil. Disinformation and propaganda each may be used for good or evil purposes. What is considered good and what evil will depend on the assessor's viewpoint.

The two labels have remarkably parallel births, though three centuries apart. Propaganda derives from the name of a new body created by the Catholic Church in 1622 as part of the Counter-Reformation. This was called the Congregatio de Propanda Fide (Congregation for Propagating the Faith). Its aim was to propagate the Catholic faith in non-Catholic countries. From the 1790s onwards, the label has been also used to describe secular activities of a similar sort. Disinformation is the English rendering of a Russian word (transliterated as dezinformatsiya) which described the KGB black propaganda division set up by Stalin in 1923 to undermine capitalism and foster communism, which continued through both the Second World War and the Cold War. Disinformation was recognised as pervasive internationally in politics by the late 1980s and a major tactic of intelligence agencies worldwide.

While the genesis of the two labels can be traced to discrete moments and organisations in history, the concepts and methods to which they refer have been deployed throughout history. They are both essentially tactics of persuasion. Both rely on using information selectively to shape how people think, feel and act. In practice, the difference between them fades. Propaganda may incorporate disinformation and be considered the overarching concept. However, disinformation is probably used colloquially more frequently in the early 21st century because it has been so intimately associated with online misrepresentation and manipulation.

Taylor (2003), in an update of a book he originally wrote in 1990 and revised previously twice, examines the manifestations of propaganda from the Ancient World to a new era of information disorder. He focuses on its use in warfare through these ages. He draws attention to the many possible forms of propaganda objects that have been used historically. One of the earliest recognisable were the elongated, rectangular stone monuments, known as stelae, depicting a king with his god or with a subjugated enemy used during the time of interstate warfare between cities in ancient Mesopotamia. These stones evolved into potent visible symbols of a military forces' power and were strategically located reminders to the defeated that it was pointless to rebel. Later civilisations sometimes used mobile objects to disseminate their version of history. For instance, the Greeks used vases, the Romans used sculptures.

Early propaganda also took the form of heroic military poems or hymns. A form useful because it was designed for public consumption and intended for oral recitation before large and illiterate crowds. These poems, composed sometimes long after a battle, were post-event celebratory war propaganda. Anticipatory propaganda about the outcome of war also grew; omens, prophesies and oracles, marshalled by the priesthood, shaped expectations of success (or failure) – raising morale (or mistrust). Taylor argues religion was used cynically to promote loyalty and fear among the ruled and suggests this provided the conceptual origins of modern day psychological warfare. It is notable that these early forms of propaganda often involved disinformation of one sort or another (such as the rigged pronouncements of the oracles or the inflated number of enemies overthrown). All involve the communication of information designed to lead the audience to believe a particular representation of what is or should become real.

Powerful imagery is often vital in the success of propaganda. The images do not have to be visual but it helps if they are since they are the means to overcoming linguistic barriers. The stelae of Mesopotamia (c.2550 BCE); the Bayeux tapestry (after AD 1066); the TV pictures of the first man on the Moon erecting the US flag (20 July 1969); the street murals of the fall of the Berlin Wall (9 November 1989); the real-time streaming of the collapse of the Twin Towers in New York (11 September 2001); the ultrastructural morphology exhibited by coronaviruses when viewed electron microscopically (December 2020); and the ice blue, stealthy march of a melting glacier on satellite recordings (now) all tell a story. They are all iconic images. Moreover, they all have propaganda value because they can be used to show where power lies, who is the enemy, what is the danger, and signal the emotions that should be felt. They tell a story but they can also have stories told about them. The interpretation of the image is not totally predetermined. It is malleable; it is rich enough to have many social representations woven around it. It depends on who is the narrator.

The art of a great propagandist lies in using the image to build a representation of what has happened or could happen that will motivate people to accept it and then share it. The image is the hook on which the propaganda is hung. The image might be amenable to many different narratives. For instance, the Saxon and the Norman chroniclers would probably use the Bayeux tapestry rather differently to represent the implications of the Norman Conquest. Equally, the melting glacier image would be used differently by anthropomorphic climate change deniers from those representing the scientific consensus on the impact of human activity on weather patterns. The object of propaganda (whether in conflict or commerce) is to induce people to assimilate a specific new interpretation of an image into their broader system of social representations. Once assimilated, it can act like a virus; it will be shared, infecting others.

These examples ranging from stone stelae to satellite pictures are chosen to illustrate that the medium of communicating an image may have changed beyond all imagining over the millennia but the uses to which it may be put have striking similarities. The fact that the images themselves now can be manipulated by the artful propagandist using digital doctoring adds a further dimension to their usefulness. The image itself is important, often because it is memorable and emotionally charged, but the narrative attached to it by propaganda techniques does most of the work because it specifies what the image actually should be understood to mean.

Propaganda Techniques and Processes of Persuasion

The techniques of propaganda and the processes of persuasion are reasonably well documented. Propaganda is thought to generally follow a pattern starting with diagnosis (what is wrong), prognosis (what needs to be done) and rationale (who should do it and why) (Wilson, 1973). However, the actual form that propaganda takes varies greatly according to who controls it and whom they wish to control. The forms are customised to suit the purposes and the channels of their communication evolve with technology and societal structures. Most of these forms seem to involve disinformation in some guise.

Many social psychologists have written about the techniques of propaganda, emerging particularly after the First World War and again after the Second World War. It is important in reading their work to recognise that they, like all social scientists, were creatures of their own time, influenced by their own life experiences and the socio-political imperatives around them. It is an area of research that inevitably seems to become politicised. These researchers often made value judgements about the use of propaganda, acting as apologists under some circumstances and condemning it in others. Nevertheless, they created a vast body of work on propaganda techniques and on the processes of persuasion that underpinned them. Smith and Lasswell (2015) produced a comprehensive bibliography of the research.

Lasswell (1927) had many years before produced a classic book on propaganda techniques in warfare. He defined propaganda as the technique of influencing human action by the manipulation of representations and noted that these representations may take spoken, written, pictorial or musical form. According to Lasswell, propaganda is a type of communication characterised by distorting the representation of reality. Of course, Lasswell was writing before the advent of a social constructionist interpretation of the concept of reality. He was, in fact, effectively referring to the manipulation of what Moscovici (1981, 1988 & 2001) called social representations. His theory has been described briefly in earlier chapters. In fact, SRT was evolved, in part, because Moscovici was trying to understand how social influence processes work. He was particularly interested in minority influence processes. These involve the techniques that a minority of individuals in a group can use to bring about changes in the way the majority in the group think, feel and act. In a series of classic experiments, Moscovici and his co-workers (e.g. Moscovici, Mugny & van Avermaet, 1985; Moscovici & Nemeth, 1974) showed the power of minorities in small groups. Minorities that made a judgement at variance with the majority judgement, as long as all members of the minority said the same thing consistently and repeatedly, were able to establish doubt in a significant percentage of the majority concerning their own initial judgement. The doubt was sufficient for them to change. The intriguing thing about these experiments was that such changes occurred not only in judgements about attitudes, they also occurred in relation to the perception tasks. Some people shown a card that was clearly blue would say it was green once they heard a minority of other participants say it was green (Moscovici & Personnaz, 1980). The minorities in these experiments were using a most basic propaganda technique: the delivery of the same disinformation from a number of sources apparently without their collusion and without any apparent ulterior motive. Moscovici used these experiments, together with qualitative analyses of growth in understanding and acceptance of certain technological and theoretical innovations (including Freudian theory) to build SRT. He showed that minorities are able to direct the course of social representation processes even though their influence is sometimes hidden (Maass & Clark, 1984). It is important to note that while minorities may have little resource or positional power, they can be powerful through their propaganda, that is through their ability to shape social representations.

One important ingredient in propaganda is the promulgation of disinformation. However, in propaganda, when disinformation is used it is woven into wider and deeper patterns of communication that deliver the desired persuasive effect. These patterns of communication involve the following elements to varying degrees.

Undermine the Opposition

The object is to silence or discredit people who disagree with the propaganda message. The primary purpose is to make other people at least to mistrust the target. This can involve direct false accusations against their morals (e.g. that they are liars, cheats or thieves) or their competence (e.g. that they have a history of failure). This is likely to be more effective if the accusation can be rooted in some scintilla of evidence, but even this is not essential because, if they are repeated and difficult to disprove, 'smears' will stick to the target. They will be remembered, out of context, and influence attitudes towards the target. Discrediting can also involve quoting the target out of context (to suggest their views are unsubstantiated, extremist or self-contradictory). 'Guilt by association' is also used. This involves linking an opponent in some way to a person or thing that is unacceptable. For instance, it may claim that a politician has attended the same party as someone convicted of a sex crime. The claim may not be true, it helps if it is, but the important thing is to associate the target with something that plants the seed of doubt about this person's judgement or moral rectitude. Similarly, associating the target with a symbol which carries strong emotive connotations (e.g. daubing the Nazi Swastika over an opponent's campaign posters) deposits in the memory of observers a residue of doubt. Propaganda campaigns will sometimes bombard the target with attacks. They can continue a long time and they can be resurrected when necessary. The bombardment technique is aimed at demonising and demoralising the target. Long-term propaganda campaigns against an individual can induce significant loss of self-esteem and self-efficacy. This may be a collateral advantage for the propagandists who are mainly interested in cauterising the positive effect the target might otherwise have upon the people they themselves wish to manipulate.

Disguise the Message Source

The object is to optimise the apparent source of the propaganda message. Propagandists will often not wish to be seen to be the source of their own messages. This is usually apparently true of secret services using the techniques. The KGB Disinformation Agency, according to reports of comments made by William Colby (once a Director of the US Central Intelligence Agency), would plant a false report in a minor left-leaning newspaper, then it would be repeated in a Communist periodical, then published in a Soviet newspaper, which would say its sources were undisclosed individuals. It is rather like criminal money laundering; the more bona fide hands it passes through the better for the anonymity of the source. Recent research on propaganda has shown how general this tactic has been. For example, Pena-Rodríguez (2020) analysed the way members of the Spanish fascist party became the 'black embassy', the diplomatic legation, of General Franco to Portugal during the Spanish Civil War. From Portugal, the embassy was the base for propaganda disseminated to the US, Latin America and across Europe, using multiple media conduits and intermediaries. Pena-Rodriguez shows that, in order to legitimise internationally the military coup, attract recruits to fight and donations to fund them, and to give voice to Franco's 'new' Spain, the 'black embassy' carried out intense media activity which included the spreading of false information, institutional declarations, press releases and photo montages.

Online presentation now makes the identification of the originating source of a message enormously difficult. The use of 'botnets' makes identification particularly problematic – at least for the average citizen. A botnet is a network of computers, sometimes arranged hierarchically, infected by malware that are under the control of a single operator. The identity of the operator is typically invisible. The botnets may be used in many ways, to steal data for instance, but they can also be used to disseminate messages.

Governments, secret service agencies, terrorist groups and commercial operations all now have the capacity to 'sow' their messages internationally and simultaneously to mass publics with anonymised impunity. Of course, there is also intense competition to develop propaganda detection algorithms. These flowered during 2020 in response to the disinformation circulating online about the COVID-19 pandemic. For instance, Khanday, Khan & Rabani (2020) report machine learning techniques for identifying propaganda in tweets about the virus. Sadly, these detectors alert users to the presence of propaganda techniques, they do not typically identify the source. However, the methods are being refined. Increasingly, they are able to identify users that have a very active role in the diffusion of different propaganda and disinformation items, and they can identify topological clusters of users and which users are playing a 'central' role in the network (see e.g. Guarino et al., 2020).

Some ways of masking the source are less elaborate. Many propaganda campaigns will involve individuals that 'front' the message. The object is to associate the message with trusted, well-known or authoritative figures. This does not always mean hiding the organisation behind the 'front'. In 2020, with the development of effective vaccines against COVID-19, governments globally needed to get people to agree to be vaccinated. One key plank in the persuasion technique they adopted was initially to have older media personalities, generally liked and respected for their independence and common sense, publicise that they would be having the vaccination. Using older figures in this way first was tactical because it was older people in the general population, and who were most at risk, who needed to agree to vaccination first. At the same time (December 2020), in the UK, there was a media 'leak' that the Queen and her husband, Prince Philip, both in their nineties, would be having the vaccination – but they would 'wait their turn and not jump the queue' for it. For many in the UK, this would have carried a number of subtle messages about the positive value of the vaccination. It is doubtful that endorsement of the vaccine simply by the political or medical elites would have the same effect. This sort of approach also says something about propagandists manipulating mistrust. Choosing the right 'front' is significantly about minimising mistrust of the message and the motives behind it.

Craft the Content

How the message is presented is crucial. Bearing in mind that we are rarely talking about a single message broadcast only once, certain presentational techniques are typical:

- *Use of simple slogans that are memorable and repeated through every medium available.* For instance, the UK government during the COVID-19 pandemic in March 2020, when a national lockdown lasting 4 months was instituted, told people they were giving one simple instruction – you *must* stay at home – 'Stay at home, Protect the NHS, Save Lives'. A letter to this effect was sent on headed notepaper from the Prime Minister to every household. After a second shorter lockdown, in December 2020, the government told the public: 'There are three simple actions we must all do to keep on protecting each other – wash hands, cover face and make space.' Since hygiene was an important break on spreading the infection, the message on hand washing had been amplified. People were told they should wash their hands with soap and for as long as it would take them to sing two verses of 'Happy Birthday to you'. Rather memorable for most people.
- *Use of stretching the truth or half-truths.* This involves linking what is said to something verifiable but going beyond it to claim something that is not true. Exaggeration from a slender database is an example of this technique. An aligned technique entails the selective omission of information that refutes the claims that are being made. The misuse of statistics and distortion of data in propaganda messages is common. Graphics can be wilfully made misleading. When arguments emanate from some sources (e.g. campaigners or advertisers), the public is already sensitised to the likelihood of sleight of hand in the use of data and, on occasion, this mistrust will be justified. The problem is that mistrust of data bandied about in the midst of a conflict

or crisis can be indiscriminate. People get disillusioned with the presentation of 'facts' because they have come to regard nothing to be objectively factual. Propagandists have an uphill battle ahead; naivety in the face of stretched- or half-truths is now a rare commodity (Nguyen, 2017). Mistrust of facts as represented through most media is an everyday reality. No percentages from opinion polls that could substantiate this assertion are presented here – since, if the assertion were correct, why would you take any notice of them?

- *Tell people how to belong.* Propaganda appeals can be based on a message that offers people the chance to stay in or become part of a group of like-minded and/or important people. The basic structure of the message is simple at one level – join us, we are like you, we understand you, and we will deliver what you want. At the next level, it says to belong you must think, feel and act in ways that we prescribe. Radicalisation propaganda often uses this message structure. This sort of message is aimed at using identity processes. It offers opportunities to raise self-esteem, prove self-efficacy, develop a deeper sense of continuity of self through time by linking to a strong religious or socio-political heritage, and, thereby initiates a greater sense of positive distinctiveness. Schlegel (2019) explored how homegrown extremists' beliefs about their own abilities to change their situation are directly shaped by the online ISIS propaganda they consumed. She concluded that online-propaganda seeks to increase perceived personal self-efficacy in order to inspire terrorist action. Similarly, Biswas and Deylami (2019) conclude from Islamic State's English-language propaganda materials that the group's appeals to women across the West relied on discourses of empowerment and agency. The Islamic State propaganda reimagined Muslim women, not simply as mothers and wives, but as public agents of change in creating and shaping the global caliphate. The offer made to women who are potential foreign terrorist recruits was not only belonging, it was also the chance to achieve something. This then has to be weighed by those targeted against other, more negative, implications for identity, or, indeed, for longevity.

- *Arouse emotions.* Propaganda messages may be designed to arouse an emotional response that will precipitate people into a desired way of thinking and/or acting. Few rely solely on the force of logical argument to achieve their objective. Propaganda most often mobilises negative emotions – fear, hatred, anger. For instance, the fear message says: if you do not do this, something very bad will happen. This message is designed to generate or intensify fear. The hatred message says: you are justified in your hatred and the people you hate deserve what we are asking you to do. This message is designed to highlight awareness that the supposed hatred is there in you, it may even instigate it by offering that such hatred is justified. The anger message says: if you do this, you will not feel so angry anymore. This message is designed to assert that the anger exists and at the same time offer an escape from it. It all sounds easy, but it certainly is not. Manipulating with any precision the emotions of a single person at a time is hard enough. Moving large numbers in the same direction in concert is horrendously difficult. Moreover, emotions once triggered have a bad habit of being uncontrollable. This is why propaganda campaigns need to be long-lived and need to be refreshed to match changing responsiveness in the target populations.

- *Using demoralisation and euphoria.* Propaganda may be a blunt or unwieldy instrument when focused on a specific emotion; it has, however, been shown to have the power to induce an emotional tone in large groups. War propaganda has been used both to demoralise the enemy and to inculcate euphoria on the home front. Demoralising and euphoria both rely heavily upon disinformation. Feeding an enemy a heavy diet of bad news (even if false, and announced to be so by the enemy leaders) has an impact on morale. Sustaining allies with tales of success and hopes of new victories can lift hearts and increase effort. This has always been known and used by war leaders. It is more difficult now because people have so many ways of corroborating or disproving the assertions of leadership. So now, manipulating mistrust of alternative sources of information becomes increasingly important to all parties in a conflict.
- *Instil confusion and self-doubt.* Sometimes the manipulation of emotions and psychological state is taken to extremes. Typically, this can only be achieved if the propagandist has significant control over the targets' environment. It involves disorientation, for instance by bombarding the targets with information from many channels that is inconsistent or contradictory, so that self-doubt and confusion emerges concerning the facts or the motivations of the source. It can involve serial denials of the targets' perception of events, misdirection in 'evidence' presented, together with a convoluted series of lies. Often this will be conducted amidst protestations of goodwill and concern about the target's evident 'confusion' and 'instability'. Sometimes this technique, which is aimed at making people question their own memory, perception or judgement, is called 'gaslighting'. Its use is mainly feasible in closed communities or close relationships. It reflects the way propaganda can blend into what is called brainwashing.

Designing the presentation of a propaganda message involves consideration of each of these elements: the representation of the opposition, the proponents that voice the message, the specific content, the emotions it evokes and mobilises, and the arousal of self-doubt.

Control the Channels of Information Transmission

Closing down competing messengers, physically or by effectively gagging, is often vital to the effective delivery of propaganda. Powerful elites have always striven to control the conduits of communication – the language to be used, access to literacy, ownership of the print media, and now control of mass media and online platforms. Managing news – that is, controlling which events are presented and the way those events are represented – is fundamental to effective propaganda. However, this only matters if people on average have faith in the news presented. The conundrum facing propagandists now is to keep mistrust at bay sufficiently to allow propaganda to continue in business.

To Summarise

Propaganda, which entails manipulating prevailing social representations of current reality, is a process that involves undermining the opposition; manufacturing the message source; crafting the message content; and controlling the channels of information transmission. To be effective, propaganda must manage mistrust. If its sources, messages or media of communication come to be mistrusted, the capacity to control the effects of propaganda is eroded. Therefore, mistrust is typically something that propagandists need to mobilise against others but keep well away from themselves and their works. In the climate of febrile information exchange that the digital age has heralded, shielding against mistrust is not easy and can be hazardous.

The Disinformation Crisis

Rothkopf (1999) pronounced that we are in the 'disinformation age'. He was reflecting on the fact that the information age, far from crystalizing the harmonic convergence of free markets, democratization, and a communication revolution, had failed to release the reliable flow of valid information. Rothkopf, who was particularly interested in financial systems, said old habits of secrecy and a system rigged by insiders to serve their own needs were reinforced. Over two decades later, having experienced the financial crisis of 2008 and the global coronavirus pandemic of 2020, it is evident that his diagnosis was correct but probably too optimistic.

   We are now at a point where fear of disinformation is influencing most aspects of life. We have come to mistrust, if not totally distrust, virtually all information presented to us. We no longer believe the evidence of our senses when it comes to mediated text, audio, still images or video. People in general know just enough about the way communication systems can be manipulated and their content edited to know that they must doubt the veracity of what they provide. People are just ignorant enough about the technologies to feel at risk of unconscious imperceptible manipulation, harking back to the use of subliminal techniques as propaganda tools (Bornstein, 1989). This is a global phenomenon. This is the disinformation crisis.

The Roots of the Crisis

How has this come about? There are three prime roots of the disinformation crisis. First, the discovery and publicising of very serious and systematic breaches in major information systems. Second, the proliferation of criminal activity that is dependent upon using disinformation. Third, advent of random disinformation attacks on individuals and organisations.

Breaches in information systems

The first root of the disinformation crisis is well illustrated by instances of significant attacks upon political systems. Perhaps the most widely discussed examples of interference via digital technologies concern interference in political and democratic processes. Schia and Gjesvik (2020) label this 'hacking democracy'. It is the process of disrupting political discourse. It can involve everything from simply giving false information to inflaming political divisions by rigging poll data collection and feedback on a grand scale using botnets. Probably the most recognised example comes from the so-called 'RussiaGate' controversy (Boyd-Barrett, 2019). Since the 2016 Presidential election in the US, investigations, congressional hearings, academic research and myriad news stories have detailed the spreading of false information on social media platforms. The Russian government was accused of seeking to benefit the Republican Party by creating fraudulent accounts on social media sites such as Twitter and Facebook and using them to polarise and disenfranchise particular groups; discredit or promote particular candidates; and suppress turn-out to the vote. The latter aim being linked to messages circulated on social media in the days before the election that Hilary Clinton had died. The actual outcome of the complex and lengthy investigations that followed these accusations, and that left many questions unresolved, is probably less important than the fact that they consumed so much space and time in the public mind internationally. The RussiaGate phenomenon symbolised the weakness of the system to protect itself against disinformation. Ironically, the heated polemical blame game, following the unveiling of the supposed disinformation attack itself, probably initiated as much mistrust as the success of any attack itself might have done. Indeed, this might have been a core aim of any such attack.

State disinformation campaigns are not new (as we have seen in relation to the historical instances of propaganda) and they are not infrequent or limited to a small number of agents (Lukito, 2020). They are also creative in their use of techniques. For example, linking human curation with automations by using state-sponsored trolls alongside botnets (Zannettou et al., 2019); talk shows rigged to create an illusion of equal representation among guests with opposing views (Gulenko & Dolgova, 2020); and, fake news coverage of 'leaks' purporting to come from key figures in order to discredit them (Hintz, 2019). However, other actors now also use disinformation in subtle ways.

The use of disinformation by violent extremists to justify their actions and recruit new followers has been described above and has been examined further by Ritzmann (2017). Digital communication platforms are also used in the aftermath of terrorist attacks to amplify or constrain the social impacts and consequences of politically motivated violence. Innes, Dobreva and Innes (2019) monitored social media platforms following four terrorist attacks in the UK in 2017 during a period of three months. Their analyses concerned the role of 'soft facts' (rumours/conspiracy theories/fake news/propaganda) in influencing public understandings and definitions of the situation (i.e. social representations in Moscovici's terms). They identified three prime techniques that were being used: 'spoofing', 'truthing' and 'social proofing'.

Spoofing primarily entailed either identity spoofing or information spoofing. Identity spoofing refers to an individual claiming falsely to be someone or to have some social position. Information spoofing involves misrepresenting data, through falsification, omission or amplification. Often these spoof messages ask the reader to share them with others or call for help. In post-attack contexts, emotional spoof appeals can further inflame anger and fear but also confuse. In contrast, *truthing* relies on claiming to be offering the audience the 'real facts'. Supposedly official statistics or statements are used to substantiate the 'truth' on offer. This can work to discredit police or government representations of events or counter the advice they give. They are most effective when they incorporate references to things that are common knowledge or presented in a format that is expected or predictable. Truthing techniques are frequently used by conspiracy theorists. *Social proofing* is a concept derived from social psychological studies of persuasion (Cialdini, 2009). It refers to the way people use the experience and views of others as a reference point for their own conduct and beliefs. Where they believe others will do or think a thing they are more likely to accept and act in accordance with it – especially if they think the 'others' are similar to themselves in important ways. Social media provide an environment where it is possible to create the illusion (e.g. using bots) that significant numbers of other people believe or do something. So it is possible to manipulate social proofing evidence and lead a user to believe they are part of a like-minded group. This can then result in genuine users sharing the fake information or taking other action. Social media likes, re-shares and 'favouriting' are important because they imply social validation and thereby impute value or accuracy to a communication (Confessor et al., 2018).

It is notable that the role of these soft facts circulating on social media after serious atrocities were typically contrary to, or misrepresented, the official representations of what was happening. It is hard to know what influence they had upon widespread public acceptance of the police and government reports. Innes, Dobreva and Innes (2019) do describe push-back on social media from users who supported the police stance. What happened does illustrate two aspects of mistrust that are at work when disinformation is used. On one hand, there is the mistrust engendered about the authorities' reportage and handling of the situation by the 'soft facts'. On the other, there is the mistrust of 'soft facts' and their producers. Either way, the mistrust mill goes round and round but always grinds on.

The production and pedalling of soft facts need not be the preserve of organised groups. Actually, any motivated individual or group wishing to promote a particular worldview can use the digitization of disinformation to manipulate across geographic boundaries. 'Deepfakes' – videos artificially created to misrepresent – could be made using tools available to almost anyone with a laptop and access to the Internet (Chesney & Citron, 2019). Only lack of imagination limits the chaos of disinformation that can be wrought. As more people have access to the technology that makes this possible, probably the more obvious the threat becomes to them. However, there is some evidence that people are not conscious of the effects of disinformation on their own behaviour (Bastick, 2021). However, there is ample evidence that people do now mistrust social media content, even as they increasingly consume it (Park et al., 2020). Simultaneously, greater exposure to social media fosters mistrust of traditional news sources and of societal institutions (Lupu, Bustamante & Zechmeister, 2020). The mistrust mill grinds on.

Looking into the future, Morgan (2018) emphasised that the concentration of power and money held by internet platforms that are not regulated in the same ways as media companies or public utilities opens a door to transform whole sectors of the economy, just as it has already revolutionised journalism and the news. That transition may have been accelerated with the global dependence on online purchases that the 2020 pandemic quarantining and lockdowns have brought about. Many more people have been exposed to the digital economy as a result. They have seen what it can deliver (literally) but also what risks it entails – especially in relation to misrepresentation of both products and the service offered.

Criminal uses of disinformation

This takes us to the second root of the disinformation crisis. This is the proliferation of criminal activity reliant upon disinformation. Cyber frauds, scams, phishing, identity theft are all now everyday concepts. Not all involve complex technologies. A telephone call purporting to come from your internet provider saying that your account is about to be immediately blocked because irregular traffic has been identified on it. The scammer asks for remote access to your computer, supposedly to run a diagnostic test. This gives them numerous options – they can ask payment for their technical support, they can install malware on your machine, and they can steal data from the machine. Similarly, you can get scammed by following a request to call a phone number, usually this purports to be a request from some authority figure (e.g. the tax authorities, the police). This scam, also known as port-out or SIM splitting fraud, allows criminals to hijack your mobile phone number. Once they have your number, they can try to get into your bank account, suborn your email, delete your data or take over your social media profiles. We are all increasingly aware of these techniques. Phishing, which involves getting individuals to reveal personal information such as passwords or credit card numbers, is probably the most notorious and well-known. While we are aware, nevertheless the scams multiply and when new are difficult to spot.

Simply knowing that all this is going on raises the mistrust temperature. Yet, in addition, we are all asked to protect ourselves against these forms of theft. The organisations that employ us require us to defend them against cybercrime and impose safety protocols that restrict our behaviour. Our workplaces and our personal digital dependencies open us to attack. To protect ourselves we increasingly have to build barriers to access. Double and triple authentication systems for account access proliferate. It is important to acknowledge that many of these attacks revolve around attempts at digital identity theft. This need to defend oneself causes generalised anxiety and fear, in addition to inconvenience and doubt about the capacity of those owning the systems to control them. The message to the public is one that emphasises their responsibility for their own safety. The locus for the possibility of theft has shifted from the public to the private and domestic sphere. Picking up the telephone puts you at risk because you have no way of assuring the intentions of your caller. Moreover, you have no way of avoiding that exposure (short of abandoning the telephone). Such crimes, especially those involving more complex digital manipulations, introduce a pervasive mistrust of the systems at the heart of our economies.

Random disinformation attacks

The third root of the disinformation crisis rests in what appear to be random disinformation attacks. These are not strategically motivated or co-ordinated. People doing this may have no other motivation than knowing that they can do it or for a prank or pay back. Anyone can have the means to digitally claim something has happened or is about to happen. Trolling may fall into this category – though it is rarely purely randomised. Policing random attacks is beyond the capacity of most systems that are reliant on pattern detection in content. They can be taken down from social media or refuted retrospectively but by then the damage often has been done – mistrust is further justified. This sort of disinformation should be recognised as a root of the crisis because, for those affected, it is inexplicable and unpredicted. The uncertainty it generates acts as an accelerant for mistrust not just of the platforms that admit disinformation but also of the authorities that cannot eradicate it.

These three roots of the disinformation crisis sustain the growth of societal mistrust. Indeed, it is a crisis precisely because it is not under control and it has stimulated such mountains of mistrust.

The Disinformation Spreader

While people are sensitised now to the omnipresence of disinformation and are very concerned about it, they still have a tendency to pass on disinformation. They tell others about it – even if they say it is not correct, they pass it on. If message and context are held constant (as in an experiment), some people are more likely than others to spread a message that contains disinformation.

Profiling disinformation spreaders, and particularly fake news spreaders, is now a popular pastime for researchers, especially since competitions to find reliable techniques for identifying spreaders have been established (e.g. Rangel et al., 2020). Stylometry (the writing style of the user), personality (inferred from the user's behaviour on social media), emotion (the amount of emotion conveyed in a message) and embeddings (the type of topics they include) are all typically examined. They mostly use artificial intelligence (AI) systems with models built around specifying what is expected in the personality or behaviour of fake news generators (Cardaioli et al., 2020; Fersini, Armanini & D'Intorni, 2020). These use psychological findings to suggest the behavioural, cognitive and affective evidence that signals that a user is spreading fake news or other disinformation. However, this work is not focused on further developing psychological theories that explain or predict disinformation spreading. It is more focused on developing the tools to detect faking and the sources of faking. The distinction between the producer of the story and the distributor of that story is important. Understanding something about the distributor/user from the style of the message, emotion or embeddings may be difficult unless the distributor changes the message before spreading it. Of course, they do embellish and/or edit messages sometimes. This means a whole new layer of models would appear to be necessary.

Meanwhile, there have been various attempts from a psychological perspective to determine why some individuals pass on disinformation. Buchanan (2020) argued that much of the spread of false information online was a result of human action, rather than being AI facilitated. He conducted a series of studies on the self-reported likelihood of spreading examples of disinformation and of past participation in spreading such material. Between studies, there was some diversity and inconsistency in the results. However, those findings that were consistent indicate that likelihood of sharing was not influenced by authoritativeness of the source of the material, nor indicators of how many other people had previously engaged with it. Participants' level of digital literacy had little effect on their responses. Across his studies, personality traits such as lower Agreeableness and Conscientiousness, higher Extraversion and Neuroticism, and demographic variables (male gender, lower age and lower education) were weakly and inconsistently associated with self-reported likelihood of sharing. Consistently, the people reporting the greatest likelihood of sharing disinformation were those who thought it likely to be true, or who had pre-existing attitudes consistent with it. They were also more likely to have seen the content before.

From this, it would appear that some of the factors that social psychology has in the past linked with being open to persuasion and compliance are not explaining the spreading of disinformation. Particular personality constellations, seeking to join a consensus supporting the message, or the characteristics of the source of the message, for example, are not sufficient to explain disinformation flows. From Buchanan's studies, it would seem that people spread disinformation if they are familiar with it already, agree with its message, and think it is true. It is important here to remember that his object was not to assess whether the disinformation was influencing or persuading participants, he was interested in predicting likelihood of spreading the disinformation. Yet it is also notable, across his studies, that the strongest predictor of likelihood of participants spreading was whether they believed the content. This is a somewhat perplexing result to interpret because, if they believed the message content, from their perspective they were not spreading disinformation. So could they be accused of being spreaders of disinformation? The answer is positive only if you ignore their viewpoint. Buchanan's work suggests it would be interesting to look at the characteristics of those who believe the message is untrue and still spread it.

Chadwick and Vaccari (2019) reported that in a large sample of UK users of social media 43% reported sharing problematic (made up or exaggerated) material, and this included 25% who thought the story entirely fabricated and 29% who shared a story they later found was made up. Those sharing problematic material most often said they did so 'in order to express my feelings'. It is clear that people are sharing material that they suspect or know to be false for their own purposes (these include informing and influencing others, finding out what others would think about it, provoking discussion and making people laugh). In general, people are more likely to share information online that arouses a strong emotional response (Berger, 2011; Berger & Milkman, 2012). Vosoughi, Roy and Aral (2018) reported that false news spreads faster than true news online. They used data of rumour cascades on Twitter from 2006 to 2017, involving 126,000 rumours spread by more than 3 million people. False news diffused to more people and more quickly. The researchers showed that false news was more novel and inspired greater fear, disgust and surprise. True stories inspired anticipation, sadness, joy and trust. In false news, novelty encourages spreading, so does inspiring intense negative emotions.

Despite large percentages of people reporting they had experience of inaccurate or misleading content, in the Chadwick and Vaccari study only one-fifth reported trying to correct those who shared it. Being criticised directly for sharing such content is relatively rare. People do not typically wish to challenge disinformation merchants. They inadvertently condone the global disinformation system. Even if they do take action, there is little likelihood that they will have decisive impact. Walter and Tukachinsky (2020) conducted a meta-analysis of 32 studies (with a number of participants totalling over 6,500) and showed that on average correction does not entirely eliminate the effect of misinformation (including some errors and inadvertent falsehood). Corrective messages were found to be more successful when they are coherent, consistent with the audience's worldview, and delivered by the source of the misinformation itself. Corrections are less effective if the misinformation was initially attributed to a credible source, the misinformation has been repeated multiple times prior to correction, or when there was a time lag between the delivery of the misinformation and the correction.

As a whole, the studies of disinformation spreaders suggest that more people do it than might be expected. They suggest people are not keen to quell the spread of disinformation by taking corrective action. There are no significant or consistent correlations between socio-demographical characteristics, personality and willingness to spread disinformation. In fact, there is no coherent pattern linking social media usage and disinformation spreading. Really, it all seems to depend on the characteristics of the disinformation itself. If it has strong negative emotional connotations, people will be more likely to spread it. If it resonates with their personal beliefs, feelings and aims, they will be more likely to spread it. If it echoes or chimes with something familiar, they will be more likely to spread it.

It is as if in this arena social responsibility is laid aside. At the same time that people fear the disinformation that affects them and arouses their mistrust, they perpetuate it through their own actions. Vast numbers of ordinary people, with no particular motive or goal in mind, will participate in the maintenance of the distrust–mistrust merry-go-round every day. Some researchers (e.g. Pennycook & Rand, 2019) have said this happens because people are not attending to the material they pass on, they are 'lazy, not biased'. This probably underestimates the guile of those who produce the disinformation. Everything we have reviewed suggests that both disinformation and its big brother, propaganda, are well-honed products. They are designed to be shared. The people who share them are doing what they are meant to do. They do not seem to be identifiable by some peculiar vulnerability. Given the right disinformation, we are all vulnerable.

Defending against Disinformation

Apart from asking individuals to be aware, use protection and avoid sources (rather like the advice to the public during the COVID-19 pandemic), the defences against disinformation have largely involved either fact-checking or identifying and eliminating systematic manipulation of digital platforms, particularly those created by AI algorithms.

Fact-checking is now a way of life. Since a lot of information available is now tinged with mistrust, fact-checking is a service that is flourishing and comes in many forms. It is usual now in news reports to have a commentary after material is presented (e.g. by a government minister in a radio interview) that examines whether the assertions and data that were included are accurate. Fact-checking reports targeted at posts online often become newsworthy themselves. For instance, posts falsely claimed that the first COVID-19 vaccine recipient in the UK in December 2020 was actually a 'crisis actor'. Caldera (2020) found that in 24 hours, over 475,000 Twitter users were potentially exposed to a single tweet that made this allegation. Caldera stated categorically that there was no credible evidence that the vaccine recipient was a crisis actor and provided photographic evidence that assertions made and proofs offered in the posts were totally false. Fact-checking of this sort is now fast and, importantly, tends to provide evidence of falsehood rather than just rebuttals of online disinformation. Agencies such as Reuters have ongoing sifting of platforms to pick up messages that misrepresent events. For instance, in December 2020 Reuters reported how a video of Bill Gates explaining how a COVID-19 vaccine works was used to misrepresent his remarks so as to suggest that the COVID-19 vaccine 'will change our DNA forever' (Reuters, 2020). Reuters not only presented fully what Gates had said but also backed up their rebuttal of the false claim with evidence from the US Centre for Disease Control and from a series of scientific and medical experts.

The difficulty that fact-checkers have is to penetrate the unwillingness of the disinformation spreaders to accept that their claims have been disproven. They have a tendency to dismiss the evidence that undermines their claims. The refrain 'who fact-checks the fact-checkers' lingers in the air. Fact-checking can help the social media user who is not producing disinformation and who is genuinely uncertain about what to trust. However, a user would need to be alert to the availability of the service and not seduced into feeling that these too should be mistrusted.

The second protection against disinformation lies in the rapid growth of AI systems designed to identify and then close down manipulation of digital platforms. It is not important here to go into the technicalities of these very complex systems. The relevant factor for this examination of mistrust is where the control of these systems sits. Predominantly, they are designed for and operated by State agencies or by the organisations that own media and online platforms. This immediately gives rise to a potential tension between calls for complete freedom of expression and those for the protection of the public against dangerous misrepresentation. A public, already mistrustful, may find this sort of 'protection' a cause for further suspicion. Doubtless, there will be agents that will actively seek to incite such mistrust. The opportunity to arouse concern is furthered when AI is given a key role in shaping the protection offered. Mistrust of AI is itself already significant – science fiction has a lot to answer for.

Is Mistrust Weaponised?

Mistrust is analogous to gunpowder. Gunpowder is the earliest known chemical explosive, a mixture of sulphur, charcoal and potassium nitrate. The balance of these three chemicals in the mixture determines its behaviour. Gunpowder has had many uses. Some were benign and constructive – for instance, its use in pyrotechnics or in rock clearance in quarrying or mining. Many were destructive – for instance, the use as a propellant in firearms, artillery and rockets. Similarly, mistrust has several key ingredients (such as uncertainty, suspicion and fear) which, if present in different quantities, will produce different thoughts, feelings and action. Mistrust may be constructive – for instance, instigating avoidance of danger. It may also be destructive in two directions. Internally, it can harm the person experiencing mistrust – for instance, by eroding self-esteem or threatening valued relationships. Externally, it can harm others – for instance, by causing the person to desert or attack others. There is one other similarity between mistrust and gunpowder. When properly stored, the modern successor to gunpowder, smokeless powder, has an indefinite shelf life. Mistrust shares such longevity.

To weaponise something is to adapt it for use as a weapon. Mistrust can be weaponised in the same way that smokeless powder can be weaponised – to be a fuel for other weapons and to be a weapon in its own right. Both propaganda and disinformation can act to weaponise mistrust. This is because they operate at two levels simultaneously. First, they seek to rewrite social representations: they alter understandings of the physical and social world and they reshape the causal paths of argument and meaning. Second, they undermine the bases for assigning trust and allow mistrust to grow, encouraging all its negative emotional connotations (such as outrage, anger and depression). This moulds a public to be more open to suggestion, misdirection, protest, and rebellion against the status quo or violence against outgroups. Mistrust can detach individuals and groups from the norms and social rules that typically constrain them. Mistrust can result in rejection of authorities and their doctrines. Propaganda and disinformation that arouses such mistrust is making it into a weapon. This mistrust is a weapon that harms the people that assimilate it – threatening their identity resilience and challenging the social representations they use to make sense of their world. Also, through the actions of those people, it can harm targets chosen by the organisations or individuals that originally spread the propaganda or disinformation. To weaponise mistrust it has to be manipulated to make it dangerous preferably at two levels. At one level, it must have a clarity of purpose and target. At another, the meta-level, it just has to be omnipresent and capable of precipitating generalised social uncertainty and lack of acceptance of the possibility of certainty, expertise or authority. A sort of anarchy of will.

CHAPTER 9
CONSPIRACY THEORIES

Having discussed how mistrust is incited through gossip and rumour, and weaponised through propaganda and disinformation, it is only logical to consider the relationship between mistrust and conspiracy theories. Conspiracy theories are bred of uncertainty and mistrust but they are also a stimulant for the next generation of mistrust. They are part of the social context that propels the formation of mistrust. A social context that is in turn reshaped by the decisions and actions that mistrust motivates.

Conspiracy theories are now commonplace and have found fertile ground in the mass and social media. This chapter examines what constitutes a conspiracy theory. It describes how and why they come about, focusing upon the role of mistrust. It also analyses why conspiracy theories survive efforts to disprove them. It explores why people believe conspiracy theories. The function they serve in generating and channelling mistrust is presented. Case studies of well-established conspiracy theories are used to illustrate how complex the social psychological processes are that underly their longevity. The particular significance of social representation and identity processes is emphasised.

What is a Conspiracy Theory?

A conspiracy theory is an explanation of an event or situation in terms of the covert motives and actions of some person or grouping of people. The person or grouping (that can actually be merely a chimera) typically is said to have considerable power. The motives and actions attributed to them are usually sinister. A conspiracy theory can emerge even when other, more plausible, explanations for what is happening can be provided or are already available. In fact, conspiracy theories will often deny the validity of other explanations that are supported by the consensus of experts (e.g. scientists, medics or historians).

Conspiracy theories are usually purposive. They offer an explanation that is meant to manipulate responses and serve an ulterior goal – for instance, it may be to motivate a particular reaction, to attack an opponent, or to protect an ally. They can be both offensive and defensive in objective. Of course, some explanations that centre on a narrative about a supposed conspiracy appear that have no ulterior motive. An individual believing that she has observed a pattern surrounding an unexplained event might spontaneously propose why it has happened and this could involve behind-the-scenes machinations of people with power. She does this not to effect a response in others but to satisfy her own need to make sense of the world. She is not producing a conspiracy theory designed to have another purpose. Yet, if communicated to others, it can change their understandings and acquire different purposes. The difference between what might be called speculative conspiracy theories and manipulative conspiracy theories may be a bit blurred at the edges but it is definitely the manipulative variety that is the focus for this chapter. We treat conspiracy theories as purposive, recognising that they have many different types of purpose and that their purposes will morph with use.

It is also important to differentiate theories about bona fide conspiracies from conspiracy theories (Douglas et al., 2019). Obviously, there can be theories that are proposed to explain what has been agreed to be a verified conspiracy. When Marcus Brutus, Gaius Cassius and Decimus Brutus, and circa 60 other senators came together secretly in 44 BCE to plot the murder of Julius Caesar, they were embroiled in a conspiracy. Theories to explain that conspiracy have been posited, including the desire of the conspirators to restore the institutions of the Roman Republic and their desire to further their own ambitions. However, they are not the sort of theories about a conspiracy that are labelled 'conspiracy theories' nowadays. The label 'conspiracy theory' now tends to be used when someone argues a conspiracy exists or existed when verifiable and uncontested evidence for its existence is unavailable.

The conspiracy theory label is used to derogate and undermine an explanation. It is used to suggest that the explanation is based on prejudice, wilful ignorance or self-interest rather than objective evidence. It suggests the explanation is being used to manipulate others and as a way to justify the activities of those promulgating it. Nevertheless, just because an explanation is called a conspiracy theory does not automatically mean that it is false or in error. It may be that the people labelling it a conspiracy theory do so because they wish it to be believed to be wrong. Where 'conspiracy theories' are concerned, there are always at least two sides to the story. Conspiracy theories sit in the midst of controversy and conflict – justly, and occasionally unjustly, attacked and derided – but always embattled.

Conspiracy theories flourish best when there is uncertainty. For instance, they frequently emerge when the circumstances of the death of a prominent public figure are open to question. The assassination of the US President John F. Kennedy, shrouded with accusations of crucial missing information, was probably the most prolific source of conspiracy theories. They ranged from accusing the CIA, the Mafia, the KGB and Fidel Castro to the Vice President Lyndon B. Johnson (or some combination thereof) of masterminding the assassination. The death of Diana, Princess of Wales in a car crash while being chased by paparazzi in Paris in 1997 also stimulated many conspiracy theories. A British inquest jury returned a verdict of 'unlawful killing' in 2008, after a special Metropolitan Police inquiry team had investigated at least 175 conspiracy theories, none of which were supported. This has not convinced or silenced those who believed the theories. Other events, where uncertainty prevails about their actual causes, are also targets for conspiracy theories. For instance, the disappearance of Malaysia Airlines Flight 370 in Southeast Asia in 2014, without probable cause, has given rise to many explanations. One proposed that the Boeing Honeywell Uninterruptible Autopilot (that was supposedly installed on board) had been hacked and the plane piloted remotely to Antarctica. Public interest in the mysterious disappearance of the plane has continued. Media stories of wreckage from the plane washing up on beaches of islands in the western Indian Ocean or scattered over jungle in Cambodia continued for more than a decade. Mysteries like this are the lifeblood of conspiracy theories.

However, not all are tied to specific events. Some of the longest lasting are derived from attempts to explain more broadly why the world and the social order are what they are. These offer an inclusive explanation for a variety of events, which often have no apparent connection with each other. They are brought together as the product of some overarching, dastardly plot. These often accuse a social category (such as Muslims, Jews, Catholics or communists) or fringe protest movements (such as anti-vaxxers or birthers) of being the culprits (Uscinski & Parent, 2014). Choice of culprit seems heavily influenced by the dominant folk devils of the culture from which the conspiracy theory springs. Folk devils are usually outsiders or flaunt social norms or arouse mistrust and/or fear, especially if they have some sort of power. Uscinski and Parent concluded that power asymmetries are the main drivers of conspiracy theories. They suggest those at the bottom of power hierarchies have a strategic interest in blaming those at the top. Though this does not explain why minority groups are so often targeted for blame in conspiracy theories, it does suggests that conspiracy theories are the vehicles for transmitting blame and mistrust between socio-economic classes and across national boundaries. Byford (2011) describes a conspiracy theory, widely published in China, that the Rothschild family, a wealthy Jewish family originally from Frankfurt, Germany, planned the rise of Hitler, the 1997 Asian financial crisis and climate change, and that all these influenced the direction of China's currency policy. The Rothschild family, which is now synonymous with money and power, has frequently been the subject of conspiracy theories, such as claims that the family controls the world's wealth and financial institutions or that it has shaped the course of wars. Many of these theories have anti-Semitic and/or anti-capitalist origins.

Characteristics of Conspiracy Theories

A mystery or uncertainty offers one sort of opportunity for a conspiracy theory but it does not dictate its underlying structure. While conspiracy theories vary widely in degree of elaboration and complexity, they are typically characterised by certain common features:

- They identify what needs to be explained ('this is happening or has happened') and this usually involves problematising the happening ('this really needs explaining') or locating it in a pattern of happenings that emphasise its importance ('it has happened before and is important').
- There are explanations ('it is because').
- They posit some secret coalition as the source of the thing explained ('there is a hidden consortium of forces causing this').
- They attribute blame ('these are the people who are guilty of this').
- They attribute motive ('they are doing this because').
- They attribute objective or purpose ('they are doing this in order to').
- They identify who is affected ('it will change things for').
- They claim everyone needs to know about this ('even if people try to stop you, you should listen').
- They detail why people should believe (it is important to you because').
- They weave into aspects of their structure features designed to arouse negative emotional reactions ('this is a terrifying situation and you are personally at risk of serious harm from the behind-the-scenes machinations of this corrupt and hateful band of').
- They suggest the explanation should be passed on ('you really should tell others').

Together these features form a potent weapon for arousing and directing mistrust. They pinpoint whom or what are suspect.

As a by-product of their structure, conspiracy theories actually impose certainty and predictability upon the uncertain. They may also include a clear exhortation for action (beyond just telling others). This is certainly present in many of the conspiracy theories concerning health issues. Oliver and Wood (2014) examined several medical conspiracy narratives in the US. These included:

- Health officials know that cell (mobile) phones cause cancer but are doing nothing to stop it because large corporations will not let them.
- The global production and sale of genetically modified foods by Monsanto Inc. is part of a secret program, called Agenda 21, launched by the Rockefeller and Ford Foundations to shrink the world's population.
- Public water fluoridation is really just a secret way for chemical companies to dump the dangerous by-products of phosphate mines.
- The US Food and Drug Administration is deliberately preventing the public from getting natural cures for cancer and other diseases because of pressure from drug companies.

The actions advocated in the narratives range from 'participate in public protests' to 'use/avoid certain products'. What they all share is a clear finger pointed at culprits who increase the health risks that people face and a message that the authorities tasked with looking after public health should be mistrusted. Alongside raising mistrust, exposure to such medical conspiracy theories increases anxiety levels. They have been correlated with the sort of health worries people report, such as gastro-intestinal disorders (Lahrach & Furnham, 2017).

Conspiracy Theories are Social Representations

Birchall (2006) described conspiracy theory as a 'unique form of popular knowledge or interpretation'. Similarly, it might be considered a unique form of social represen-tation. Moscovici (1987) considered the relationship between social representations and conspiracy 'mentality'. He links conspiracy theories to works of fiction and sug-gests there are common principles that explain their popularity. In a lecture in 2006, published posthumously (Moscovici, 2020), he notes four 'themata' common to con-spiracy stories. These were: the prohibition of knowledge; the dichotomy between ignorant masses and enlightened minorities; the search for a common origin for the past and the present (similar to a Goethean 'ur-phenomenon' – the hidden relation-ship of parts that explains how one form can transform into another while being part of an underlying archetypal form); and the valorisation of tradition as a bulwark against modernity. Later, Graumann and Moscovici (2012) argued that conspiracy theory has played a central role in our epoch with very serious consequences. The obsession with conspiracy has spread to such an extent that it continuously crops up at all levels of society. They point to the striking paradox that in the past, society was governed by a small number of men, at times by one individual, who, within tradi-tional limits, imposed his will on the multitude. Today, they argue, this is no longer the case. Power is divided among parties and spread throughout society. So, power flows, changes hands and affects opinion, which no one controls and no one rep-resents entirely. Conspiracy theories explain and influence both the power vacuum and the struggle for power.

The advantage of introducing SRT is that it explains the processes whereby a con-spiracy theory can be generated by one or a few theorists but then become accepted as an agreed, though perhaps contested, explanation by many people. Whether the conspiracy theory is merely a 'best guess', an error or a deliberate pack of lies is not at issue. Social representational processes will work just as well with all these possi-bilities. They are meant to interpret new ideas and allow people to become familiar with them. They were introduced by Moscovici to explain how theories (in his case, psychoanalysis) become accepted or rejected. In the abstract, these processes are non-evaluative. They happen as a fundamental part of creating meaning in social life. Over time, they can winnow out the incredible or unacceptable, but only through cycles of iterative communication and negotiation that are heavily dependent upon the power differentials between the various actors.

Conspiracy theories often manifest signs of having gone through social representational processing. They become 'anchored' in prior explanatory systems to make them more credible. They become 'objectified' in over-simplified illustrations and embodied in memorable slogans in order to make them intelligible. Both features make them easier to pass on to other people. Like most social representations, conspiracy theories evolve. It is necessary to think of conspiracy theories over time – they mutate, they marry, interact and merge. New conspiracy theories can sit on the shoulders of their earlier counterparts. They actually behave like any other theory, whether in science or economics.

Recognising that conspiracy theories are built through a social process and depend upon the work of many hands and minds interacting over time, raises the question of who is 'the' conspiracy theorist? Can they be profiled? Is there a type of person that is the weaver of webs, the seer of patterns and connections in disparate fragments of evidence? Undoubtedly, sometimes the originator – the first sower of the seeds of doubt – the 'discoverer' – will be identifiable, but it is rare. Even where a single scientist signals there is a question mark about the safety of a vaccine, it would be hard to identify that person as the sole originator of a conspiracy theory that then grew around the initial assertion. The conspiracy theory is manufactured by iterative social representation of the original argument. These manufacturers do not need to be self-consciously part of some group or recognisable category. They can be inputting to the manufacturing process independently, especially now that social media offers many channels for contribution. Indeed, the manufacturers may not even label themselves as participating in the process, let alone identifying with it.

The prevalence of these processes of social representation undermines the notion that conspiracy theories are the product of a leading mind. Even in cases where a key figure is identified, as in the case of William Cooper described below, it often turns out that the conspiracy theory being broadcast is an elaboration or concatenation of pre-existent stories. However, such figures can be vital in calling attention to a particular slant on more commonly held assumptions and surmises. It is notable how often those currently identified as conspiracy theorists work, or have worked, in the mass media. They have a social position and a platform that enable them not only to profess their beliefs but also to call on other people to accept them. There is an important feedback loop in this part of the social representational process. A person who already has enough social caché to attract an audience in the first place will further enhance their attractiveness as followers come to accept that the conspiracy might be real. The power of the person, and any acolytes, to direct the social representational processes is then enhanced. When this happens, the processes become less spontaneous, fragmented or diverse and increase in purposiveness. In behaving like this, conspiracy theories again echo the ways that other explanatory and belief systems evolve.

The idea that conspiracy theories can be the product of ordinary social representational processes where people who do not identify consciously with the process and have no personal investment in it may seem intuitively unlikely. This may be a result of the way conspiracy theorists are treated regularly as a 'type' or a 'group' by other people who view them as crack-brained or malevolent. So individuals can be labelled as conspiracy theorists or as a type characterised by 'conspiracist ideation' (Brotherton, French & Pickering, 2013) without ever identifying with the category themselves.

Labelling in this way is useful for anyone who wishes to discredit or marginalise the conspiracy theory and its apparent proponents. The tactics are well established: identify, label, homogenise, caricature, undermine and dismiss. It is a well-worn route. Of course, these tactics can be used with the best of intentions. Conspiracy theories after all can be dangerous. They can waste time and energy. They can mislead people into danger. They can whip up emotions and public dissent or disorder. It is hardly surprising, since this happens, that those labelled will often reject or deny the category membership. This is reminiscent of the 'conceptual grouping' phenomenon described in an earlier chapter.

Convenience categorisations of this sort are used all the time. They reduce individuality. Instead, they homogenise a range of people who may be very different and be engaging in social representation processes and in actions derived from them in disparate ways. The consequences may be significant. We considered earlier in the book the backlash against the BAME categorisation that has developed. Conspiracy theory 'followers' show some similar responses when they are arbitrarily assigned to an undifferentiated and derogated 'type' of people. This is particularly likely since most would argue that they are not just theorists who hypothesise what might be true; they are describing what is true without doubt. Convenience categorisation is potentially a threat to the identity of a conspiracy theory follower on two counts: it allocates them to a conceptual group to which they feel they do not belong, and it misinterprets the 'truth' status of their beliefs. Consequently, it potentially threatens identity continuity, self-esteem and distinctiveness (the latter through deindividuation). We will return to the effects of this identity threat in a later section of this chapter but the other implication of such categorisation is that it will affect how those labelled interact with social representation processes. Identifying them as a 'type' may motivate them to become more engaged in the conspiracy theory or to detach themselves from it. Reactance to the labelling will depend on many factors. However, the fact of being labelled, and thereby castigated, is particularly likely to arouse further mistrust of the power elites seen to be core to the conspiracy.

Resistant to Refutation

Unlike most standard scientific theories, conspiracy theories are resistant to disproof. They are convoluted models, with many moving parts. Counter-evidence can be dismissed as irrelevant because it is based on a misunderstanding of the theory's basic propositions. It can be dismissed as originating from the very people who are leading the conspiracy. It can be incorporated as support for the theory by a process of extending or elaborating the initial parameters of the theory. Moreover, some conspiracy theories are so inchoate but multiplex that comprehensive evidence to disprove them would be nigh on impossible to gather, even though exposés of their originators can be compiled. The theories that include reference to extra-terrestrial life, UFOs and the Illuminati would seem to fit into this last category. The more florid, elaborate and incredible the conspiracy theory, the less evidence or rebuttal seem relevant. It all becomes a matter of what you choose to believe.

The works of Cooper (1991), a radio broadcaster and author, illustrate how florid and elaborate conspiracy theories can get (incidentally, there is no suggestion that they were merely meant as spoofs). In these, Cooper 'revealed' that AIDS was a result of a conspiracy to decrease the populations of Blacks, Hispanics and homosexuals; the US leadership had secretly signed a treaty with extra-terrestrials, who now manipulate the human race through secret societies, religions, magic, witchcraft and the occult; Kennedy was assassinated because he was about to reveal that extraterrestrials were about to take over the Earth and, under their influence, it was the President's own limousine driver who was the 'second shooter'; and that the Illuminati, a secret international organisation involving a cabal of senior government officials and scientists, with others, including aliens, conspired to establish a 'New World Order' – essentially a totalitarian world government, replacing sovereign states. Trying to unpick all of this and then systematically categorically disproving it seems both hopeless and pointless.

Of course, Cooper was hardly the first conspiracy theorist to refer to plots to establish a New World Order. Christian thinkers of the 19th century concerned with the ultimate destiny of humanity based on their interpretation of the Bible talked of a global conspiracy to impose a New World Order. From earlier still, Freemasons were alleged to have conspired to bring about a world government controlled by themselves. The Order of the Illuminati, a secret society founded in 1776 and suppressed shortly thereafter, have regularly been resurrected in conspiracy theories that have them play a role in innumerable plots to create a New World Order through a one-world government. Were they alive to see it, this must all have been especially galling for the founders of the Illuminati who advocated freethought, secularism, liberalism, republicanism and gender-equality. So New World Order conspiracy theories are not new. In fact, their history illustrates that conspiracy theories are certainly not new phenomena.

In its modern incarnation, New World Order conspiracism has proven enormously influential, galvanising support across a wide range of people who were disillusioned with political elites. These included, in the US, Fundamentalist Christian groups and the secular far right but also gathered in more diverse left-wing anti-elite agitators. The New World Order 'superordinate' conspiracy theory that could enfold many smaller, more specific, theories has proven resistant to refutation. In fact, it gets regular re-invigoration by the use of the phrase 'new world order' by politicians. It was used by many in the late 2000s, when facing a global financial crisis, to point to the need for reform and the extent of change needed. Believers in the conspiracy saw this as evidence that the cabal still exists. New World Order (NWO) is now a meme in its own right. It is a phrase that triggers a constellation of anti-elitist, anti-globalism sympathies. During the early phases of the COVID-19 pandemic of 2020, facing a new global threat, politicians avoided the phrase. They talked about the 'New Normal' instead. The New Normal now has its own conspiracy theories, but we should come to that later.

Put simply, conspiracy theories are structured to defend themselves. They have built-in get-out-of-jail clauses. They can be impossible to prove wrong through rational argument or through empirical data because they build in the explanations for why such data will be false, corrupted or misrepresented. In order to achieve this, conspiracy theories have two faces: the simple front statement (like an advertising jingle) so that people have something concrete to grasp and the convoluted backstage system of arguments and melange of justifications that incorporate the self-defence mechanisms; and the 'back door' escape routes. It is notable that social representations of novel phenomena or unanticipated events, even when no conspiracy element is included in them, can be two-sided or, indeed, many-layered. Take the example of the components of the social representation that evolved during 2020 to explain how the COVID-19 infection spread might be controlled. On one side, the supremely simple slogan: Wash Hands, Cover Face, Make Space. On the other side, the cocktail of complex constructs – vaccination, herd immunity, tiered lockdown, international quarantines, self-isolation, track and trace and so on. The example is particularly useful because it shows how a social representation once publicly available can develop in unexpected ways. The complexities of the social representation support self-defence because they allow a proponent to switch between justifications of the explanation. They also can be weaknesses that allow opponents to reinterpret and misuse the social representation. Every element in the complex layers of the COVID-19 social representation was first promulgated by formal governmental, scientific or medical authorities but was subsequently annexed and woven into elaborate conspiracy theories, each using their own underlying anchoring and objectification.

Why Believe in Conspiracy Theories?

We have established that conspiracy theories flourish in times of heightened uncertainty, mistrust, paranoia and fear – what Van Prooijen and Douglas (2017) call societal crisis situations. They emerge when people feel that something, usually some danger or mystery, needs to be explained and someone needs to be held responsible. However, this does not explain why some people believe in a conspiracy theory and others dismiss it. Furthermore, it does not explain why so many people are attracted to conspiracy explanations. Consequently, a significant number of research studies have been designed to determine why some believe in conspiracy theories.

Explanations range over a series of factors, not all of which are as robust as they appear at first sight, as described below.

Prior Political Beliefs or Attitudes

People have been found to gravitate toward conspiracy theories that affirm or validate their existing right- or left-wing political views. Thus, in the US, some studies showed that Republican voters were vastly more likely than Democrats to believe the Obama 'birther' theory (i.e. that Barack Obama was not born in the US and was ineligible to be President) or that climate change is a hoax. Democrats are more likely to believe that Trump's campaign for the Presidency 'colluded' with the Russians. However, Enders, Smallpage and Lupton (2020) suggested a more nuanced relationship. They found in the US that beliefs in a variety of specific conspiracy theories are simultaneously, but differentially, the product of both a general tendency toward conspiratorial thinking and left/right political orientations. They report that partisan and ideological self-identifications are more important than any other variable in predicting 'birther' beliefs, while conspiratorial thinking (see below) is most important in predicting conspiracy beliefs about the assassination of John F. Kennedy and the 9/11 terrorist attacks. This study suggests that, where a conspiracy theory is relevant to prior ideological orientation, beliefs will predict acceptance of the theory. Not startling in itself, the conclusion is important in emphasising that blanket generalisations about the political persuasion of those who believe in conspiracy theories are misleading. One generalisation that does hold is that conspiracy theories that support people's cherished beliefs are more likely to gain their support. The link to prejudices and long-term intergroup antagonism is marked.

Personality Traits

Goreis and Voracek (2019) did a systematic review and meta-analysis of 96 psychological research studies on conspiracy beliefs to examine their relationship with personality traits. They found that the psychological literature on predictors of conspiracy beliefs could be divided into two broad approaches. One had a pathological focus (e.g. paranoia), the other a socio-political focus (e.g. perceived powerlessness). Their meta analysis revealed that only disagreeableness (normally linked with suspicion and antagonism) and openness to experience (linked to willingness to seek out unusual and novel ideas) from the Big Five personality traits are systematically significantly associated with conspiracy beliefs. Goreis and Voracek usefully explored the variety of indices that are used to measure conspiracy belief. Some are concerned with beliefs in specific conspiracy theories (Douglas & Sutton, 2011); others are focused generic conspiracist beliefs (Brotherton, French & Pickering, 2013). The diversity in approaches to operationalisation of conspiracist beliefs make comparability of results across studies questionable. Swami et al. (2017) also found when reassessing the psychometric properties of the most frequently used scales that there were inadequacies in factorial structure and convergent validity. It is notable that Goreis and Voracek did not find the link to paranoia or to powerlessness typically mentioned in characterising conspiracy believers.

Motives

Douglas, Sutton and Cichocka (2017) report that belief in conspiracy theories is driven by three sorts of motive: epistemic (e.g. the desire for understanding, accuracy and subjective certainty), existential (e.g. the desire for control and security) and social (e.g. the desire to maintain a positive image of the self or group). These categories easily encompass the specific motives that are usually mentioned for conspiracist belief – such as seeking to gain power, self-justification, blame-shifting or material disadvantaging of opponents. Douglas and her colleagues emphasise that, while the three prime types of motive may propel people to accept a conspiracy theory, there is little evidence to indicate that these desires are satisfied by involvement. Nevertheless, they do not dismiss the possibility that engagement with conspiracist beliefs can have both damaging and constructive effects. The damaging effects are all too obvious (e.g. the health risks of failure to support MMR vaccination, or carbon emissions reduction, or AIDS/HIV transmission precautions). The constructive effects are less stark. For instance, they point out that individuals who are already alienated from society or disempowered may find a way of subverting the status quo by coming together through shared conspiracist beliefs and, at the same time, gain a sense of belonging and a common understanding of their world.

Conspiracist Ideation (Sometimes Called Conspiratorial Thinking)

This notion is based on the assumption that cognitive biases may play a role in determining whether someone endorses conspiracy theories. Essentially, the argument is that, for instance, individuals who are biased towards inferring intentional explanations for ambiguous actions are more likely to endorse conspiracy theories, which portray events as the exclusive product of intentional agency. This attributional bias is seen as co-existing alongside other cognitive strategies or biases such as the conjunction fallacy, illusory pattern perception, proportionality bias and projection as characteristics of what is known by the rather grand label of conspiracist ideation (Brotherton & French, 2015). The details of each type of bias are not presented here but they all lay the individual open to greater susceptibility to accepting a conspiracy theory with the exception of projection, which can work in either direction. Douglas and Sutton (2011) found that people were more likely to believe a conspiracy theory if they could project themselves into the position of the presumed conspirators and believed that they would have engaged in the alleged conspiracy if they had been there. If conspiracist ideation is a key determiner of believing in conspiracy theories it could help to explain why there is a tendency for people who endorse one theory to also believe in others. Goertzel (1994), who first reported this tendency in US samples, suggested it arises because conspiracy beliefs comprise part of a 'monological belief system' – an exclusive network of ideas that support each other. This could arise because the people who harbour such a network apply the same cognitive biases to uncertainties about different issues or, more likely, towards uncertainties in issues they perceive as inter-related (also because of their cognitive biases).

Media Use

It is not yet clear what impact the Internet is having on who chooses to follow conspiracy theories. However, it is clear that it makes conspiracy theories more visible and more easily available and is associated with an acceleration of their circulation. We have already seen that disinformation spreads more quickly and widely than factual corrections of it. It would seem possible that following conspiracy theories is linked to use of social media. This may be exaggerated if the recommendation algorithms of platforms like YouTube quickly lead viewers into a spiral of similar or more extreme content. If this notion were confirmed, it seems likely the algorithms would be amended. In any case, there is limited evidence about whether social media engagement with conspiracy theories causes, or is caused by, endorsement of the theory. It could be either. There are also certainly cases where circulating a conspiracy story is associated with opposition to it. For instance, the rise of alt-right trolling has used the spreading of conspiracy theories to provoke a negative reaction (Eckstrand, 2018). DeCook (2020) describes the ironic use of the technique by these right-wing extremists. Hodge and Hallgrimsdottir (2020) also consider how within alt-right online communities the debates about the acceptability of alt-right language and imagery are effectively a process of laying claim to cultural borders around online communities. In SRT terms, they are creating their own social representation system that involves evicting explanatory systems that are unacceptable. Hence their attempts to expose and undermine conspiracy theories that do not conform to their own. However, their representations of conspiracy theories, which are sometimes outrageous and caricaturing cartoons, may be attention snatching for people who would otherwise not seek out the alt-right rhetoric. So, while the idea that social media usage leads to conspiracy belief is alluring, there is by no means a simple association. In fact, in order to make it useful or predictive, the proposition would need to be so caveated as to transform it into something quite different. For instance, the prior predictors of media usage would need to be factored into the equation, in addition to the type of usage and purpose of use.

The search for individual differences that explain differential belief in conspiracy theories is interesting because it shows how diverse the foundation of such belief may be. It is also clear that it is an area where much remains to be discovered. It would be useful to know what differences there are between those who initiate a conspiracy theory and those who subsequently become adherents. It would be useful to establish whether there are differences between the early adopters of the conspiracy theory and late adopters (parallel to the distinctions pertaining to lags in acceptance of innovations, Rogers, 1995). The life cycle of believers would be useful to know (how do people change over their time of attachment to the conspiracy beliefs). Equally, it could be valuable to establish if those who are faithful to only one conspiracy theory (perhaps they could be called monogamous) differ from those who are more promiscuous or serially monogamous. Answers to some of these questions might help for those building responses to conspiracy social representations. It might be particularly advantageous to know what factors encourage someone to switch from being casually interested in, or aware of, a conspiracy theory to being an ardent believer and evangelist.

Identity, Emotions and Conspiracy Beliefs

From what we already know it is evident that individual differences in inclination to endorse conspiracy beliefs are a product of a complex interaction of personality, motives, cognitive style, prejudices and social attitudes, and exposure to conspiracy communications. IPT would also suggest that people are influenced to support conspiracy theories specifically by their need to optimise their self-esteem, self-efficacy, continuity and positive distinctiveness. These motivate every engagement with all forms of social representation (Breakwell, 2014c) and conspiracy theories are no different. In keeping with this proposition, Lantian et al. (2017) found that the tendency to believe in conspiracy theories was associated with the need for uniqueness (i.e. distinctiveness via being 'in the know'). Lantian et al. (2017) say that 'People who believe in conspiracy theories can feel "special," in a positive sense, because they may feel that they are more informed than others about important social and political events' (p. 162). Billig (1987) had earlier signalled that conspiracy theories offer a chance to assume greater self-efficacy and self-esteem because they provide 'the chance of hidden, important, and immediate knowledge, so that the believer can become an expert, possessed of a knowledge not held even by the so-called experts' (p. 132).

IPT explains why people will engage with conspiracy theories in general. However, in interaction with SRT it also explains which particular conspiracy theories an individual will gravitate towards. An individual seeking to optimise self-efficacy, self-esteem, continuity and positive distinctiveness, and thus maintain identity resilience, will be attracted by a conspiracy theory if it provides grounds for protecting or improving resilience. Where identity resilience is already high and stable, conspiracist engagement will be low. Where identity resilience is under threat, perhaps due to some new physical or social hazard, vulnerability to conspiracist narratives will be greater. Other factors will act as an accelerant to engagement with the conspiracist narratives when identity threat occurs. Most notable are two factors: existing levels of personal mistrust of the capacity of 'the authorities' to eliminate the hazard, and the extent to which the conspiracists have anchored their case in relevant social representations accepted by the individual. Above all, the conspiracy theory must be perceived to offer a protection for at least some aspect of identity. Some of these propositions have been tested in relation to responses to the risk of COVID-19 infection and the conspiracy theories that have surrounded it and interventions to deal with it. These studies are described later in this chapter.

The list of factors influencing endorsement of conspiracy theories considered above notably omits the effects of emotion, though Douglas, Cichocka and Sutton (2020) do look at emotions in the context of motivation effects and Byford (2011) explains their general significance in conspiracist activity. Given that one of the common features of conspiracy theories is their attempt to inflame and manipulate emotions, particularly outrage, fear and anger, it would seem likely that emotional state will affect susceptibility. Emotion probably plays a vital role both in initiating involvement in a conspiracy belief and in maintaining it in the face of refutation attempts. For instance, fear of something may drive the individual to explore what a conspiracy theory has to say about the source of the fear and then generate anger when they are criticised for believing in the conspiracy, resulting in greater adherence. This is illustrated by studies of parents who endorse vaccine conspiracy beliefs. Tomljenovic, Bubic and Erceg (2020) found that negative emotions related to vaccination and lower analytically rational thinking were associated with vaccine conspiracy beliefs in parents and predicted more refusal of vaccine by them for their children. It is notable that it was not a general positive or negative emotional outlook that predicted conspiracy beliefs, it was a specific negative emotional reaction to vaccination. This suggests we are not dealing with the manifestation of an underlying stable personality trait (such as optimism-pessimistic) nor a generalised attribution style. The emotion that matters is that attached to the topic of the conspiracy theory.

Emotional reactions also play a role in moderating responses to identity threat. Feeling afraid in the context of uncertainty is significantly linked to both experiencing identity threat, mistrusting experts and resorting to alternative sources of guidance and reassurance. Breakwell and Jaspal (2020), surveying responses of adults in the UK to COVID-19, found that fearing COVID-19 was associated with lower identity resilience, and that this was linked to uncertainty about who to trust to give self-protection guidance. The less trust they had in science and scientists, the more they mistrusted the medical advice they were given. This study did not directly index conspiracy beliefs. It did illustrate that identity processes have an impact on behaviour in high stakes and uncertain contexts that arouse emotional reactions and that then influences decisions about who to trust. In a different conspiracy theory domain, Mashuri et al. (2016) examined how intergroup threats and negative emotions mould conspiratorial beliefs, and how this is dependent upon the level of Muslims' perceived identity subversion (i.e. a sense that the Western ways of life have fundamentally changed Islamic identity). Indonesian Muslims' willingness to believe in conspiracy theories that claim the West is behind terrorist attacks in Indonesia was greater if they perceived realistic or symbolic intergroup threats from the West and were experiencing emotions of dejection-agitation. However, the capacity of this general emotional state to drive conspiracist belief was only present in those with perceived identity subversion. This is an interesting finding since it suggests that feeling a specific type of identity threat channels negative emotions in the direction that best may reconcile the threat.

Seeing endorsement of conspiracy theories from the perspective of identity processes will always require us to consider whether the individual differences in belief are some predictable function of group identifications that contribute to the overall structure of a person's identity. In the case of some conspiracy theories, this will be inevitable because the conspiracy beliefs are centred on intergroup contact and power struggles. Members of a group whose position in a conflict is explained and justified by an intergroup conspiracy theory might find endorsement of the theory advantageous for their group and a fillip for their own identity. In order to recruit followers, the originators of conspiracy theories would do well to make intergroup antagonisms salient in their narratives. Many do exactly this, and if antagonisms do not already actually exist, they conjure them up. The more important the group is to a member, the more motivated that member will be to pay attention when a conspiracy theory 'reveals' a threat to that group. The salience of the group membership for the individual's identity and the centrality of the group in the conspiracy narrative are key factors in determining how involved in it that individual will become. This is not simply because the conspiracy story echoes the individual's or the group's ideology or goals. It is because the group itself, with all its identifying features, is an important aspect of the individual's sense of identity. Protecting the group equates to protecting the self.

Channelling Mistrust

We said earlier that the characteristic form of a conspiracy theory is a potent weapon for arousing and directing mistrust. It identifies the arena in which mistrust operates by revealing what has to be explained. It goes on to provide the explanation in a way that attributes blame and signifies the motive and purpose behind the actions. It says who will be harmed. It specifies and condones the appropriate emotional reaction.

It offers a recipe for action and an exhortation to tell others. Underlying all, there is the idea that these forces are acting in secret, doing things that are immoral if not illegal. Conspiracy theories can create a social representation of a phenomenon that is penetrated at every level with mistrust. It exhorts the believer to mistrust others. It offers 'certainty' but at the cost of accepting the need to mistrust many prior under-standings and certitudes.

Essentially, the conspiracy theory is a tool for channelling mistrust. In this con-text, channelling is about directing mistrust at particular targets. Like propaganda and disinformation, it uses mistrust to its own ends, or rather to the ends of those many minds that shape it. Reifying the conspiracy theory as an actor in its own right would be an error. Even when it has outlived its initiator, like other social representations, it is not autonomous. It is influenced to a greater or lesser degree by those it attempts to influence, and is open to restructuring as it is shared. As it spreads, like a virus, it mutates. These mutations are not in its own control. They may well obey some evolutionary law of survival. As such, many variants will prove untenable – due primarily to changes in the host community or environment. The capacity to continue to channel mistrust is likely to be a prime evolutionary advantage.

It helps if the conspiracy story does not have to instigate mistrust from scratch. It helps if there is existing mistrust that can be refreshed and re-used. In this con-text, channelling is about marshalling or pooling residues of mistrust that linger in societal memory and myth. This dynamic process is reliant on the patterns of communication between people who are exposed to the theory. Conspiracy the-ories often mould together past wrongs that engendered mistrust to fashion a hybrid multi-layered, stronger reason to mistrust. This is easier than it might sound because every contributor to the conspiracy narrative can unload into it recollec-tions of reasons for mistrust. This may make the narrative objectively incoherent but subjectively rich in mistrust. In any case, the social representational processes will cast out elements that have low evolutionary value. Once the mistrust associ-ated with a memory is uploaded, even if the memory is edited out, the mistrust it carried remains. Once channelled, the mistrust can be disconnected from its original reason and associated with some other that is central to the purpose of the conspiracy theory. Consequently, the amalgamation of apparently different conspiracy theories may have considerable advantages. Each brings its mistrust contribution. So long as they are not fundamentally, or manifestly, incompatible, the result can be a powerful way to channel mistrust. They do not even have to be amalgamated to have this synergistic mistrust developing. Different conspiracy theories that deal with the same societal crisis can co-exist and feed off each other's impact on mistrust. While they have different narratives to offer, each has its own contribution to make to the public perception of uncertainty, emotional agitation and mistrust. The turmoil is even greater if they each call for different responses on the part of the public.

Roots of COVID-19 Conspiracies

To understand in technicolour what conspiracy theories can mean in a major societal crisis it is useful to look at what has happened during the coronavirus pandemic. In the 12 months from December 2019, when it was first identified in Wuhan, China, the SARS-CoV-2 virus was reckoned to have been implicated in the deaths of 1,613,671 people and had infected 71,554,018 people worldwide (European Centre for Disease Prevention and Control, 2020). These were probably conservative estimates given the limitations of data gathering in some countries.

Without doubt, COVID-19 had precipitated a global societal crisis and, without doubt, it was a dream come true for conspiracy theorists. Why? Conspiracy theories thrive in times of uncertainty, fear and personal threat. Coronavirus (SARS-CoV-2) provided all three:

- It arrived out of the blue – no warning, no slow-burn anticipation of disaster.
- It spread rapidly.
- It could be spread by people who were not symptomatic.
- It killed indiscriminately and painfully.
- It was not controlled by existing vaccines.
- It drove whole nations into a state of self-imposed paralysis.
- It evoked the basis for a panoply of dystopian fears surrounding the curtailment of civil liberties (occurring as a result of efforts to limit the spread of the virus).
- It laid waste the global economy.
- It mutated many times, to become more virulent just as vaccines were rolled out to contain it.

The ideal conditions for conspiracy theories were created. People wanted explanations and answers. How did the virus originate? Who would be its victims? How could it be stopped? What should they do to protect themselves and their loved ones? A further layer of questions emerged as the pandemic progressed. Could blame for the virus be laid anywhere? What inequities existed in how people were being supported or treated during the crisis? Were governments capable of dealing with the financial implications of the scale of the crisis? Who was benefitting from the pandemic and the measures put in place to handle it? Did anyone, especially the 'experts', actually know what to do to control the virus? Could science and scientists be trusted? Were political leaders self-interested, ignorant and incompetent? Could anyone be trusted to be virus-free? After 12 months of death and disruption, other questions came to the fore, particularly as new, more virulent, variants of the virus were identified. How long can this go on? How long can we continue to live with these restrictions? Does no one have answers that we can understand and trust?

People were being asked to make great sacrifices in order to control the virus. Constraints were imposed upon their interactions with family and friends; upon whether and where they could work, shop and get education or medical treatment;

and upon their mobility locally, regionally and internationally. In addition, as the pandemic continued, the constraints imposed by governments changed (sometimes being relaxed and at others becoming more stringent; applied in some places but not others; some policed, others not). Perceived inconsistencies and caveated advice or guidance became more prevalent. New measures such as test and trace (using mobile apps to identify where people had been and with whom they had been co-located) were introduced. Measures that were initially adopted voluntarily were made compulsory but only in some contexts (such as face covering). The changes, their variability and their intrinsic complexities, over time instigated some confusion and greater uncertainty but also a degree of non-compliance and outright resistance. Moreover, established political leaders, across party lines, challenged government policies and offered a justification for protest movements to act.

Against this backdrop, people wanted their questions answered and felt they had a right to get answers. However, the tenor and substance of the questions themselves reveals the depth and breadth of the mistrust that the pandemic aroused. Answers, even when forthcoming, were likely to be viewed with suspicion. The conspiracy theories that emerged tied themselves to various parts in the battery of questions then, inevitably, channelled and accentuated mistrust. What happened represents a classic example, on a grand scale, of the genesis and evolution of conspiracy theorising. It illustrates many of the social psychological processes described earlier in this chapter. It also illustrates the effects of false rumours and fake news discussed in Chapter 8. What makes this example of the effects of conspiracy theories unique is the emotional context. Members of the public, across age groups, were facing very significant, for many unprecedented, amounts of stress. They were afraid of the virus for themselves and for others. Daily life was disrupted totally. Old habitual certainties disappeared (e.g. school attendance, or the freedom to hold a funeral ceremony, or celebrate a wedding). Mistrust and stress were united in this situation.

COVID-19 Conspiracies

The conspiracy theories began as soon as the SARS-CoV-2 virus was identified. Most have focused on its origin in one way or another. They have suggested:

- It was deliberately produced by humans and/or it escaped from a laboratory (the organisation blamed for this varies across conspiracy theories - e.g. US President Trump's administration accused the Chinese government; China's Internet carries theories accusing the CIA or the US Army). Many other conspiracy theories have explained disease outbreaks as being caused by a biological weapon designed to target enemies of their creator (e.g. AIDS/HIV and Zika). In relation to COVID-19, there were persistent calls for China to allow an independent international investigation into how the virus originated. In December 2020 it was announced that the World

Health Organisation would be allowed to send 10 international scientists to Wuhan in January 2021 to conduct investigations. Conspiracy theorists asked why this had not been allowed earlier.

- It was engineered by someone or some organisation to create a situation where other actions, with ulterior motives, would be justified. For example, one circulated in the Arabic press that suggested COVID-19, like SARS and the swine flu virus, was deliberately created to stimulate vaccine sales, and it is part of an economic and psychological war waged by the US against China with the aim of weakening it and presenting it as a backward country and a source of diseases. In another, Bill Gates was said to have known in advance that the pandemic would happen and to be using it to introduce a global vaccination programme that would allow him to plant microchips in people in order to control them. The idea that mass vaccination is a Trojan horse plot to allow the introduction of a totalitarian world government also makes an appearance in the story. Another ingredient is money. Gates, together with Anthony Fauci, the director of the US National Institute of Allergy and Infectious Diseases, was also accused of seeking financial gain from the vaccine. So were major pharmaceutical companies. The money theme plays out in many of the theories. Notably, the way it is structured follows the status of intergroup relations. Users on social media in the Muslim world suggested that Jews had manufactured COVID-19 to precipitate a global stock market collapse and thereby profit via insider trading.

It should be noted that the scientific consensus internationally, based on the virus DNA sequence, was that it evolved naturally in animals, probably first in bats and eventually jumped to humans – that is, it is a zoonotic disease (Liu et al., 2020).

- 5G caused COVID-19. This is associated with the claim that 5G weakens the immune system's cellular defences, making people more vulnerable to COVID-19. The rollout of the 5G network and new telecommunication masts being built just prior to the outbreak was used to support the theory. Publicity for the conspiracy theory was followed by telecommunications masts in several parts of the UK being the subject of arson attacks and vandalisation.

It should be noted that while ionising radiation (such as UVA and UVB rays in sunlight) can damage DNA and that repeated DNA damage can lead to cancer, non-ionising radiation, such as that used in 5G technology, is not powerful enough to penetrate and damage DNA (Belluz, 2018). Furthermore, the geographic pattern of the rollout of 5G would not explain the pattern of the spread of the disease.

The 5G conspiracy theory links to an earlier accusation, based on evidence later shown to be flawed, that mobile phone radiation was a cause of cancer. Stewart (2000) in a major independent inquiry in the UK had concluded that the evidence did not suggest mobile phone technologies put the health of the general population of the UK at risk. However, it also said there was some preliminary evidence that outputs from mobile phone technologies may cause, in some cases, subtle biological effects, although, importantly, these do not necessarily mean that health is affected.

They also pointed out that in some cases people's wellbeing may be adversely affected by the insensitive siting of base stations. They proposed a 'precautionary approach', particularly for children under 16 using cellular (mobile) phones, and called for subsequent continuing review. In fact, they avoided any simple or non-nuanced categorical denial of any health effects of the technology. They particularly asked manufacturers to provide more information on the radiation emissions of their phones. It seems that the precautionary approach advocated was enough to allow mobile mast conspiracy theories to persist throughout the next 20 years.

- COVID-19 is a plot to remove a President and its severity is a hoax ('less deadly than the common cold' – echoing President Trump's own attitude to the virus in the early months of the outbreak). A five-minute clip posted on Facebook on 11 November 2020, which was deleted a day later, was captioned 'The Four Year Plan to Overthrow an Elected President'. It claimed that the release of COVID-19 was planned to remove President Trump from office and had been a plot in the making for four years since his election. The timing of the release of this story coincided with the end of the 2020 Presidential election that it also claimed was rigged so that Trump would fail.

This is an odd example of an 'origin conspiracy theory'. While it has some of the standard ingredients (e.g. the secret plotting by the powerful in that it refers to the prescience of both Fauci and Gates in predicting pandemics would occur), it has an uneasy juxtaposition of two elements (COVID-19 is capable of removing President Trump, and COVID-19 is not so dangerous after all so people are wrong to fear). If the latter were true, could COVID-19 achieve the former? Also, if the plot was known to exist for four years, why wait until eleven months after the pandemic began to reveal it? Origin conspiracy theories are best placed close to the start of the crisis when people are most in need of the causal explanation.

- An attack on freedom. National or regional lockdowns and COVID-19 testing and systems for tracing contacts are just tactics for reducing civil liberties. The policies impinge differentially upon different sub-groups of people (e.g. in the UK between those in the North and those in the South of England). This reflects a lack of equality and inclusiveness. Consequently, civil disobedience is justified. This is not an origin conspiracy theory. It is a conspiracy theory to explain why certain measures to control the virus are introduced but also to justify action against them. It is a fine example of how prevailing mistrust of those who make political decisions will shape an interpretation of their behaviour. They are not being given the benefit of the doubt. They are assumed to be self-interested. Adherence to this particular variant of COVID-19 conspiracy theory is likely to be associated with prior political views. Yet it will also be associated with how the effects of the control measures are objectively evaluated.

It is easy to see that most of the theories tied to COVID-19 are repurposed models that have been used before. They follow the common structure for origin and blame conspiracy theories that are targeted at opponents and power elites. The other type of conspiracy theory evident in relation to COVID-19 is that which attacks vaccination. It is evident in the references to Bill Gates above but it emerges in several forms. The object is to discredit the efficacy or safety of the vaccine, to encourage people to refuse vaccination. It is also designed to attack the moral standing and motives of those who support vaccination. They are dismissed as being motivated by self-interest.

The warning signalled by the impact of the conspiracy theories surrounding the MMR vaccine and autism (Breakwell, 2020b) cannot be ignored. Many people refused to have their children vaccinated and the incidence of measles rose rapidly. Anti-vaxxers have a following. They are concerned not only with undermining one type of vaccination but in challenging the value of them all. Scare stories, which are part-conspiracy theories, around the development of the COVID-19 vaccine were widespread. There were many hooks for them to hang on. The vaccines were developed more rapidly than would traditionally have been expected. Consequently, suspicions that corners had been cut in the clinical trialling and authorisation were raised – though there was absolutely no evidence that this was the case. When the first vaccine to be authorised in Europe was found to initiate an allergic reaction in two people who were very early recipients of the vaccine and were known allergy sufferers, mistrust was alerted. People waited for the next cases of negative side effects. Indeed, by Spring 2021, there were claims that at least two of the vaccines were associated with very rare cases of unusual blood clots. This delayed authorisation of their use in some countries and for some populations. Another thing that raised suspicions was that different international research groups came up with quite different structures and bases for their vaccines. Could they all be right? Were the public being told the truth about the risks? What did the data on the efficacy of the vaccines really mean? Why were two vaccine doses needed and why did the period between them need to be different for different vaccines?

The questions indicate both uncertainty and mistrust. The complexities underlying vaccine development and the nature of clinical trials were difficult to explain in a non-scientific, non-technical way that would be persuasive. The counter-rhetoric of the conspiracy theorists was simple and direct – these things are not safe, you can rely on us, why would we mislead you? Dealing with this sort of conspiracy appeal is hard unless the public has reason to trust those who reject the appeal. Acceptance of vaccination for COVID-19 is strongly associated with perceived personal risk and generic trust in science and scientists (Jaspal & Breakwell, 2021). This is also associated with high levels of identity resilience, having supportive social networks and feeling a belonging to a social group that is powerful (Breakwell, Jaspal & Fino, 2021).

It is evident that the various conspiracy theories surrounding COVID-19 have different roots and purposes. However, they all interact in the production of social representations that motivate people to think, feel and act differently. It was notable in Autumn 2020, as protesters gathered, with or without face masks, in public places in major cities internationally and in considerable numbers, to protest against governmental guidelines, to show their antipathy towards the way they were being treated, that their banners amalgamated messages from the full spectrum of conspiracy theories. One, carried by a teenager, said simply: NO VACCINES, NO GMO, NO MASKS, NO 5G, NO NOW.

It should be remembered that these protests were not simply driven by conspiracy theories, though the 'attack on freedom' theory may have had a strong part to play. They were, to some extent, a result of frustration against lockdowns and the implications that job losses and education disruption had for the future. The protests were also driven by mistrust of those people with power in this situation. Mistrust of their motives and of their competence. In relation to COVID-19 the role of the conspiracy theories was clearly to channel the frustration and mistrust generated by the real crisis situation.

Mistrust: The Allure of Conspiracy Theories

This chapter examined what constitutes a conspiracy theory and how and why they come about. It illustrated how conspiracy theories survive efforts to disprove them and explored the individual differences that explain variability in belief in conspiracy theories. The way they generate and channel mistrust was considered. COVID-19 was used as an exemplar of how conspiracy theories serve the interests of diverse groups and individuals with different objectives. The complex social psychological processes that underlie the interactions and longevity of conspiracy theories are outlined. The particular significance of social representation and identity processes has been emphasised. The need to maintain identity resilience through developing self-esteem, self-efficacy, continuity and positive distinctiveness is explained.

The thing missing is a direct answer to the question: why are conspiracy theories so alluring? Against the backdrop of the social psychological theories presented, the response is not so surprising. Conspiracy theories attract because they explain the inexplicable, they evict uncertainty, and, they permit retribution and offer justification. They offer a route to identity resilience. Most importantly, they promise the road out of doubt and mistrust. This is the lure of the conspiracy theory. Inevitably, the promise offered is rarely delivered.

CHAPTER 10
MODELLING MISTRUST PROCESSES

Mistrust is Normal

It must be acknowledged that some parts of this book seem to paint mistrust as a villain, and to represent it as dangerous, especially when used deliberately to manipulate others. In this guise, mistrust can be seen to lead to psychological distress and behavioural problems for individuals, and discrimination and conflict for communities. However, before going on to describe a model of mistrust processes, it is important to note that this is not the only way to think about mistrust.

Feeling mistrust is part of being human. Quintessentially, it is about suspicion and doubt. It is a by-product of being aware, inquisitive, seeking explanations and attempting predictions of the future. It is a corollary of being creative and attuned to the motives and needs of others. It is a core ingredient of self-protection. Seen in this way, the evolutionary inevitability and advantages of mistrust are highlighted. Mistrust has a survival value – for individuals, and for communities. Consequently, mistrust has become systemic, embedded in our societal mores and structures because we have recognised that we have to live with it.

In practice, mistrust may simultaneously both help and hinder, protect and harm. In any specific exchange, how you evaluate the outcomes of mistrust will depend on many factors. However, for an individual and society, both the gains and losses accruing from mistrust operating in any particular situation need to be taken into account. Typically, in interpersonal relationships, there is an ongoing, primarily subliminal, calculation of the trade-off between mistrust gains and losses. The balancing of profit and loss becomes more overt in large-scale interorganisational or international relations. Translating the mistrust tally into negotiating positions is the art of diplomacy and commercial deals. In most cases, the reckoning will influence how far mistrust is freed to determine action.

Acknowledging that mistrust is an abiding characteristic of humanity changes how we need to think about interventions to mitigate its more adverse effects. This is acutely necessary at a time in the 21st century when mistrust has emerged as a major societal concern. Mistrust is now increasingly seen to be out of control. The old institutions and belief systems that allowed us to live with it seem to be crumbling. Mistrust has more channels of expression (including new forms of violence and protest) and a greater diversity of targets than ever before. Therefore, the idea that mistrust is remediable with a range of simple, separate treatments, whether through changes in leadership styles, information provision or power redistribution or any number of other fixes that have been suggested, has to be treated with suspicion (i.e. mistrust). An alternative is to consider the system of psychological and societal processes within which mistrust resides. Based on understanding this complex system of interacting elements, it may be possible to influence the extent and direction of mistrust.

However, even with such a systemic approach, intervention may have unpredicted, limited or transient impact. The point was made in Chapter 1 that the trusting process involves ongoing cognitive and emotional activity that may entail, in quick succession and in any order, mistrust, distrust and trust, but will not necessarily produce a stable outcome. The stream of incoming information shifts the needle back and forth on the metaphorical trust barometer. However, this barometer spans multiple dimensions. It is not a unidimensional scale with trust at one end and distrust at the other with mistrust somewhere in between. The sentiments we call trust, distrust and mistrust each have many facets and these do not covary perfectly. Consequently, the measurement used must be multidimensional and collected separately for trust and mistrust. Furthermore, measurement should be iterative. While the capacity to mistrust is an abiding characteristic, the existence of specific incarnations of mistrust are unstable. Interventions to adjust levels of mistrust (e.g. to correct the effects of disinformation or conspiracy theories) may have an impact but this may be eroded by the next incoming data or, indeed, by the way in which mistrust morphs. Therefore, measurement of mistrust should not only be able to capture the different facets of the mistrust construct (e.g. behavioural, purposive, emotional and evaluative), it must also be capable of monitoring changes in the forms mistrust takes over time. Managing mistrust is probably best understood as a perpetual labour, and certainly more demanding than the 12 set for Hercules (Encyclopaedia Britannica, 2021).

A Model of Mistrust Processes for the Individual in Social Context

This book offers a primarily social psychological analysis of some of the dynamic processes that generate and maintain mistrust. It has focused on certain key aspects of these processes: the purposes mistrust serves; the perception and evaluation of risk and uncertainty; the effects of emotions and identity motives; the role of leadership styles and organisation cultures; the images and treatment of those mistrusted; and the tactics for inciting, channelling and justifying mistrust. It has been particularly concerned with the roles that identity and social representational processes play in creating and shaping mistrust.

Any integrative model that can capture the interactions of the forces that are at work will be necessarily complex. It needs to operate on several levels of analysis. We have seen in earlier chapters that mistrust is a product of intrapsychic, interpersonal, intra- and inter-group, and societal processes. Mistrust processes exist at the level of the individual and macro-society (and within that in other social categories that vary in scale, from small groups to nation states). Capturing how mistrust processes interact across all these levels in a single flowchart is impractical, therefore the model presented in Figure 10.1 is concerned with the interactions between the individual and the social context mistrust processes. The important influences of group processes are not represented separately. Intra-group and inter-group effects are an integral part of the processes (risk evaluation, societal uncertainty and social representation) that are highlighted in the figure to represent the social context. Key aspects of those group processes have been discussed in earlier chapters. While the figure does not include a box signifying group processes, the theoretical model of mistrust proposed here recognises that group processes permeate how any social context is constructed and influences individuals.

The conceptual model proposed here relies upon IPT and SRT. Both of the theories explicitly acknowledge the importance of group dynamics in shaping individual and shared thought, feelings and behaviour. The basic tenets of these theories have been presented earlier so we will present the model without reiterating them. Here we will focus only on how those theories help to explain mistrust processes. Figure 10.1 presents a schematic of the model. It comprises two main boxes with dashed outlines. The top box contains the three elements of the social context that are posited to be prime influences upon mistrust. It is recognised that this is not an exhaustive catalogue of influences. The bottom box represents the individual intra-psychic and behavioural elements of mistrust processes. The elements included in the model have all been discussed in earlier chapters. The purpose of the figure is to present an integrative framework bringing the elements together. Not all of the interactions between the elements are marked in the figure but they will be discussed.

It is important to note that this two-dimensional representation cannot capture the dynamism of the constructs and the processes involved. In reality, they are constantly changing. Furthermore, the figure does not reflect the way their interactions occur iteratively and through time. It is frustrating that this glorious complexity cannot be visualised using traditional methods. Improving the way we visualise dynamic systems in social psychology has to be a stepping-stone to better theory. Multivariate data analysis and predictive analytics, with the aid of AI, are enabling

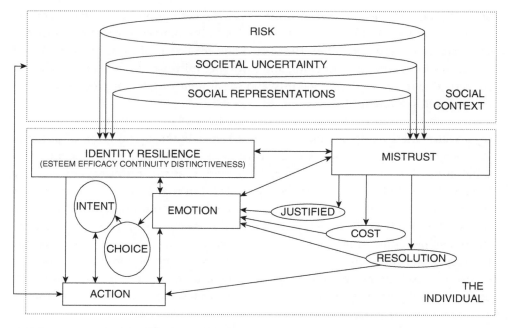

Figure 10.1   Model of Mistrust Processes

us to grasp some of the complexity but we have to improve the methods available for conceptualising and communicating it. Meanwhile, we resort to one of the traditional methods.

The Social Context

In Figures 4.1, 4.2 and 4.3, social context was represented but not broken into its key constituents. The social context factors influencing mistrust are numerous. However, three superordinate forces within the social context that encompass many of these factors are particularly identified in this model. They are risk, societal uncertainty and social representation processes. Each has been described at length in earlier chapters. They are central to the genesis and maintenance of individual mistrust. Risk refers to both the possibility that harm will occur and the extent of the likely damage. Social contexts vary in the level and forms of risk they harbour at any one time and over time. The model is capable of encompassing the role of risk attached to a specific hazard and, more usefully, the generic sense of risk produced by the concatenation of a number of hazards. Societal uncertainty refers, in part, to the sense of shared doubt and indecision experienced in the face of hazards that create this risk. Societal uncertainty also refers to the shared sense that institutions and ideologies that might have previously offered assurance and certitude are fading or gone. Perhaps this form of uncertainty is best captured in the phrase 'We do not know and nobody knows'.

The pertinent social representation processes for the model are those that actively describe the risk and uncertainty, but also try to explain them and imply how they should be evaluated and what actions are appropriate. Many types of interaction underlie social representation processes. In earlier chapters, the way social representations are negotiated and communicated, for instance through gossip, rumour, disinformation, propaganda and conspiracy theories, has been examined.

Risk, societal uncertainty and social representation are treated here as a system of interacting processes. Each may independently instigate and channel mistrust experienced by an individual. However, in practice, the tripartite system works in concert to precipitate the mistrust that the individual experiences. For visual clarity, the flowchart does not include the two-way arrows that tie all three processes together. It is important to note that the flow of influence is not unidirectional (and no significance should be attached to their relative position in the flowchart). Risk can influence uncertainty and social representations. Social representations can initiate cognitive, emotional and behavioural changes that radically alter both the objective nature of a risk and the way it is perceived or evaluated. They can also redirect the focus of societal uncertainty. Similarly, societal uncertainty will influence both social representations and risk. Interacting, these three processes within the social context will shape individual mistrust.

However, individual mistrust is also a product of the characteristics of the person experiencing it. The individual is a part of this social context and actively assimilates and accommodates to the three processes. Individuals differ greatly in their responses to these processes. For instance, Chapter 2 described how reactions to both risk and uncertainty are influenced by the biases and heuristics the individual employs in making decisions. Evaluation of risk and uncertainty information is also affected by personal cognitive biases (such as the self-serving, optimistic or hindsight biases). The ways social representations (i.e. through the phenomena of stereotyping, gossip, rumour, disinformation, propaganda and conspiracy theories) influence mistrust will also depend upon the individual's active interpretation of them. Individuals are not passive recipients of social representations. First, they are purposive in what they allow themselves to be exposed to. Second, they will edit and select content from the social representations to which they are exposed. Third, they will attend differentially to that content which they retain. An analogy can be found in fishing: there are many fish in the sea but the angler decides which species to target (say trout, bass or perch); having hauled in the catch, many of the smaller specimens are discarded, and, among those kept, only those likely to be the tastiest are served at dinner. Social representations that suit the individual's tastes are most likely to be consumed. That does not discount the possibility that a shark-like social representation may consume the unwary or ill-equipped angler. Some hegemonic social representations will be hard for an individual to resist.

Essentially, individuals have agency in responding to risk, uncertainty and social representations. It is, however, worth noting that the model clearly indicates that individual identity processes are also influenced by these three processes, both directly and indirectly through their effects on mistrust. The individual responding to these three processes of the social context is over time, in part, also a product of them.

The communication channels through which the individual experiences risk, societal uncertainty and social representations are not depicted in the figure. However, there has been a great emphasis throughout the book that mass media, social media and other online and virtual interactions are now vital channels for their transmission. These channels are also the environments where representations of risk and uncertainty, together with the responses appropriate to them, evolve and mutate. In fact, the channels themselves can be as important as the content they carry. It is not quite as simple as saying that the medium is the message. It is more that the medium inevitably adulterates the meaning of the message. It does this by determining: who has access; who generates the content; how it is structured; the amount and type of interaction with recipients; and the frequency of revision of the message. The channels vary in how far they can determine each of these. As we saw in Chapter 7, some channels are more influential than others at inciting mistrust. Social media are now powerful channels for inciting and, indeed, weaponising mistrust. To go back to the fishing analogy, each channel baits, hooks and cooks the fish in its own way.

The Individual

The second box with a dashed outline encompasses the features of the individual that are central to mistrust processes. These are: mistrust awareness; evaluation of justification, cost and resolution; emotional reactions; decision making regarding action; identity resilience; and action.

The box labelled 'mistrust' represents the individual's awareness that mistrust is a potentially appropriate response given their situation. The social context, through risk, societal uncertainty and social representation processes, has an influence on whether the situation is deemed to merit mistrust. However, the personal circumstances of the individual will also play a role. Chapter 1 described the circumstances when an individual experiences mistrust. It argued that the circumstances capable of initiating mistrust fall into three clusters: unfulfilled expectations; being warned; and echoes in the situation of past experiences that signal danger or trigger habitual mistrust. This indicates that, for the individual, mistrust is a state that can be useful because it identifies the possibility of harm (ranging from momentary disappointment to some life-threatening catastrophe) and it sets in train cognitive and emotional processes that may stimulate avoidance of that harm. Equally, unjustified or misdirected mistrust can undermine self-protection or cause the individual to fall into danger. Much has been said earlier in the book about the way conspiracy theories can incite unjustified mistrust and lead people to choose to act in ways that endanger themselves (e.g. conspiracy theories causing mistrust of vaccines and resulting in refusal to vaccinate).

While the model in Figure 10.1 represents how an individual reacts to the experience of mistrust, it is worth saying that this occurs within the broader social context. This means that other people may be reacting with mistrust to the same circumstantial cues at virtually the same time. Consequently, the reaction to, and expression of, mistrust may be shared with others. The social representations that shape the experience of mistrust for one person will also be at work upon others. People sharing this experience will often communicate with each other, creating new ripples of influence in the social context. Of course, there is also the feedback from actions of individuals into the social context, perhaps changing not only social representations but also the evaluation of risk and the nature of societal uncertainty. This feedback is schematically indicated in the model by the two-way arrow linking the overall social context box with the individual action box.

Action may be seen as the outcome for the individual of experiencing mistrust but it is evident in the model that there is no inevitability about their relationship. A number of mediating processes are identified in Figure 10.1. In Chapter 4, these were described in detail. The model posits that mistrust arouses emotional reactions (notably fear, anger, anxiety and sadness). The form of emotion and its severity depends on three broad types of factors. First, whether the individual believes the mistrust to be justified (based on evidence judged subjectively as meriting mistrust). Robust justification for their suspicions is likely to lead to more extreme emotions. The second factor is the perceived cost or damage of the incident that precipitates mistrust. The greater the estimated cost, the more extreme the emotional reaction is likely to be. This effect is conceptually independent of whether there is evidence that the incident merits mistrust. However, justification and cost can interact to magnify the emotional effect. Cost estimation will be subjective but influenced by social context. Moreover, emotion, once triggered, may change the attributions of both justification and cost. The third factor deals with the possibility of resolution of mistrust by removing the suspicion or doubt that the incident creates and, thereby, assuaging the emotional reaction. Such resolution of suspicion, because it may confirm distrust is appropriate, will also sometimes still precipitate strong emotional reactions. Even the effort to achieve certainty can itself generate considerable emotional turmoil.

While these three mediating processes will largely determine the emotional reaction to instigation of mistrust, they also, simultaneously, involve the individual constructing a clearer image of what their mistrust means for them. The conceptualisation of this particular instance of mistrust is made clearer by the analyses these processes entail. These three processes have a part in moving the individual from having only an inkling of mistrust to substantiating or crystallising that mistrust. Essentially, this is the cognitive processing that allows the individual to determine whether the possibility of mistrust should be converted into the existence of mistrust.

The assessment of justification, cost and options for resolution typically involve significant effort and thought. They shape both the conceptualisation of the mistrust and its emotional consequences. In the model, it is indicated that the consideration of options for resolution will also be directly associated with action decisions. This action may involve the search for evidence that eradicates doubt but it may also include efforts to extricate oneself from the situation engendering mistrust. For instance, if the mistrust concerns the probity of an employer, the individual may seek more information to assuage the doubts or choose to leave the workplace. Attempts to escape from mistrust take many routes. Sadly, many of these routes will prove dead-ends.

Besides shaping emotional reactions through the operation of the three assessment subroutines, the mere experience of mistrust can release an emotional response. Figure 10.1 indicates a two-way route between emotion and mistrust that does not require any significant conscious cognitive processing. Mistrust, especially extreme mistrust, may behave as a stressor and can elicit physiological and pharmacological effects that directly moderate mood and, additionally, may intervene to reduce cognitive efficiency (Yaribeygi et al., 2017; Lupien et al., 2007). The fact that this is a two-way process matters because emotional changes can modify the way incidents precipitating mistrust are interpreted and, therefore, shift the level and meaning of mistrust experienced. Emotional instability will open the possibility of generating new domains of mistrust for the individual.

There are a number of drivers of action included in the model. The effect of attempts at resolving mistrust have already been mentioned. In addition, emotional state will influence action directly. For instance, mistrust that triggers fear may lead to flight without much, if any, rational evaluation of alternative action options. The action taken can equally have a direct reciprocal effect on emotion. However, emotional reactions stimulated by mistrust will mostly be contemporaneous with the operation of other processes that shape action.

The model represents these as choice and intent. This is shorthand for the large array of cognitive processes involved in decision making. Choice here is used to refer to the individual's preferred or desired course of action. Choices (preferences) and intentions are treated as distinct because they need not be identical or rationally related. Emotions may precipitate a choice/preference that implies a particular intention; however, past actions may militate against this intention. For instance, a person angered by mistrust of the motives of authorities imposing a lockdown during a pandemic may choose/desire to take part in a public protest, but this may not materialise as an intention to protest because they have already received a police warning resulting from previous involvement in a protest. Past actions, and their implications, will moderate the impacts of emotion upon intentions.

Identity processes will also drive intention and action, besides influencing mistrust. In Figure 10.1, identity processes are symbolised by the identity resilience box. Chapter 4 considered the relationship between various identity processes and the experience of mistrust. It specifically differentiated extreme mistrustfulness as a trait, from 'common' mistrust as a state initiated as a reaction to some temporally proximate experience. The model of mistrust processes depicted in Figure 10.1 does not describe the extreme mistrustfulness that is treated as symptomatic of various psychiatric conditions (including paranoia and borderline personality disorder). Such extreme mistrustfulness requires a different model that would include clinical, as well as social psychological, analysis. Nevertheless, extreme mistrust, like its 'common' counterpart, is influenced by identity processes, particularly self-efficacy and self-doubt.

The model of mistrust processes presented here emphasises the significance of identity resilience in moderating the influence of the social context (in respect to risk, societal uncertainty and social representations) upon the mistrust experience, emotional responses and action taken. Identity resilience refers to the extent to which an identity can cope with experiences that would damage its coherence (stability and consistency), continuity and positivity (reflected in self-esteem, self-efficacy and optimised distinctiveness). A resilient identity will optimise adaptation to changed conditions by reconciling it with needs for continuity, avoidance of rigidity, and coherence in the identity structure.

Many influences affect identity resilience. Social context certainly affects identity resilience, and this is indicated in the model. However, through its influence upon action, identity resilience also contributes to the evolution of that social context. It will change the way the individual interacts with risk, societal uncertainty and social representations. Like the butterfly effect, the consequences of these individual, identity-derived, idiosyncrasies of interaction permeate the social context. The characteristics of identity also permeate how mistrust experiences are interpreted. It was explained in Chapter 4 that the effects of identity resilience on mistrust are not simple and will depend particularly upon the significance the object of mistrust has for self-esteem, self-efficacy, continuity and distinctiveness levels. This reflects the fact that mistrust itself will impact identity resilience. The feedback loop in the model is important.

The model indicates that identity resilience affects emotional reactions to mistrust and, in turn, is affected by them. Identity resilience may dampen or accelerate the emotion aroused by mistrust. For instance, someone becomes angry because he suspects a friend has lied. If he has high self-esteem he could interpret this as a personal sleight that should be punished and become incensed, or he could regard it as a childish error not worthy of his concern and become amused. Either way, the incident is interpreted in a way that bolsters self-esteem. A mistrust experience also may have a major effect upon identity processes through the emotion it arouses. For instance, feeling fear because you mistrust the health system that is meant to support you during an illness can undermine your sense of self-efficacy. In this situation, the mistrust has a direct effect on self-efficacy because it indicates that you are less well equipped to deal with the problem than you expected. But additionally, the fear this mistrust generates has a corollary effect on self-efficacy. The fact that you feel afraid makes you feel less in control and less capable, besides impeding problem-solving abilities.

Finally, the model indicates that identity processes (reflected in identity resilience) will influence the actions that follow mistrust being awakened. Besides their indirect effects upon action through mistrust and emotion, identity processes will have a direct influence upon action. Both type and extent of action will be affected. The specific nature of the relationship between identity processes and action in the context of mistrust will crucially depend upon the social context in which the action is to occur, the particular characteristics of the mistrust (including justification, cost and resolution) and the emotions it arouses.

Limitations and Elaborations of the Model

The model that is presented is an attempt to indicate some of the key processes at work when mistrust is aroused. It brings together many of the themes that have been introduced in this book. These themes have been considered more thoroughly earlier. The model can be considered simply as a way of systematising their complex interactions. It is a structural model summarising the associations between theoretical constructs. This model is not the sort that predicts the magnitude of effects. In some of the interactions, it does not even suggest the direction of the effect. To do that, it needs to be applied to a particular mistrust situation, where dependent and independent variables based on the theoretical constructs in the model can be estimated.

However, as it stands, it could be viewed as a sort of map for orienteering in the territory of mistrust. It suggests what you need minimally to consider when thinking about analysing mistrust phenomena. In this sense, it is a good basis for designing an integrative programme of research. A model is needed because disparate, uncoordinated studies tackling fragments of the mistrust domain do not provide the basis for systematic advances in our understanding of it.

The model here does not focus on everything that might be considered relevant to mistrust. It does not elaborate on group processes (intra- or inter-group), though they are embedded in the discussions of risk, societal uncertainty and social representations. Within the chapters on leadership and images of the mistrusted, group processes were discussed and they are unavoidable when discussing disinformation, propaganda and conspiracy theories. So it can be argued that the model, seen against the backdrop of the entire book, does consider group processes. When the model is used in designing an empirical study in a specific mistrust situation, it will be necessary to specify which group processes are significant and should be independently indexed.

Similarly, the model is primarily concerned with the mistrustful rather than the mistrusted, but Chapter 5, which focuses on the mistrusted, is the antidote for that limitation. Understanding what happens to the mistrusted and how they respond is a fundamental part of grasping the personal and societal significance of mistrust.

Currently, the construct is assumed within the social context box because identification of the mistrusted is part of the mistrust message carried by social representation processes. In fact, there is a case for elaborating the model to include the mistrusted explicitly. It would highlight that the mistrusted may actively influence mistrust processes through their own responses.

If it were included in the model, the 'mistrusted' construct would sit as a new dashed-line box alongside the social context and the individual. The mistrusted is a category identified through societal judgements of risk and uncertainty and described through social representations. It is also a categorisation attributed to others by individuals based on their own motives and experience; they do not necessarily perfectly echo what society says. The societal images of the mistrusted are communicated to individuals as part of the process of channelling mistrust. Therefore, the actions of individuals and the social context that are appropriate towards the mistrusted are determined in concert.

Once the mistrusted are explicitly included in the model, it is necessary also to consider how they will respond to being labelled and to the actions directed at them. It seems reasonable to assume there would be a parallel set of processes to those operating for the individual who is mistrusting. The mistrusted will consider the justification, cost and resolution options for being mistrusted and this will affect emotion and action. Identity resilience of those who are mistrusted will play a role in their reactions, similar to that in the individual who is mistrusting them. The mistrusted will normally respond specifically to the accusations against them. Consequently, they will have an impact on the system described in the original model. Their action may change, even if not deliberately, the prevalence of specific risk, uncertainty and social representations in the social context, and/or modify how individuals interpret the circumstances instigating mistrust. It can be seen that an extension of the original flow diagram of the theoretical model to include the mistrusted does have advantages. It emphasises that the mistrust process always involves the mistrusting and the mistrusted as well as those that would influence them. Figure 10.2 includes the mistrusted in the flow diagram representing the theoretical model. The dashed-line box representing the mistrusted includes a summarised version of the identity–emotion–action interactions linking to being mistrusted. Actions of the mistrusted are shown as affecting both the social context and the individuals who mistrust. It is worth remembering that the mistrusted may be an individual but often they are an identifiable minority. The action an individual can take to affect change in social representations and uncertainties, let alone the evaluation of major risks, is limited. However, minorities can wield influence, depending upon their tactics and their initial power base. The effect of the mistrusted should not be underestimated. Besides showing the significance of the actions of the mistrusted, the flow diagram suggests that the social processes that create and maintain mistrust in some individuals simultaneously identify others as mistrusted. Whether deliberate or accidental, feeding mistrust erects the mistrusting–mistrusted dichotomy. Both then become agents in the ongoing mistrust system.

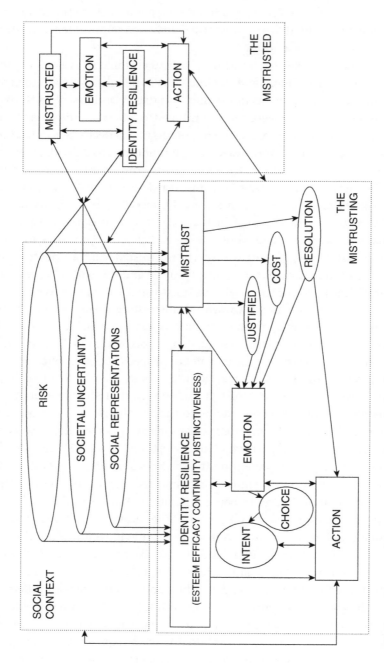

Figure 10.2 Model of Mistrust Processes including the Mistrusted

Another limitation of the model of mistrust processes presented in this chapter is that it does not unpack the relationships between the various activities that are used to promulgate mistrust. These include gossip, rumour, disinformation, propaganda and conspiracy theories. The model uses social context as a cipher for all these sorts of activities and indicates they become incorporated into social representations. These activities and the communication channels in which they reside (ranging from social and mass media to barbershops and school gates) are described in Chapters 7, 8 and 9. Furthermore, the roles of identity and social representation processes in the operation of these activities are outlined in those chapters. Essentially, the substrate for their inclusion in the theoretical model has been presented but they are not drawn into the flow diagram – it would probably be a bridge too far.

Things to Remember and to Question

Ending a book on mistrust turns out to be difficult. Every day, some new example of how it is manifested appears. It is tempting to analyse yet another twist on some ongoing health scare conspiracy theory, or the latest rumour about the replacement of the President of some country with a body double generated as part of an international disinformation campaign, or some new data on the doubts septuagenarians have about the faithfulness of their spouses. There is always something new to learn about mistrust. Of course, there are also things we have learned already and are worth remembering. Some are so obvious they are difficult to forget; others are contentious and open to question. In summarising a few of these take-home messages, the emphasis here is upon whether they actually help individuals or society in coping with mistrust:

- The theoretical model of mistrust processes presented here can be used as an orienteering map. However, to help in coping with mistrust, it is most useful when applied in specific mistrust circumstances where the constructs in the model can be measured and their effects upon each other monitored.
- Identity processes and social representation processes can be used effectively to explain what happens in a variety of different mistrust scenarios. It is most useful to analyse the effects of the interactions of these two types of process. Explaining how mistrust occurred in the past can support prediction of the course it may run in the future. Patterns of mistrust recur. In individuals, they appear as habits in choices that place the person into situations that precipitate mistrust. In a community, they appear in recurrent attacks on stigmatised groups. The patterns, once understood, offer a way to change when, how and whether mistrust happens.
- At a personal level, knowing how your own requirements for self-esteem, self-efficacy, continuity and distinctiveness were affected either by feeling mistrustful or by being mistrusted in the past is enormously helpful in anticipating how you will react in any future mistrust experience. You can design your own early warning system.

- Perceiving that a risk exists and that the appropriate response is to be mistrustful is significantly affected by the way heuristics and biases influence decision making. You can learn what heuristics and biases most characterise your own thinking and, thereby, perhaps be alert to potential errors of judgement.
- Mistrust is much influenced by pre-existing beliefs and values. It helps in coping with mistrust at individual or group levels to know how the subject of mistrust relates to prior attitudes, beliefs or values.
- Mistrust is very resilient to amelioration. If you are trying to manage mistrust and it persists, it is worth remembering this is probably no reflection upon your skills. However, take some solace from knowing which aspects of mistrust processes may be most malleable. Addressing the justification, cost and resolution issues associated with mistrust conceptualisation can be helpful. Focusing effort on influencing one or more of these may pay off in affecting emotional reactions to mistrust and directly affect action. Through emotional responses, it might also affect identity resilience.
- Leaders must expect to have to deal with mistrust. Like people, organisations sometimes develop mistrust cultures to aid their survival. Leaders should not ignore how mistrust is channelled in their own organisation or the effects that it has.
- Feeling mistrust or feeling mistrusted arouses emotions that will affect cognitive performance and decision making, and thus action. In coping with mistrust reactions, expect irrationality. However, being able to identify the sources of mistrust (whether in the social context influences or in individual experiences) helps to lay bare where the boundaries of realism and irrationality fall. Knowing this supports appropriate interventions (e.g. it will guide what new information should be given or the communication channel most likely to be effective).
- People who are mistrusted may be damaged psychologically or materially by the experience. They often will seek redress, involving hostility. This also makes managing mistrust difficult. The management task involves dealing with both the mistrusting and the mistrusted.
- Knowing how mistrust can be incited and weaponised creates temptations. It is evident that the means for mounting mistrust campaigns are now, in the social media era, commonly available. However, before falling for the temptation and trying to use any of these techniques, it is important to recognise that arousing mistrust is easier than either directing it or controlling its consequences. Once released mistrust can turn against the very individuals or agencies that aroused and released it. Putting it mildly, the backlash against those who deliberately incite mistrust can be very unpleasant indeed.

This is just some of what we have learned about mistrust processes that may assist in coping with it. It is important not to assume that the control of mistrust is ever likely to be perfected, but equally there is no reason for despair. There have been giant strides in recording and modelling the effects of mistrust. Many of the methods for growing mistrust have been described and their effects explained. Perhaps the most significant development that has been the basis for others is the conceptual leap that centres on treating mistrust as a multidimensional process in its own right, worthy of research programmes that do not conflate it with either trust or distrust. Mistrust is, in essence, much more akin to feelings of risk and uncertainty. Mistrust comprises doubts and suspicions that can shape affect and motivate action. It deserves to be a continuing object of social psychological analyses and theory. After all, much of human experience involves secrets, mystery, suspicion and doubt.

REFERENCES

Abric, J. C. (1996). Specific processes of social representations. *Papers on Social Representations*, *5*, 77–80.

Aghababaei, N., Mohammadtabar, S., & Saffarinia, M. (2014). Dirty Dozen vs. the H factor: Comparison of the Dark Triad and honesty–humility in prosociality, religiosity, and happiness. *Personality and Individual Differences*, *67*, 6–10.

Albarghouthi, S. I., & Klempe, S. H. (2019). 'Al-Khabith' – the malignant cunning disease: Sociocultural complexity and social representations of cancer in the occupied Palestinian territory. *Culture & Psychology*, *25*(1), 99–131.

Allcott, H., & Gentzkow, M. (2017). Social media and fake news in the 2016 election. *Journal of Economic Perspectives*, *31*(2), 211–236.

Allport, G. W., & Postman, L. (1947). *The psychology of rumor*. New York: Russell & Russell.

American Psychiatric Association (APA) (2013). *Diagnostic and Statistical Manual of Mental Disorders*, 5th Edition (DSM-5). New York: APA.

Arkes, H. R., Faust, D., Guilmette, T. J., & Hart, K. (1988). Eliminating the hindsight bias. *Journal of Applied Psychology*, *73*(2), 305.

Arun, K., & Kahraman Gedik, N. (2020). Impact of Asian cultural values upon leadership roles and styles. *International Review of Administrative Sciences*, DOI: 0020852320935982.

Asad, S., & Sadler-Smith, E. (2020). Differentiating leader hubris and narcissism on the basis of power. *Leadership*, *16*(1), 39–61.

Audrezet, A., de Kerviler, G., & Moulard, J. G. (2020). Authenticity under threat: When social media influencers need to go beyond self-presentation. *Journal of Business Research*, *117*, 557–569.

Ayman, R., Chemers, M. M., & Fiedler, F. (1995). The contingency model of leadership effectiveness: Its levels of analysis. *The Leadership Quarterly*, *6*(2), 147–167.

Bach, B., & Lobbestael, J. (2018). Elucidating DSM-5 and ICD-11 diagnostic features of borderline personality disorder using schemas and modes. *Psychopathology*, *51*(6), 400–407.

Bandura, A. (1977). Self-efficacy: Toward a unifying theory of behavioral change. *Psychological Review*, *84*(2), 191–215.

Banfield, E. C. (1958). *The moral basis of a backward society*. New York: Free Press.

Banks, G. C., McCauley, K. D., Gardner, W. L., & Guler, C. E. (2016). A meta-analytic review of authentic and transformational leadership: A test for redundancy. *The Leadership Quarterly, 27*(4), 634–652.

Baral, G., & Arachchilage, N. A. G. (2019). *Building confidence not to be phished through a gamified approach: Conceptualising user's self-efficacy in phishing threat avoidance behaviour*. In 2019 Cybersecurity and Cyberforensics Conference (CCC) (pp. 102–110). New York: Institute of Electrical and Electronics Engineers.

Barnes, T. D., Beaulieu, E., & Saxton, G. W. (2018). Restoring trust in the police: Why female officers reduce suspicions of corruption. *Governance, 31*(1), 143–161.

Barnett, J., & Breakwell, G. M. (2001). Risk perception and experience: Hazard personality profiles and individual differences. *Risk Analysis, 21*(1), 171–178.

Barnett, J., & Breakwell, G. M. (2003). The social amplification of risk and the hazard sequence: The October 1995 oral contraceptive pill scare. *Health, Risk and Society, 5*(3), 301–313.

Barreto, N., & Hogg, M. A. (2017). Evaluation of and support for group prototypical leaders: A meta-analysis of twenty years of empirical research. *Social Influence, 12*(1), 41–55. DOI: 10.1080/15534510.2017.1316771.

Bartlett, F. C. (1932). *Remembering: A study in experimental and social psychology*. Cambridge: Cambridge University Press.

Bastick, Z. (2021). Would you notice if fake news changed your behavior? An experiment on the unconscious effects of disinformation. *Computers in Human Behavior*, Vol. *116*. DOI: 10.1016/j.chb.2020.106633

Beck, U. (1992). From industrial society to the risk society: Questions of survival, social structure and ecological enlightenment. *Theory, Culture & Society, 9*(1), 97–123.

Beersma, B., & Van Kleef, G. A. (2011). How the grapevine keeps you in line: Gossip increases contributions to the group. *Social Psychological and Personality Science, 2*(6), 642–649.

Belluz, J. (2018). A comprehensive guide to the messy, frustrating science of cellphones and health. *Vox*, 2 November. Available at www.vox.com/2018/7/16/17067214/cellphone-cancer-5g-evidence-studies (accessed 11 March, 2021).

Berger, J. (2011). Arousal increases social transmission of information, *Psychological Science, 22*(7), 181.

Berger, J., & Milkman, K. L. (2012). What makes online content viral?, *Journal of Marketing Research, 49*(2), 192–205.

Bernardes, S. F., & Lima, M. L. (2005). Comparative optimism and perceived control over health in adolescence: Are there any age differences? *Estudos de Psicologia (Natal), 10*(3), 335–344.

Bernstein, D. M., Aßfalg, A., Kumar, R., & Ackerman, R. (2016). Looking backward and forward on hindsight bias. In J. Dunlosky & S. K. Tauber (Eds), Oxford library of psychology. *The Oxford handbook of metamemory* (pp. 289–304). Oxford: Oxford University Press.

Billig, M. (1987). Anti-semitic themes and the British far left: Some social-psychological observations on indirect aspects of the conspiracy tradition. In C. Graumann & S. Moscovici (Eds), *Changing conceptions of conspiracy* (pp. 115–136). New York: Springer.

Birchall, C. (2006). Cultural studies on/as conspiracy theory. In C. Birchall (Ed.), *Knowledge goes pop from conspiracy theory to gossip* (pp. 65–90). Oxford: Berg.

Biswas, B., & Deylami, S. (2019). Radicalizing female empowerment: Gender, agency, and affective appeals in Islamic State propaganda. *Small Wars & Insurgencies, 30*(6–7), 1193–1213.

Blank, H., & Nestler, S. (2007). Cognitive process models of hindsight bias. *Social Cognition, 25*(1), 132–146.

Bonaiuto, M., Breakwell, G. M., & Cano, I. (1996). Identity processes and environmental threat: The effects of nationalism and local identity upon perception of beach pollution. *Journal of Community & Applied Social Psychology, 6*(3), 157–175.

Bornstein, R. F. (1989). Subliminal techniques as propaganda tools: Review and critique. *The Journal of Mind and Behavior, 10*(3), 231–262.

Bostrom, A., Hayes, A. L., & Crosman, K. M. (2019). Efficacy, action, and support for reducing climate change risks. *Risk Analysis, 39*(4), 805–828.

Boyd-Barrett, O. (2019). Fake news and 'RussiaGate' discourses: Propaganda in the post-truth era. *Journalism, 20*(1), 87–91.

Bradfield, A., & Wells, G. L. (2005). Not the same old hindsight bias: Outcome information distorts a broad range of retrospective judgments. *Memory & Cognition, 33*(1), 120–130.

Bradshaw, S., & Howard, P. (2017). *Troops, trolls and troublemakers: A global inventory of organized social media manipulation*, Vol. 12 (pp. 1–37). Oxford: Oxford Internet Institute.

Breakwell, G. M. (1978). Groups for sale. *New Society, 45*, 66–68.

Breakwell, G. M. (1979). Woman: Group and identity? *Women's Studies International Quarterly, 2*(1), 9–17.

Breakwell, G. M. (1983). Identities and conflicts. In G. M. Breakwell (Ed.), *Threatened identities* (pp. 189–214). Chichester: Wiley.

Breakwell, G. M. (1986). *Coping with Threatened Identities*. London and New York: Methuen.

Breakwell, G. M. (1988). Strategies adopted when identity is threatened. *Revue Internationale de Psychologie Sociale, 1*(2), 189–204.

Breakwell, G. M. (1992). Processes of self-evaluation: Efficacy and estrangement. In G. M. Breakwell (Ed.), *Social psychology of identity and the self concept* (pp. 35–55). London: Academic Press.

Breakwell, G. M. (1993). Social representations and social identity. *Papers on Social Representations, 2*(3), 198–217.

Breakwell, G. M. (1996). Identity processes and social changes. In G. M. Breakwell & E. Lyons (Eds), *Changing European identities: Social psychological analyses of change* (pp. 13–27). Oxford: Butterworth-Heineman.

Breakwell, G. M. (2001a). Social representational constraints upon identity processes. In K. Deaux & G. Philogene (Eds), *Representations of the social: Bridging theoretical traditions* (pp. 271–284). Oxford: Blackwell.

Breakwell, G. M. (2001b). Promoting individual and social change. In F. Butera & G. Mugny (Eds), *Social influence in social reality* (pp. 344–357). Goettingen: Hogrefe & Huber.

Breakwell, G. M. (2010). Resisting representations and identity processes. *Papers in Social Representations, 19*, 6.1–6.11.

Breakwell, G. M. (2011). Empirical approaches to social representations and identity processes: 20 years on. *Papers on Social Representations, 20*, 17.11–17.14.

Breakwell, G. M. (2014a). Identity process theory: Clarifications and elaborations. In R. Jaspal & G. M. Breakwell (Eds), *Identity process theory* (pp. 20–39). Cambridge: Cambridge University Press.

Breakwell, G. M. (2014b). *The psychology of risk*. Cambridge: Cambridge University Press.

Breakwell, G. M. (2014c). Identity and social representations. In R. Jaspal & G. M. Breakwell (Eds), *Identity process theory* (pp. 118–134). Cambridge: Cambridge University Press.

Breakwell, G. M. (2015a). *Coping with threatened identities*. Hove: Psychology Press.

Breakwell, G. M. (2015b). Identity process theory. In G. Sammut, E. Andreouli, G. Gaskell, & J. Valsiner (Eds), *The Cambridge handbook of social representations* (pp. 250–268). Cambridge: Cambridge University Press.

Breakwell, G. M. (2020a). In the age of societal uncertainty, the era of threat. In D. Jodelet, J. Vala, & E. Drozda-Senkowska (Eds), *Societies under threat: A pluri-disciplinary approach* (pp. 55–74). New York: Springer-Nature.

Breakwell, G. M. (2020b). Mistrust, uncertainty and health risks. *Contemporary Social Science*, 1–13. DOI: 10.1080/21582041.2020.1804070.

Breakwell, G. M., & Canter, D. V. (Eds) (1993). *Empirical Approaches to Social Representations*. Oxford: Oxford University Press.

Breakwell, G. M., & Fife-Schaw, C. R. (1994). Using longitudinal cohort sequential designs to study changes in sexual behaviour. In M. Boulton (Ed.), *Challenge and innovation: Methodological advances in social research on HIV/AIDS* (pp. 25–38). London: Taylor & Francis.

Breakwell, G. M., & Jaspal, R. (2020). Identity change, uncertainty and mistrust in relation to fear and risk of COVID-19. *Journal of Risk Research*. DOI: 10.1080/13669877.2020.1864011.

Breakwell, G. M., Jaspal, R., & Fino, E. (2021). COVID-19 preventive behaviours in White British and Black, Asian and Minority Ethnic (BAME) people in the UK. *Journal of Health Psychology*, DOI: https://doi.org/10.1177/13591053211017208

Breakwell, G. M., Wright, D. B., & Barnett, J. (Eds), (2020). *Research methods in psychology* (5th ed.). London: SAGE.

Brewer, M. B. (2019). Intergroup relations. In E. J. Finkel & R. F. Baumeister (Eds), *Advanced social psychology: The state of the science* (pp. 249–274). Oxford: Oxford University Press.

Brooking, E. T., & Singer, P. W. (2016). War goes viral. *The Atlantic, 318*(4), 70–83.

Brooks, R. T., & Hopkins, R. (2017). Cultural mistrust and health care utilization: The effects of a culturally responsive cognitive intervention. *Journal of Black Studies, 48*(8), 816–834.

Brotherton, R., & French, C. C. (2015). Intention seekers: Conspiracist ideation and biased attributions of intentionality. *PLOS One, 10*(5), e0124125.

Brotherton, R., French, C. C., & Pickering, A. D. (2013). Measuring belief in conspiracy theories: The generic conspiracist beliefs scale. *Frontiers in Psychology, 4,* 279.

Brown, D. (2020). Amber Heard accuses Johnny Depp of online 'smear campaign' to get her fired from Aquaman sequel. *The Times,* 13 November. Available at www.thetimes.co.uk›article›amber-heard-accus (accessed 11 March, 2021).

Buchanan, T. (2020). Why do people spread false information online? The effects of message and viewer characteristics on self-reported likelihood of sharing social media disinformation. *PLOS One, 15*(10), e0239666.

Burgess, A. (2015). Social construction of risk. In H. Cho, T. Reimer, & K. McComas (Eds). *The SAGE handbook of risk communication* (pp. 56–68). Thousand Oaks, CA: SAGE.

Byford, J. (2011). *Conspiracy theories: A critical introduction.* New York: Palgrave Macmillan.

Byung-Chul, H. (2017). *Psych-politics: Neo-liberalism and new technologies of power.* London: Verso.

Caldera, C. (2020). Fact check: Posts falsely claim first vaccine recipients in the UK are 'crisis actors'. *USA Today,* 10 December. Available at https://www.usatoday.com/story/news/factcheck/2020/12/10/fact-check-posts-falsely-claim-vaccine-recipients-uk-actors/3882553001/ (accessed 23 April, 2021).

Campbell, J. D., & Tesser, A. (1983). Motivational interpretations of hindsight bias: An individual difference analysis. *Journal of Personality, 51*(4), 605–620.

Campbell, L. F., & Stewart, A. E. (1992). Effects of group membership on perception of risk for AIDS. *Psychological Reports, 70*(3), 1075–1092.

Caponecchia, C. (2012). Relative risk perception for terrorism: Implications for preparedness and risk communication. *Risk Analysis: An International Journal, 32*(9), 1524–1534.

Cardaioli, M., Cecconello, S., Conti, M., Pajola, L., & Turrin, F. (2020). Fake news spreaders profiling through behavioural analysis. In L. Cappellato, C. Eickhoff, N. Ferro, & A. Névéol (Eds), Working Notes of CLEF 2020 – Conference and Labs of the Evaluation Forum, Thessaloniki, Greece, 22–25 September.

Carey, M. (2017). *Mistrust: An ethnographic theory.* Chicago, IL: Hau Books.

Carli, L. L., & Eagly, A. H. (2016). Women face a labyrinth: An examination of metaphors for women leaders. *Gender in Management, 31*(8), 514–527.

Chadwick, A., & Vaccari, C. (2019). News sharing on UK social media: Misinformation, disinformation, and correction. *Survey Report.* Available at https://repository.lboro.ac.uk/articles/News_sharing_on_UK_social_media_misinformation_disinformation_and_correction/9471269 (accessed 11 March, 2021).

Chambers, J. R., & Melnyk, D. (2006). Why do I hate thee? Conflict misperceptions and intergroup mistrust. *Personality and Social Psychology Bulletin*, *32*(10), 1295–1311.

Chesney, R., & Citron, D. (2019). Deepfakes and the new disinformation war: The coming age of post-truth geopolitics. *Foreign Affairs*, *98*, 147.

Cialdini, R. B. (2009). *Influence: Science and practice*. New York: William Morrow.

Clark, C., Davila, A., Regis, M., & Kraus, S. (2020). Predictors of COVID-19 voluntary compliance behaviors: An international investigation. *Global Transitions*, *2*, 76–82.

Confessor, N., Dance, G. J. X., Harris, R., & Hansen, M. (2018). The follower factory. *New York Times*, 27 January. Available at www.nytimes.com/interactive/2018/01/27/technology/social-media-bots.html (accessed 11 March, 2021).

Cooper, M. W. (1991). *Behold a pale horse*. Flagstaff, AZ: Light Technology Publishing.

Cort, M. A. (2004). Cultural mistrust and use of hospice care: Challenges and remedies. *Journal of Palliative Medicine*, *7*(1), 63–71.

Council of Europe (2011). European media and anti-Gypsy stereotypes. Available at www.coe.int/en/web/commissioner/-/european-media-and-anti-gypsy-stereotyp-1 (accessed 11 March, 2021).

Covey, S. R., & Merrill, R. R. (2006). *The speed of trust: The one thing that changes everything*. London: Simon and Schuster.

Cuevas, A. G., O'Brien, K., & Saha, S. (2019). Can patient-centred communication reduce the effects of medical mistrust on patients' decision making? *Health Psychology*, *38*(4), 325.

Cumming, G. S., Barnes, G., Perz, S., Schmink, M., Sieving, K. E., Southworth, J., ... & Van Holt, T. (2005). An exploratory framework for the empirical measurement of resilience. *Ecosystems*, *8*(8), 975–987.

Cunningham, S. B. (2002). *The idea of propaganda: A reconstruction*. Westport, CT: Greenwood Publishing.

da Silva Rebelo, M. J., Fernández, M., & Achotegui, J. (2018). Mistrust, anger, and hostility in refugees, asylum seekers, and immigrants: A systematic review. *Canadian Psychology/Psychologie canadienne*, *59*(3), 239–251.

David, E. J. R. (2010). Cultural mistrust and mental health help-seeking attitudes among Filipino Americans. *Asian American Journal of Psychology*, *1*(1), 57.

Davis, J. L., Bynum, S. A., Katz, R. V., Buchanan, K., & Green, B. L. (2012). Sociodemographic differences in fears and mistrust contributing to unwillingness to participate in cancer screenings. *Journal of Health Care for the Poor and Underserved*, *23*(40), 67.

Day, C. (2018). Professional identity matters: Agency, emotions, and resilience. In P. Schutz, J. Hong, & D. Cross Francis (Eds), *Research on teacher identity*. Cham: Springer, Cham. DOI: org/10.1007/978–3-319–93836–3_6.

de Berker, A., Rutledge, R., Mathys, C., Marshall, L., Cross, G. F., Dolan, R. J., & Bestmann, S. (2016). Computations of uncertainty mediate acute stress responses in humans. *Nature Communications*, *7*, 10996.

DeCook, J. R. (2020). Trust me, I'm trolling: Irony and the alt-right's political aesthetic. *M/C Journal*, *23*(3). Available at https://doi.org/10.5204/mcj.1655 (accessed 11 July, 2021).

Deer, B. (2020). *The doctor who fooled the world: Science, deception, and the war on vaccines*. Baltimore, MD: Johns Hopkins University Press.

Dekker, S. W. (2004). The hindsight bias is not a bias and not about history. *Human Factors and Aerospace Safety*, *4*(2), 87–99.

Descartes, R. (1641 [1978]). Meditations on first philosophy in focus (pp. 221). Psychology Press.

Dickens, D. D., Womack, V. Y., & Dimes, T. (2019). Managing hypervisibility: An exploration of theory and research on identity shifting strategies in the workplace among Black women. *Journal of Vocational Behavior*, *113*, 153–163.

Dietz, G. (2011). Going back to the source: Why do people trust each other?, *Journal of Trust Research*, *1*(2), 215–222.

Dirks, K. T., & Ferrin, D. L. (2002). Trust in leadership: Meta-analytic findings and implications for research and practice. *Journal of Applied Psychology*, *87*(4), 611.

Dolinski, D., Gromski, W., & Zawisza, E. (1987). Unrealistic pessimism. *The Journal of Social Psychology*, *127*(5), 511–516.

Douglas, K. M., Cichocka, A., & Sutton, R. M. (2020). Motivations, emotions and belief in conspiracy theories. In M. Butter & P. Knight (Eds), *Routledge handbook of conspiracy theories* (pp. 181–191). London: Routledge.

Douglas, K. M., & Sutton, R. M. (2011). Does it take one to know one? Endorsement of conspiracy theories is influenced by personal willingness to conspire. *British Journal of Social Psychology*, *50*(3), 544–552.

Douglas, K. M., Sutton, R. M., & Cichocka, A. (2017). The psychology of conspiracy theories. *Current Directions in Psychological Science*, *26*(6), 538–542.

Douglas, K. M., Uscinski, J. E., Sutton, R. M., Cichocka, A., Nefes, T., Ang, C. S., & Deravi, F. (2019). Understanding conspiracy theories. *Political Psychology*, *40*, 3–35.

Dunbar, R. I. (2004). Gossip in evolutionary perspective. *Review of General Psychology*, *8*(2), 100–110.

Eagly, A. H., Johannesen-Schmidt, M. C., & Van Engen, M. L. (2003). Transformational, transactional, and laissez-faire leadership styles: A meta-analysis comparing women and men. *Psychological Bulletin*, *129*(4), 569.

Eagly, A. H., & Sczesny, S. (2009). Stereotypes about women, men, and leaders: Have times changed? In M. Barreto, M. K. Ryan, & M. T. Schmitt (Eds), *Psychology of women book series. The glass ceiling in the 21st century: Understanding barriers to gender equality* (pp. 21–47). Washington, D.C.: American Psychological Association.

Eckstrand, N. (2018). The ugliness of trolls: Comparing the strategies/methods of the alt-right and the Ku Klux Klan. *Cosmopolitan Civil Societies: An Interdisciplinary Journal*, *10*(3), 1–20.

Emler, N. (1994). Gossip, reputation, and social adaptation. In R. F. Goodman & A. Ben-Ze'ev (Eds), *Good gossip* (pp. 117–138). Lawrence, KS: University Press of Kansas.

Encyclopaedia Britannica (2021). Heracles classical mythology. Available at www.britannica.com/topic/Heracles (accessed 11 March, 2021).

Enders, A. M., Smallpage, S. M., & Lupton, R. N. (2020). Are all 'birthers' conspiracy theorists? On the relationship between conspiratorial thinking and political orientations. *British Journal of Political Science*, *50*(3), 849–866.

Engelmann, J. M., Herrmann, E., & Tomasello, M. (2016). Preschoolers affect others' reputations through prosocial gossip. *British Journal of Developmental Psychology*, *34*(3), 447–460.

Erikson, E. H. (1963). *Childhood and society* (2nd ed.). New York: Norton.

European Centre for Disease Prevention and Control (2020). Situation Updates on COVID-19: Weekly Surveillance. https://www.ecdc.europa.eu/en/covid-19/situation-updates (accessed 1 April, 2021).

Evans, C. (2018). Risky photography in National Parks: An examination of the role of online identity management in wildlife risk perceptions. PhD dissertation, Colorado State University.

Fan, L., Yu, H., & Yin, Z. (2020). Stigmatization in social media: Documenting and analyzing hate speech for COVID-19 on Twitter. *Proceedings of the Association for Information Science and Technology*, *57*(1), e313.

Farquharson, W. H., & Thornton, C. J. (2020). Debate: Exposing the most serious infirmity – racism's impact on health in the era of COVID-19. *Child and Adolescent Mental Health*, *25*(3), 182–183.

Fernandez, A. A., & Shaw, G. P. (2020). Academic leadership in a time of crisis: The coronavirus and COVID-19. *Journal of Leadership Studies*, *14*(1), 39–45.

Fersini, E., Armanini, J., & D'Intorni, M. (2020). Profiling fake news spreaders: Stylometry, personality, emotions and embeddings. In L. Cappellato, C. Eickhoff, N. Ferro, & A. Névéol (Eds), Working Notes of CLEF 2020 – Conference and Labs of the Evaluation Forum, Thessaloniki, Greece, 22–25 September.

Fertuck, E. A., Fischer, S., & Beeney, J. (2018). Social cognition and borderline personality disorder: Splitting and trust impairment findings. *Psychiatric Clinics*, *41*(4), 613–632.

Fiedler, F. E. (1967). *A theory of leadership effectiveness*. New York: McGraw-Hill.

Fine, G. A. (1977). Social components of children's gossip. *Journal of Communication*, *27*(1), 181–185.

Fischhoff, B. (1975). Hindsight is not equal to foresight: The effect of outcome knowledge on judgment under uncertainty. *Journal of Experimental Psychology: Human perception and performance*, *1*(3), 288.

Fischhoff, B., Gonzalez, R. M., Lerner, J. S., & Small, D. A. (2005). Evolving judgments of terror risks: Foresight, hindsight, and emotion. *Journal of Experimental Psychology: Applied*, *11*(2), 124.

Fischhoff, B., & Kadvany, J. (2011). *Risk*. Oxford: Oxford University Press.

Flew, T., Dulleck, U., Park, S., Fisher, C., & Isler, O. (2020). Trust and mistrust in Australian news media. Brisbane: Queensland University of Technology. Available at https://eprints.qut.edu.au/199132/ (accessed 11 March, 2021).

Foner, E., & Garraty, J. A. (Eds) (1991). *The reader's companion to American history*. Boston, MA: Houghton Mifflin Harcourt.

Freberg, K., Graham, K., McGaughey, K., & Freberg, L. A. (2011). Who are the social media influencers? A study of public perceptions of personality. *Public Relations Review, 37*(1), 90–92.

Fulmer, C. A., & Ostroff, C. (2017). Trust in direct leaders and top leaders: A trickle-up model. *Journal of Applied Psychology, 102*(4), 648.

Furnham, A. (2010). *The elephant in the boardroom: The causes of leadership derailment.* Basingstoke: Palgrave MacMillan.

Furnham, A. (2018). *Management failure and derailment.* In P. Garrard (Ed.), *The leadership hubris epidemic* (pp. 69–92). Cham: Palgrave Macmillan.

Furnham, A., Boo, H. C., & McClelland, A. (2012). Individual differences and the susceptibility to the influence of anchoring cues. *Journal of Individual Differences, 33*, 89–93.

Furnham, A., Richards, S. C., & Paulhus, D. L. (2013). The Dark Triad of personality: A 10-year review. *Social and Personality Psychology Compass, 7*(3), 199–216.

Furtner, M. R., Maran T., & Rauthmann J. F. (2017). Dark leadership: The role of leaders' Dark Triad personality traits. In M. Clark & C. Gruber (Eds), *Leader development deconstructed: Annals of theoretical psychology*, Vol. *15* (pp. 75–99). Cham: Springer.

Galbraith, J. K. (1977). *The age of uncertainty*. Boston, MA: Houghton Mifflin Harcourt.

Gardner, W. L., Cogliser, C. C., Davis, K. M., & Dickens, M. P. (2011). Authentic leadership: A review of the literature and research agenda. *The Leadership Quarterly, 22*(6), 1120–1145.

Gaspar, R., Gorjao, S., Seibt, B., Lima, L., Barnett, J., Moss, A., & Wills, J. (2014). Tweeting during food crises: A psychosocial analysis of threat coping expressions in Spain, during the 2011 European EHEC outbreak. *International Journal of Human-Computer Studies, 72*(2), 239–254.

Gibson, B. L., Rochat, P., Tone, E. B., & Baron, A. S. (2017). Sources of implicit and explicit intergroup race bias among African-American children and young adults. *PLOS One, 12*(9), e0183015.

Giddens, A. (1984). *The Constitution of Society: Outline of the Theory of Structuration.* Cambridge: Polity Press.

Giddens, A. (1991). *Modernity and self-identity: Self and society in the late modern age.* Palo Alto, CA: Stanford University Press.

Gilmore, D. (1978). Varieties of gossip in a Spanish rural community. *Ethnology, 17*(1), 89–99.

Glover, H. (1984). Themes of mistrust and the posttraumatic stress disorder in Vietnam veterans. *American Journal of Psychotherapy, 38*(3), 445–452.

Gluckman, M. (1963). Gossip and scandal. *Current Anthropology, 4*, 307–316.

Goertzel, T. (1994). Belief in conspiracy theories. *Political Psychology, 15*(4), 731–742.

Goldschmidt-Gjerløw, B., & Remkes, M. (2019). Frontstage and backstage in Argentina's transitional justice drama: The *Niet@s'* reconstruction of identity on social media. *International Journal of Transitional Justice, 13*(2), 349–367.

Goreis, A., & Voracek, M. (2019). A systematic review and meta-analysis of psychological research on conspiracy beliefs: Field characteristics, measurement instruments, and associations with personality traits. *Frontiers in Psychology, 10*, 205.

Görner, K., Zieliński J., & Jurczak A. (2013). Interpersonal functioning in individuals who practise extreme sports and those who prefer hazardous behaviour. *Journal of Health Sciences, 3*(13), 178–189.

Graumann, C. F., & Moscovici, S. (Eds) (2012). *Changing conceptions of conspiracy.* New York: Springer Science & Business Media.

Grewal, L., Stephen, A. T., & Coleman, N. V. (2019). When posting about products on social media backfires: The negative effects of consumer identity signaling on product interest. *Journal of Marketing Research, 56*(2), 197–210.

Groysberg, B., & Slind, M. (2012). *Talk, Inc.: How trusted leaders use conversation to power their organizations.* Boston, MA: Harvard Business Press.

Guarino, S., Trino, N., Celestini, A., Chessa, A., & Riotta, G. (2020). Characterizing networks of propaganda on Twitter: A case study. Available at *arXiv preprint arXiv:2005.10004* (accessed 11 March, 2021).

Gulenko, P., & Dolgova, Y. (2020). Evolution of interactive elements in socio-political talk shows in post-Soviet Russia. *Global Media and Communication*, July. DOI: org/10.1177.1742766520946471.

Harris, L. M., Chin, N. P., Fiscella, K., & Humiston, S. (2006). Barrier to pneumococcal and influenza vaccinations in Black elderly communities: Mistrust. *Journal of the National Medical Association, 98*(10), 1678.

Helweg-Larsen, M. (1999). (The lack of) optimistic biases in response to the 1994 Northridge earthquake: The role of personal experience. *Basic and Applied Social Psychology, 21*(2), 119–129.

Hendy, J., Lyons, E., & Breakwell, G. M. (2006). Genetic testing and the relationship between specific and general self-efficacy. *British Journal of Health Psychology, 11*(2), 221–223.

Higgins, C. (2020). *Mapping global leadership: Cross-cultural analyses of leadership styles and practices.* Amsterdam, Netherlands: CCBS Press.

Hintz, A. (2019). Leaks. *The International Encyclopedia of Journalism Studies*, 1–7.

Hodge, E., & Hallgrimsdottir, H. (2020). Networks of hate: The alt-right, 'troll culture', and the cultural geography of social movement spaces online, *Journal of Borderlands Studies, 35*(4), 563–580. DOI: 10.1080/08865655.2019.1571935.

Hodson, G., & Sorrentino, R. (1999). Uncertainty orientation and the big five personality structure. *Journal of Research in Personality, 33*(2), 253–261.

Holmberg-Wright, K., & Hribar, T. (2016). Soft skills – the missing piece for entrepreneurs to grow a business. *American Journal of Management, 16*(1).

Hölzl, E., & Kirchler, E. (2005). Causal attribution and hindsight bias for economic developments. *Journal of Applied Psychology, 90*(1), 167.

Hopp, T., Ferrucci, P., & Vargo, C. J. (2020). Why do people share ideologically extreme, false, and misleading content on social media? A self-report and trace data-based analysis of countermedia content dissemination on Facebook and Twitter. *Human Communication Research*, *46*(4), 357–384.

Hudson, J. (2006). Institutional trust and subjective well-being across the EU. *Kyklos*, *59*(1), 43–62.

Igweze, Z. N., Ekhator, O. C., & Orisakwe, O. E. (2020). A pediatric health risk assessment of children's toys imported from China into Nigeria. *Heliyon*, *6*(4), e03732.

Innes, M., Dobreva, D., & Innes, H. (2019). Disinformation and digital influencing after terrorism: Spoofing, truthing and social proofing. *Contemporary Social Science*, 1–15.

Ipsos MORI (2019). Veracity Index 2019: Trust in Professions. Available at https://www.ipsos.com/sites/default/files/ct/news/documents/2019-11/trust-in-professions-veracity-index-2019 (accessed 1 April, 2021).

Ipsos MORI (2020a). Veracity Index 2020. Available at www.ipsos.com/en-ie/ipsos-mrbi-veracity-index-2020 (accessed 11 March, 2021).

Ipsos MORI (2020b). Political Trust and the COVID-19 crisis. Available at https://www.ipsos.com/sites/default/files/ct/news/documents/2020-08/political-trust-and-the-covid-19-crisis (accessed 1 April, 2021).

Jaspal, R., & Bayley, J. (2020). Intersecting identities. In R. Jaspal & J. Bayley, *HIV and Gay Men*. Singapore: Palgrave Macmillan.

Jaspal, R., & Breakwell, G. M. (Eds) (2014). *Identity process theory: Identity, social action and social change*. Cambridge: Cambridge University Press.

Jaspal, R., & Breakwell, G. M. (2020). Socio-economic inequalities in social network, loneliness and mental health during the COVID-19 pandemic, 1–11. *International Journal of Social Psychiatry*. DOI:10.1177/0020764020976694.

Jaspal, R., & Breakwell, G. M. (2021). Social support, perceived risk, and the likelihood of COVID-19 testing and vaccination. *Current Psychology* (in press).

Jaspal, R., & Cinnirella, M. (2012). The construction of ethnic identity: Insights from identity process theory. *Ethnicities*, *12*(5), 503–530.

Jaspal, R., Fino, E., & Breakwell, G. M. (2020). The COVID-19 own risk appraisal scale (CORAS): Development and validation in two samples from the United Kingdom. *Journal of Health Psychology*, October. DOI: org/10.1177/1359105320967429.

Jaspal, R., Nerlich, B., & Cinnirella, M. (2014). Human responses to climate change: Social representation, identity and socio-psychological action. *Environmental Communication*, *8*(1), 110–130.

Jodelet, D. (2008). Social representations: The beautiful invention. *Journal for the Theory of Social Behaviour*, *38*(4), 411–430.

Jodelet, D., Vala, J., & Drozda-Senkowska, E. (2020). *Societies under threat: A pluridisciplinary approach*. New York: Springer-Nature.

Kaakinen, M., Sirola, A., Savolainen, I., & Oksanen, A. (2020). Shared identity and shared information in social media: Development and validation of the identity bubble reinforcement scale. *Media Psychology*, *23*(1), 25–51.

Kahneman, D., Slovic, S. P., Slovic, P., & Tversky, A. (Eds) (1982). *Judgment under uncertainty: Heuristics and biases*. Cambridge: Cambridge University Press.

Kay, J., & King, M. (2020). *Radical uncertainty: Decision-making for an unknowable future*. London: Bridge Street Press.

Keynes, J. M. (1937). The general theory of employment. *The Quarterly Journal of Economics, 51*(2), 209–223.

Khanday, A. M. U. D., Khan, Q. R., & Rabani, S. T. (2020). Identifying propaganda from online social networks during COVID-19 using machine learning techniques. *International Journal of Information Technology*, 1–8.

Ki, C. W. C., & Kim, Y. K. (2019). The mechanism by which social media influencers persuade consumers: The role of consumers' desire to mimic. *Psychology & Marketing, 36*(10), 905–922.

Knapp, R. A. (1944). A psychology of rumour, *Public Opinion Quarterly, 8*(1), 22–37.

Knoll, M. A., & Arkes, H. R. (2017). The effects of expertise on the hindsight bias. *Journal of Behavioral Decision Making, 30*(2), 389–399.

Kosfeld, M., Heinrichs, M., Zak, P. J., Fischbacher, U., & Fehr, E. (2005). Oxytocin increases trust in humans. *Nature, 435*(7042), 673–676.

Kumar, S., Cheng, J., Leskovec, J., & Subrahmanian, V. S. (2017). *An army of me: Sockpuppets in online discussion communities*. Proceedings of the 26th International Conference on World Wide Web (pp. 857–866).

Lahrach, Y., & Furnham, A. (2017). Are modern health worries associated with medical conspiracy theories? *Journal of Psychosomatic Research, 99*, 89–94.

Lantian, A., Muller, D., Nurra, C., & Douglas, K. M. (2017). I know things they don't know! *Social Psychology, 48*, 160–173.

Lasswell, H. D. (1927). *Propaganda techniques in the world war*. Cambridge: Ravenio Books.

Lazer, D., Baum, M., Benkler, Y., Berinsky, A. J., Greenhill, K. M., Menczer, ... & Zittrain, J. L. (2018). The Science of Fake News. *Science, 359*(6380), 1094–1096.

Lee, R. M. (2005). Resilience against discrimination: Ethnic identity and other-group orientation as protective factors for Korean Americans. *Journal of Counseling Psychology, 52*(1), 36.

Lefcourt, H. M. (Ed.) (2014). *Locus of control: Current trends in theory and research*. Hove: Psychology Press.

Levin, I. P., Schneider, S. L., & Gaeth, G. J. (1998). All frames are not created equal: A typology and critical analysis of framing effects. *Organizational Behavior and Human Decision Processes, 76*(2), 149–188.

Liberman, Z., & Shaw, A. (2020). Even his friend said he's bad: Children think personal alliances bias gossip. *Cognition, 204*, 104376.

Libório, R. M. C., & Ungar, M. (2010). Children's perspectives on their economic activity as a pathway to resilience. *Children & Society, 24*(4), 326–338.

Lieb, K., Zanarini, M. C., Schmahl, C., Linehan, M. M., & Bohus, M. (2004). Borderline personality disorder. *The Lancet, 364*(9432), 453–461.

Liu, P., Jiang, J.-Z., Wan, X.-F., Hua, Y., Li, L., Zhou, J., ... Chen, J. (2020). Are pangolins the intermediate host of the 2019 novel coronavirus (SARS-CoV-2)? *PLOS Pathog, 16*(5), e1008421.

Lonati, S. (2020). What explains cultural differences in leadership styles? On the agricultural origins of participative and directive leadership. *The Leadership Quarterly, 31*(2), 101305.

Lovric, D., & Chamorro-Premuzi, T. (2018). Why great success can bring out the worst parts of our personalities. *Harvard Business Review*, August, 09.

Lowry, P. B., Zhang, J., Wang, C., & Siponen, M. (2016). Why do adults engage in cyberbullying on social media? An integration of online disinhibition and deindividuation effects with the social structure and social learning model. *Information Systems Research, 27*(4), 962–986.

Lukito, J. (2020). Coordinating a multi-platform disinformation campaign: Internet research agency activity on three US social media platforms, 2015 to 2017. *Political Communication, 37*(2), 238–255.

Lupien, S. J., Maheu, F., Tu, M., Fiocco, A., & Schramek, T. E. (2007). The effects of stress and stress hormones on human cognition: Implications for the field of brain and cognition. *Brain and Cognition, 65*(3), 209–237.

Lupu, N., Bustamante, M. V. R., & Zechmeister, E. J. (2020). Social media disruption: Messaging mistrust in Latin America. *Journal of Democracy, 31*(3), 160–171.

Luyten, P., Campbell, C., & Fonagy, P. (2020). Borderline personality disorder, complex trauma, and problems with self and identity: A social-communicative approach. *Journal of Personality, 88*(1), 88–105.

Maass, A., & Clark, R. D. (1984). Hidden impact of minorities: Fifteen years of minority influence research. *Psychological Bulletin, 95*(3), 428.

Mahdavi, S., & Rahimian, M. A. (2017). Hindsight bias impedes learning. *Proceedings of the NIPS 2016 Workshop on Imperfect Decision Makers*, PMLR 58, 111–127.

Manning, L. K., & Bouchard, L. (2020). Encounters with adversity: A framework for understanding resilience in later life. *Aging & Mental Health, 24*(7), 1108–1115.

Marková, I. (2012). Social representations as anthropology of culture. In J. Valsiner (Ed.), *The Oxford handbook of culture and psychology* (pp. 487–509). Oxford: Oxford University Press.

Martinescu, E., Janssen, O., & Nijstad, B. A. (2019). Gossip as a resource: How and why power relationships shape gossip behavior. *Organizational Behavior and Human Decision Processes, 153*, 89–102.

Mashuri, A., Zaduqisti, E., Sukmawati, F., Sakdiah, H., & Suharini, N. (2016). The role of identity subversion in structuring the effects of intergroup threats and negative emotions on belief in anti-west conspiracy theories in Indonesia. *Psychology and Developing Societies, 28*(1), 1–28.

Masland, S. R., Schnell, S., & Shah, T. (2020). Trust beliefs, biases, and behaviors in borderline personality disorder: Empirical findings and relevance to epistemic trust. *Current Behavioral Neuroscience Reports* (in press). DOI: 10.1007/s40473-020-00220-7.

McCombie, S., Uhlmann, A. J., & Morrison, S. (2020). The US 2016 presidential election & Russia's troll farms. *Intelligence and National Security*, *35*(1), 95–114.

McIntyre, L. (2018). *Post-truth*. Cambridge, MA: MIT Press.

Merkle, C. (2017). Financial overconfidence over time: Foresight, hindsight, and insight of investors. *Journal of Banking & Finance*, *84*, 68–87.

Meyer, I. H. (2010). Identity, stress, and resilience in lesbians, gay men, and bisexuals of color. *The Counseling Psychologist*, *38*(3), 442–454.

Michelson, G., & Mouly, S. (2000). Rumour and gossip in organisations: A conceptual study. *Management Decision*, *38*(5), 339–346.

Michelson, G., & Mouly, V. S. (2002). 'You didn't hear it from us but …': Towards an understanding of rumour and gossip in organisations. *Australian Journal of Management*, *27*(1_suppl), 57–65.

Mileham, P. (2008). Teaching military ethics in the British Armed Forces. *Ethics Education in the Military*, 43–56.

Miller, V. (2018). The ethics of digital being: Vulnerability, invulnerability, and 'dangerous surprises'. In A. Lagerqvist, (Ed.), *Digital Existence: Ontology, Ethics and transcendence in Digital Culture*. Routledge Studies in Religion and Digital Culture (pp.171–186). Routledge, London, UK, . London: Routledge.

Mitchell, C. (2000). Reducing mistrust. In C. Mitchell, *Gestures of conciliation* (pp. 164–190). Basingstoke: Palgrave Macmillan.

Mittal, S. K. (2019). Behavior biases and investment decision: Theoretical and research framework. *Qualitative Research in Financial Markets*, June. DOI: org/10.1108/QRFM-09-2017-0085.

Mlambo, O. B., & Zimunya, C. T. (2016). Rumour and the politician's public image: The case of Zimbabwe. *Journal of Pan African Studies*, *9*(4).

Molina, Y., Kim, S., Berrios, N., & Calhoun, E. A. (2015). Medical mistrust and patient satisfaction with mammography: The mediating effects of perceived self-efficacy among navigated African American women. *Health Expectations*, *18*(6), 2941–2950.

Montaudon-Tomas, C. M., Montaudon-Tomas, I. M., & Lomas-Montaudon, Y. (2020). Autocratic, transactional, and servant leadership in Japan, France, and Mexico: A cross-culture theoretical analysis. In C. Dogru (Ed.), *Leadership Styles, Innovation, and Social Entrepreneurship in the Era of Digitalization* (pp. 101–133). Hershey, PA: IGI Global.

Morgan, S. (2018). Fake news, disinformation, manipulation and online tactics to undermine democracy, *Journal of Cyber Policy*, *3*(1), 39–43. DOI: 10.1080/237388 71.2018.1462395.

Morisi, D., Jost, J. T., & Singh, V. (2019). An asymmetrical 'president-in-power' effect. *American Political Science Review*, *113*(2), 614–620.

Moscovici, S. (1981). On social representations. *Social Cognition: Perspectives on Everyday Understanding*, *8*(12), 181–209.

Moscovici, S. (1987). The conspiracy mentality. In C. F. Graumann & S. Moscovici (Eds.), *Changing conceptions of conspiracy* (pp. 151–169). New York: Springer.

Moscovici, S. (1988). Notes towards a description of social representations. *European Journal of Social Psychology, 18*(3), 211–250.

Moscovici, S. (2001). *Social representations: Essays in social psychology.* New York: New York University Press.

Moscovici, S. (2020). Reflections on the popularity of 'conspiracy mentalities'. *International Review of Social Psychology, 33*(1), 9. DOI: org/10.5334/irsp.432.

Moscovici, S., & Nemeth, C. (1974). Social influence: II. Minority influence. In C. Nemeth (Ed.), *Social psychology: Classic and contemporary integrations.* Chicago, IL: Rand McNally.

Moscovici, S., & Personnaz, B. (1980). Studies in social influence v. minority influence and conversion behavior in a perceptual task. *Journal of Experimental Social Psychology, 16*(3), 270–282.

Moscovici, S., Mugny, G., & van Avermaet, E. (Eds) (1985). *Perspectives on Minority Influence* (No. 9). Cambridge: Cambridge University Press.

Murtin, F., Fleischer, L., Siegerink, V., Aassve, A., Algan, Y., Boarini, R., ... Smith, C. (2018). 'Trust and its determinants: Evidence from the Trustlab experiment', *OECD Statistics Working Papers*, No. 2018/02, OECD Publishing, Available at www.oecd-ilibrary.org/economics/trust-and-its-determinants_869ef2ec-en (accessed 11 March, 2021).

Musch, J. (2003). Personality differences in hindsight bias. *Memory, 11*(4–5), 473–489.

Napier, J. L., Suppes, A., & Bettinsoli, M. L. (2020). Denial of gender discrimination is associated with better subjective well-being among women: A system justification account. *European Journal of Social Psychology, 50*(6), 1191–1209. doi.org/10.1002/ejsp.2702

Nguyen, A. (Ed.) (2017). *News, numbers and public opinion in a data-driven world.* New York: Bloomsbury.

Norman, S. M., Avolio, B. J., & Luthans, F. (2010). The impact of positivity and transparency on trust in leaders and their perceived effectiveness. *The Leadership Quarterly, 21*(3), 350–364.

OECD (2017). OECD guidelines on measuring trust. Available at www.oecd-ilibrary.org/governance/oecd-guidelines-on-measuring-trust_9789264278219-en (accessed 11 March, 2021).

OECD (2019). Statistical insights: Trust in the United Kingdom. Available at www.oecd.org/sdd/statistical-insights-trust-in-the-united-kingdom.htm (accessed 11 March, 2021).

Oliver, J. E, & Wood, T. (2014). Medical conspiracy theories and health behaviours in the United States. *JAMA International Medicine, 174*(5), 817–818.

Owen, D., & Davidson, J. (2009). Hubris syndrome: An acquired personality disorder? A study of US Presidents and UK Prime Ministers over the last 100 years. *Brain, 132*(5), 1396–1406.

Paine, R. (1967). What is gossip about? An alternative hypothesis. *Man, 2*, 278–285.

Park, S., Fisher, C., Flew, T., & Dulleck, U. (2020). Global mistrust in news: The impact of social media on trust. *International Journal on Media Management, 22*(2), 83–96.

Parry, S. M., Miles, S., Tridente, A., Palmer, S. R., & South and East Wales Infectious Disease Group (2004). Differences in perception of risk between people who have and have not experienced Salmonella food poisoning. *Risk Analysis: An International Journal*, *24*(1), 289–299.

Pascua, E. (2019). Invisible enemies: The devastating effect of gossip in Castile at the end of the fifteenth century. *Journal of Medieval Iberian Studies*, *11*(2), 250–274.

Patev, A. J., Hood, K. B., Speed, K. J., Cartwright, P. M., & Kinman, B. A. (2019). HIV conspiracy theory beliefs mediates the connection between HIV testing attitudes and HIV prevention self-efficacy. *Journal of American College Health*, *67*(7), 661–673.

Paulhus, D. L., & Williams, K. M. (2002). The dark triad of personality: Narcissism, Machiavellianism, and psychopathy. *Journal of Research in Personality*, *36*(6), 556–563.

Pechar, E., & Mayer, F. (2015). Identity and climate change. Presented at *Bridging Divides: Spaces of Scholarship and Practice in Environmental Communication*, The Conference on Communication and Environment, Boulder, Colorado, 11–14 June. Available at https://theieca.org/coce2015 (accessed 11 March, 2021).

Pena-Rodríguez, A. (2020). Fighting from Portugal for a new Spa. In The 'Black Embassy' in Lisbon During the Spanish Civil War: Information, Press and Propaganda. *Media History*, 1–15.

Pennycook, G., & Rand, D. G. (2019). Lazy, not biased: Susceptibility to partisan fake news is better explained by lack of reasoning than by motivated reasoning. *Cognition*, *188*, 39–50.

Perrin, A. (2015). Social networking usage: 2005–2015. *Pew Research Center*, October. Available at www.pewresearch.org/internet/2015/10/08/social-networking-usage-2005-2015/ (accessed 11 March, 2021).

Pew Research Centre (2019). Public trust in Government: 1958–2019. Available at www.pewresearch.org/politics/2019/04/11/public-trust-in-government-1958-2019/ (accessed 11 March, 2021).

Phong, L. B., Hui, L., & Son, T. T. (2018). How leadership and trust in leaders foster employees' behavior toward knowledge sharing. *Social Behavior and Personality: An International Journal*, *46*(5), 705–720.

Pidgeon, N., Kasperson, R. E., & Slovic, P. (Eds) (2003). *The social amplification of risk*. Cambridge: Cambridge University Press.

Ping, H., Mujtaba, B. G., Whetten, D. A., & Wei, Y. (2012). Leader personality characteristics and upward trust: A study of employee-supervisor dyads in China. *Journal of Applied Business Research*, *28*(5), 1001–1016.

Pohl, R. F., & Hell, W. (1996). No reduction in hindsight bias after complete information and repeated testing. *Organizational Behavior and Human Decision Processes*, *67*(1), 49–58.

Potter, P. B. (2016). Lame-duck foreign policy. *Presidential Studies Quarterly*, *46*(4), 849–867.

Powell, R. (2008). Understanding the stigmatization of Gypsies: Power and the dialectics of (dis)identification. *Housing, Theory and Society*, 25(2), 87–109. DOI: org/10.1080/14036090701657462.

Rangel, F., Rosso, P., Ghanem, B., & Giachanou, A. (2020). *Profiling fake news spreaders on Twitter*. PAN@CLEF. Available at https://pan.webis.de/clef20/pan20-web/author-profiling.html#task-committee (accessed 11 March, 2021).

Redhead, K. (2011). Behavioral perspectives on client mistrust of financial services. *Journal of Financial Service Professionals*, 65(6).

Reuters (2020). Fact check: Gates was not caught on video saying the COVID-19 vaccine 'will change our DNA forever'. *Everythingnews*, 10 December. Available at www.reuters.com/article/uk-factcheck-gates-altered-video-dna-vac-idUSKBN28K2YF (accessed 11 March, 2021).

Ritzmann, A. (2017). The role of propaganda in violent extremism and how to counter it. *EUROMED Survey*, 26–32.

Roberts, L. D., Indermaur, D., & Spiranovic, C. (2013). Fear of cyber-identity theft and related fraudulent activity. *Psychiatry, Psychology and Law*, 20(3), 315–328.

Rogers, E. M. (1995). *Diffusion of innovations* (4th ed.). New York: Free Press.

Ross, A. T., Powell, A. M., & Henriksen Jr, R. C. (2016). Self-identity: A key to Black student success. Paper based on a program presented at the *2016 Texas Association of Counselor Education and Supervisors Mid-Winter Conference*, 28–29 January, Austin, TX. Available at www.researchgate.net/publication/306333051_Self-Identity_A_Key_to_Black_Student_Success (accessed 11 March, 2021).

Rothkopf, D. J. (1999). The disinformation age. *Foreign Policy*, 1.

Roush, S. (2017). 'Epistemic self-doubt'. In E. N. Zalta (Ed.), *The Stanford encyclopedia of philosophy*. Available at https://plato.stanford.edu/archives/win2017/entries/epistemic-self-doubt/ (accessed 11 March, 2021).

Rowe, W. G., Cannella Jr, A. A., Rankin, D., & Gorman, D. (2005). Leader succession and organizational performance: Integrating the common-sense, ritual scapegoating, and vicious-circle succession theories. *The Leadership Quarterly*, 16(2), 197–219.

Russell, B. (2004). *Power: A new social analysis*. Hove: Psychology Press.

Sadler-Smith, E., Akstinaite, V., Robinson, G., & Wray, T. (2017). Hubristic leadership: A review. *Leadership*, 13(5), 525–548.

Saiphoo, A. N., Halevi, L. D., & Vahedi, Z. (2020). Social networking site use and self-esteem: A meta-analytic review. *Personality and Individual Differences*, 153. DOI: org/10.1016/j.paid.2019.109639.

Sales, S., Galloway Burke, M., & Cannonier, C. (2020). African American women leadership across contexts: Examining the internal traits and external factors on women leaders' perceptions of empowerment. *Journal of Management History*, 26(3), 353–376.

Sammut, G. E., Andreouli, E. E., Gaskell, G. E., & Valsiner, J. E. (2015). *The Cambridge handbook of social representations*. Cambridge: Cambridge University Press.

Sanders, K., Schyns, B., Dietz, G., & Den Hartog, D. N. (2006). Measuring trust inside organisations. *Personnel Review*. DOI: 10.1108/00483480610682299.

Schia, N. N., & Gjesvik, L. (2020). Hacking democracy: Managing influence campaigns and disinformation in the digital age. *Journal of Cyber Policy*, 1–16.

Schlegel, L. (2019). 'Yes, I can': What is the role of perceived self-efficacy in violent online-radicalisation processes of 'homegrown' terrorists? *Dynamics of Asymmetric Conflict*, 1–18.

Schyns, B., Wisse, B., & Sanders, S. (2019). Shady strategic behavior: Recognizing strategic followership of Dark Triad followers. *Academy of Management Perspectives*, *33*(2), 234–249.

Shead, S. (2020). JK Rowling criticizes 'cancel culture' in open letter signed by 150 public figures. *CNBC*, 8 July. Available at www.cnbc.com/2020/07/08/jk-rowling-cancel-culture.html (accessed 11 March, 2021).

Shih, M., Wilton, L. S., Does, S., Goodale, B. M., & Sanchez, D. T. (2019). Multiple racial identities as sources of psychological resilience. *Social and Personality Psychology Compass*, *13*(6), e12469.

Shinohara, A., Kanakogi, Y., Okumura, Y., & Kobayashi, T. (2020). How do children evaluate the gossiper of negative gossip? *Japanese Psychological Research*, February. DOI: oi.org/10.1111/jpr.12279.

Shuper, P. A., Sorrentino, R. M., Otsubo, Y., Hodson, G., & Walker, A. M. (2004). A theory of uncertainty orientation: Implications for the study of individual differences within and across cultures. *Journal of Cross-cultural Psychology*, *35*(4), 460–480.

Simmel, G. (1950). *The Sociology of Georg Simmel*. New York: Free Press.

Sleijpen, M., Boeije, H. R., Kleber, R. J., & Mooren, T. (2016). Between power and powerlessness: A meta-ethnography of sources of resilience in young refugees. *Ethnicity & Health*, *21*(2), 158–180.

Slovic, P. E. (2000). *The perception of risk*. London: Earthscan.

Smith, B. L., & Lasswell, H. D. (2015). *Propaganda, communication and public opinion*. Princeton, NJ: Princeton University Press.

Sønderskov, K. M., & Dinesen, P. T. (2016). Trusting the state, trusting each other? The effect of institutional trust on social trust. *Political Behavior*, *38*(1), 179–202.

Sorrenti, L., Filippello, P., Buzzai, C., Buttò, C., & Costa, S. (2018). Learned helplessness and mastery orientation: The contribution of personality traits and academic beliefs. *Nordic Psychology*, *70*(1), 71–84.

Stewart, W. D. P. (2000). *Independent expert group on mobile phones (Great Britain): Mobile phones and health*. London: HMSO.

Strube, M. J., & Garcia, J. E. (1981). A meta-analytic investigation of Fiedler's contingency model of leadership effectiveness. *Psychological Bulletin*, *90*(2), 307–321. DOI: org/10.1037/0033–2909.90.2.307.

Suedfeld, P., & Rank, A. (1976). Revolutionary leaders: Long term success as a function of changes in conceptual complexity. *Journal of Personality & Social Psychology*, *34*, 169–178.

Sundermeier, J., Gersch, M., & Freiling, J. (2020). Hubristic start-up founders – the neglected bright and inevitable dark manifestations of hubristic leadership in new venture creation processes. *Journal of Management Studies, 57*(5), 1037–1067.

Sutton, A. L., He, J., Tanner, E., Edmonds, M. C., Henderson, A., de Mendoza, A. H., & Sheppard, V. B. (2019). Understanding medical mistrust in Black women at risk of BRCA 1/2 mutations. *Journal of Health Disparities Research and Practice, 12*(3), 35.

Swami, V., Barron, D., Weis, L., Voracek, M., Stieger, S., & Furnham, A. (2017). An examination of the factorial and convergent validity of four measures of conspiracist ideation, with recommendations for researchers. *PLOS One, 12*(2), e0172617.

Sweeney, P. J. (2010). Do soldiers reevaluate trust in their leaders prior to combat operations? *Military Psychology, 22*(sup1), S70–S88.

Sztompka, P. (1999). *Trust: A sociological theory*. Cambridge: Cambridge University Press.

Taleb, N. N. (2007). *The black swan: The impact of the highly improbable*. New York: Random House.

Talwar, S., Dhir, A., Singh, D., Virk, G. S., & Salo, J. (2020). Sharing of fake news on social media: Application of the honeycomb framework and the third-person effect hypothesis. *Journal of Retailing and Consumer Services, 57*, 102197.

Tanis, M., & Postmes, T. (2005). A social identity approach to trust: Interpersonal perception, group membership and trusting behaviour. *European Journal of Social Psychology, 35*(3), 413–424.

Taylor, P. M. (2003). *Munitions of the mind: A history of propaganda from the ancient world to the present era* (3rd Edn). Manchester: Manchester University Press.

Thorbjørnsrud, K., & Figenschou, T. U. (2020). The alarmed citizen: Fear, mistrust, and alternative media. *Journalism Practice*, 1–18.

Tiggemann, M., Anderberg, I., & Brown, Z. (2020). Uploading your best self: Selfie editing and body dissatisfactioned. *Body Image, 33*, 175–182.

Timotijevic, L., & Breakwell, G. M. (2000). Migration and threats to identity. *Journal of Community and Social Psychology, 10*, 355–372.

Tomljenovic, H., Bubic, A., & Erceg, N. (2020). It just doesn't feel right – the relevance of emotions and intuition for parental vaccine conspiracy beliefs and vaccination uptake. *Psychology & Health, 35*(5), 538–554.

Towler, C. C., Crawford, N. N., & Bennett, R. A. (2020). Shut up and play: Black athletes, protest politics, and Black political action. *Perspectives on Politics, 18*(1), 111–127.

Trumbo, C., Lueck, M., Marlatt, H., & Peek, L. (2011). The effect of proximity to Hurricanes Katrina and Rita on subsequent hurricane outlook and optimistic bias. *Risk Analysis: An International Journal, 31*(12), 1907–1918.

Tversky, A., & Kahneman, D. (1974). Judgment under uncertainty: Heuristics and biases. *Science, 185*(4157), 1124–1131.

Tversky, A., & Kahneman, D. (1981). The framing of decisions and the psychology of choice. *Science*, *211*(4481), 453–458.

Tversky, A., & Kahneman, D. (1992). Advances in prospect theory: Cumulative representation of uncertainty. *Journal of Risk and Uncertainty*, *5*(4), 297–323.

Tykocinski, O. E., Pick, D., & Kedmi, D. (2002). Retroactive pessimism: A different kind of hindsight bias. *European Journal of Social Psychology*, *32*(4), 577–588.

Uscinski, J. E., & Parent, J. M. (2014). *American conspiracy theories*. Oxford: Oxford University Press.

van der Velde, F., Hooykaas, C., & van der Joop, P. (1992). Risk perception and behavior: Pessimism, realism, and optimism about aids-related health behavior, *Psychology & Health*, *6*(1–2), 23–38.

van Koot, C. (2020). The role of trust in tackling coronavirus in the world's most vulnerable communities. Available at https://views-voices.oxfam.org.uk/2020/05/the-role-of-trust-in-tackling-coronavirus-in-the-worlds-most-vulnerable-communities/ (accessed 11 March, 2021).

Van Prooijen, J-W., & Douglas, K. M. (2017). Conspiracy theories as part of history: The role of societal crisis situations. *Memory Studies*, *10*(3), 323–333.

Vergara, F., Rosa, J., Orozco, C., Bertiller, E., Gallardo, M. A., Bravo, M., ... & García, M. V. (2017). Evaluation of learned helplessness, self-efficacy and disease activity, functional capacity and pain in Argentinian patients with rheumatoid arthritis. *Scandinavian Journal of Rheumatology*, *46*(1), 17–21.

Villejoubert, G. (2005). Could they have known better? *Applied Cognitive Psychology*, *19*(1), 140–143.

Vinkenburg, C. J., Van Engen, M. L., Eagly, A. H., & Johannesen-Schmidt, M. C. (2011). An exploration of stereotypical beliefs about leadership styles: Is transformational leadership a route to women's promotion? *The Leadership Quarterly*, *22*(1), 10–21.

Vosoughi, S., Roy, D., & Aral, S. (2018). The spread of true and false news online. *Science*, *359*(6380), 1146–1151.

Wald, H. S. (2015). Professional identity (trans)formation in medical education: Reflection, relationship, resilience. *Academic Medicine*, *90*(6), 701–706.

Walter, N., & Tukachinsky, R. (2020). A meta-analytic examination of the continued influence of misinformation in the face of correction: How powerful is it, why does it happen, and how to stop it? *Communication Research*, *47*(2), 155–177.

Walumbwa, F. O., Avolio, B. J., Gardner, W. L., Wernsing, T. S., & Peterson, S. J. (2008). Authentic leadership: Development and validation of a theory-based measure. *Journal of Management*, *34*(1), 89–126.

Wang, D. S., & Hsieh, C. C. (2013). The effect of authentic leadership on employee trust and employee engagement. *Social Behavior and Personality: An International Journal*, *41*(4), 613–624.

Ward, P. R., Miller, E., Pearce, A. R., & Meyer, S. B. (2016). Predictors and extent of institutional trust in government, banks, the media and religious organisations:

Evidence from cross-sectional surveys in six Asia-Pacific countries. *PLOS One*, *11*(10), e0164096.

Waterman, A. S. (2020). 'Now what do I do?': Toward a conceptual understanding of the effects of traumatic events on identity functioning. *Journal of Adolescence, 79*, 59–69.

Weinstein, N. D. (1980). Unrealistic optimism about future life events. *Journal of Personality and Social Psychology, 39*(5), 806.

Weinstein, N. D. (1989). Optimistic biases about personal risks. *Science, 246*(4935), 1232–1234.

Wellcome (2018). Trust in science and health professionals. *Wellcome Global Monitor 2018*. Available at https://wellcome.ac.uk/reports/wellcome-global-monitor/2018/chapter-3-trust-science-and-health-professionals (accessed 11 March, 2021).

Whalen, C. K., Henker, B., O'Neil, R., Hollingshead, J., Holman, A., & Moore, B. (1994). Optimism in children's judgments of health and environmental risks. *Health Psychology, 13*(4), 319.

Whaley, A. L. (2001). Cultural mistrust: An important psychological construct for diagnosis and treatment of African Americans. *Professional Psychology: Research and Practice, 32*(6), 555–562.

White, C. A., Slater, M. J., Turner, M. J., & Barker, J. B. (2020). More positive group memberships are associated with greater resilience in Royal Air Force (RAF) personnel. *British Journal of Social Psychology*. DOI: org/10.1111/bjso.12385.

Wilkes, R. (2003). *Scandal: A scurrilous history of gossip*. London: Atlantic Books.

Wilson, D. S., Wilczynski, C., Wells, A., & Weiser, L. (2000). Gossip and other aspects of language as group-level adaptations. *The Evolution of Cognition*, 347–365.

Wilson, J. (1973). *Introduction to social movements*. New York: Basic Books.

Wilson, T. D., Houston, C. E., Etling, K. M., & Brekke, N. (1996). A new look at anchoring effects: Basic anchoring and its antecedents. *Journal of Experimental Psychology: General, 125*(4), 387.

Winsper, C. (2018). The aetiology of borderline personality disorder (BPD): Contemporary theories and putative mechanisms. *Current Opinion in Psychology, 21*, 105–110.

Wittgenstein, L. (1963). *Philosophical investigations*. Oxford: Blackwell.

Wozniak, L. (2003). Rumour mills. *Far Eastern Economic Review, 166*(16), 29–29.

Wynne, B. (1982). Institutional mythologies and dual societies in the management of risk. In H. C. Kunreuther (Ed.), *The risk analysis controversy* (pp. 127–143). Berlin: Springer.

Wynne, B. (2001). Creating public alienation: Expert cultures of risk and ethics on GMOs. *Science as Culture, 10*(4), 445–481.

Wynne, B., & Dressel, K. (2001). Cultures of uncertainty – transboundary risks and BSE in Europe. In J. Linnerooth-Bayer, R. E. Löfstedt, & G. Sjöstedt (Eds), *Transboundary risk management* (pp. 135–168). London: Routledge.

Yang, Q., & Tang, W. (2010). Exploring the sources of institutional trust in China: Culture, mobilization, or performance? *Asian Politics & Policy, 2*(3), 415–436.

Yaribeygi, H., Panahi, Y., Sahraei, H., Johnston, T. P., & Sahebkar, A. (2017). The impact of stress on body function: A review. *EXCLI Journal*, *16*, 1057–1072. DOI: org/10.17179/excli2017–480.

Yu, H. C., & Miller, P. (2005). Leadership style: The X Generation and Baby Boomers compared in different cultural contexts. *Leadership and Organization Development Journal*, *26*(1), 35–50.

Zabelina, E., Tsiring, D., & Chestyunina, Y. (2018). Personal helplessness and self-reliance as predictors of small business development in Russia: Pilot study results. *International Entrepreneurship and Management Journal*, *14*(2), 279–293.

Zannettou, S., Caulfield, T., De Cristofaro, E., Sirivianos, M., Stringhini, G., & Blackburn, J. (2019). *Disinformation warfare: Understanding state-sponsored trolls on Twitter and their influence on the web*. In Companion proceedings of the 2019 World Wide Web conference (pp. 218–226).

Zheng, W., Surgevil, O., & Kark, R. (2018). Dancing on the razor's edge: How top-level women leaders manage the paradoxical tensions between agency and commu-nion. *Sex Roles*, *79*(11–12), 633–650.

Zuckerman, M. (1991). *Psychobiology of personality*. New York: Cambridge University Press.

INDEX

5G conspiracy theory 153–4
Abric, J. C. 8
absolute uncertainty 34–5
Achotegui, J. 43
adaptive advantages 2
'age of uncertainty' 29–30, 31
agency 49, 83
    modelling mistrust 161–2
    social media 107
agreeableness 80, 129
Albarghouthi, S. I. 96
Allcott, H. 113
allostatic leaders 75
Allport, G. W. 103
alt-right trolling 146
anchoring 8, 9, 14–16, 18, 32, 33, 59, 69, 143
anxiety 41
Aral, S. 130
Arkes, H. R. 24, 25
artificial intelligence (AI) 129, 131, 132
Asad, S. 84
Audrezet, 109
authentic leadership 74, 76
autocratic leadership 73, 74, 75
availability 14–16, 18
Avolio, B. J. 81

BAME 36, 141
Bandura, A. 44
Banfield, E. C. 5
Banks, G. C. 76
Barnes, T. D. 84
Barnett, J. 31–2, 67
Barreto, N. 74
Bartlett, F. C. 102, 103
Bayley, J. 85
Beaulieu, E. 84
Beersma, B. 95
Belluz, J. 153
Bennett, R. A. 44
Bernardes, S. F. 21

Bernstein, D. M. 24
bias 15, 18, 27–8, 35, 161, 170
    conspiracist ideation 145–6
    risk estimation 19–26
Billig, M. 147
Birchall, C. 139
Biswas, B. 122
Black Lives Matter movement 86
Blank, H. 24
bloggers 108–9
bogey rumour 101, 103
bombardment technique 119
Bonaiuto, M. 27
Boo, H. C. 16
borderline personality disorder (BPD)
    48–9, 52–3
Bornstein, R. F. 124
Bostrom, A. 44
botnets 112, 120, 125
Boyd-Barrett, O. 125
Bradfield, A. 24
Bradshaw, S. 111
Breakwell, G. M. 5, 7, 8–9, 11, 26, 27, 30,
    31–2, 53, 67, 147, 148–9, 155
Brexit 9, 58
Brooking, E. T. 112
Brooks, R. T. 46–7
Brotherton, R. 141, 145
Bubic, A. 148
Buchanan, T. 129–30
Burgess, A. 14
Byford, J. 137, 148
Byung-Chul, H. 33

Caldera, C. 131–2
Campbell, C. 48
Campbell, L. F. 21
cancel culture 109–11
cancer 31–2, 96, 138, 153
Cannonier, C. 86
Cano, I. 27

Caponecchia, C. 20
Carey, M. 5
caricatures 58–9, 62, 64
Carli, L. L. 85
categorisation 36, 55, 107, 140, 141, 167
celebrity gossip 108–9
Chadwick, A. 130
Chambers, J. R. 58
Chamorro-Premuzi, T. 83
channelling mistrust 149–50
Chesney, R. 126
Chestyunina, Y. 44
children 21, 58, 107, 154
    gossip 94
    toys 64
    vaccines 37, 145, 148, 155
China
    COVID 152–3
    institutional trust 66–7
    products 64
    rumours 104
Cialdini, R. B. 126
Cichocka, A. 145, 148
Cinnirella, M. 20, 27
Citron, D. 126
Clark, C. 20
Clark, R. D. 119
climate change 27, 31, 45, 89, 111, 117, 137
cognition
    hindsight bias 24
    optimistic bias 20–1
    processes 41–2
    styles 27
Colby, W. 120
Coleman, N. V. 107
collateral mistrust 100
communication 8
    channels 93–114, 162
conceptual grouping 36–7, 55, 59, 141
Confessor, N. 126
confusion 123
Congregatio de Propanda Fide 116
conscientiousness 80, 129
conspiracist ideation 145–6, 162
conspiracy theories 2, 27, 33, 100,
    135–56, 169
context 39, 41–2
    social 41–2, 93–4, 158–63, 165–9
    uncertainty 31
contingency model of leadership 75–6
continuity 5, 8–9, 26, 90–1, 165, 169
    conspiracy theories 147–8
    gossip 95
    social media 106
control 93
    hindsight bias 24

information channels 123
    learned helplessness 44
    optimistic bias 21–2, 23
Cooper, W. 140, 142
coping strategies 5, 9, 11, 20, 26, 50, 91
Cort, M. A. 46
Covey, S. R. 72
COVID pandemic 15–16, 20, 32–3, 53–4,
    60, 61–2, 87, 90, 96–7, 109, 120–1, 127,
    131–2, 143, 148–9, 151–6
Crawford, N. N. 44
Crédit Mobilier scandal 56–7
criminal uses of disinformation 127–8
Crosman, K. M. 44
Cuevas, A. G. 41
cultural influences, leadership 72, 75
cultural mistrust 46–7
Cumulative Prospect Theory 18–19
Cunningham, S. B. 115
cyberbullying 110
cybercrime 8, 127–8

Da Silva Rebelo, M. J. 43
'dark triad' 80–2, 83
David, E. J. R. 46
Davidson, J. 82, 83
Davis, J. L. 41
de Berker, A. 14
decision making 3, 12, 13–15, 17–18,
    164, 170
    emotions 41
    intuition 35
Deepfakes 126
Deer, B. 37
Defoe, D. 98
deindividuation 111, 141
Dekker, S. W. 24
democratic leadership 73, 86
demoralisation 123
Descartes, R. 45
Deylami, S. 122
Diana, Princess of Wales 137
Dickens, D. D. 86
Dietz, G. 77
Dimes, T. 86
Dinesen, P. T. 65
directive leadership 74
Dirks, K. T. 72
discrimination 43, 86, 91
disinformation 2, 31, 45, 100, 115–33, 169
    crisis 124–8
    spreaders 128–31
distinctiveness 5, 8–10, 26, 27, 90, 165, 169
    conspiracy theories 147–8
    gossip 95
    social media 106

distrust 4–5, 158
Dobreva, D. 125–6
Dolgova, Y. 125
Dolinski, D. 21
Douglas, K. M. 136, 143, 145, 146, 148
Dressel, K. 14
Drozda-Senkowska, E. 33
Dunbar, R. I. 94
Durkheim, E. 10

Eagly, A. H. 84
egocentrism 21, 22
Ekhator, O. C. 64
emancipated representation 10
Emler, N. 94
emotions 3, 4, 5, 39–54, 170
    conspiracy theories 147–9
    identity modelling 53
    identity resilience 49–53
    modelling mistrust 163–4
    propaganda 122–3
    social representations 12
Enders, A. M. 144
Engelmann, J. M. 94
entrepreneurs 75
epistemic self-doubt 45
Erceg, N. 148
Erikson, E H. 5
ethnicity 85–6
    cultural mistrust 46–7
    racism 58, 86
euphoria 123
Eurobarometer surveys 65
European Union 9, 58
Evans, C. 107
exclusion, social media 109–11
expectations 6, 162
Expected Utility Theory 17
expertise, hindsight bias 25
extraversion 80, 129
extreme mistrustfulness 47–9, 52–3, 165

fact-checking 2, 31, 131–2
fake news 2, 31, 45, 112–13, 125, 129
Fan, L. 99
Farquharson, W. H. 46
Fauci, A. 90, 153, 154
Fernandez, A. A. 75
Fernández, M. 43
Ferrin, D. L. 72
Ferrucci, P. 113
Fiedler, F. E. 75–6
Figenschou, T. U. 113
financial crisis of 2007–2008 66
financial sector 66
Fine, G. A. 94

Fino, E. 53, 155
Fischhoff, B. 15, 23
Flew, T. 113
Fonagy, P. 48
Foner, E. 56–7
frames of reference 19
framing effects 17
Franco, F. 120
Freberg, K. 109
French, C. C. 141, 145
Freud, S. 83
fronting messages 120–1
Fulmer, C. A. 73
fundamental attribution error 25
Furnham, A. 16, 80, 81, 83, 139
Furtner, M. R. 81
fuzzy stereotype 21

Galbraith, J. K. 6, 29–30
Galloway Burke, M. 86
Gardner, W. L. 74
Garraty, J. A. 56–7
Gaspar, R. 14
Gates, W. 89–90, 132, 153, 154, 155
gender
    gossip 94
    leadership 84–6
generalisation 7
Gentzkow, M. 113
Gibson, B. L. 58
Giddens, A. 3
Gilmore, D. 97
Gjesvik, L. 125
Glover, H. 47
Gluckman, M. 97
Goertzel, T. 146
Goldschmidt-Gjerløw, B. 107
Goreis, A. 144–5
Görner, K. 47
gossip 93, 94–8, 104–5, 108–9, 114, 169
    columns 93, 97–8, 108
Graumann, C. F. 139
Grewal, L. 107
Gromski, W. 21
groups 166
    identity 107
    intergroup relations 58, 149, 159, 166
    minorities 118–19
Groysberg, B. 78
guilt by association 119
Gulenko, P. 125

habit 7
hacking democracy 125
Hallgrimsdottir, H. 146
Harris, L. M. 41

hate mail/speech 99
Hayes, A. L. 44
hazard sequences/templates 31–2
health
    cultural mistrust 46–7
    decision making 41
    medical conspiracy theories 138–9,
        153–4
    oral contraceptives 31–2
    self-efficacy 44
    see also COVID pandemic
hegemonic representation 10
Hell, W. 24
helplessness 43–4, 54
Helweg-Larsen, M. 22
Hendy, J. 27
Henriksen, R. C. Jr 46
Herrmann, E. 94
heuristics 15–17, 18, 19, 27–8, 35, 161, 170
Higgins, C. 75
hindsight bias 20, 23–5
Hintz, A. 125
history repeats 6, 7
Hodge, E. 146
Hodson, G. 27
Hogg, M. A. 74
Holmberg-Wright, K. 75
Hölzl, E. 24
Hooykaas, C. 21–2
Hopkins, R. 46–7
Hopp, T. 113
Howard, P. 111
Hribar, T. 75
Hsieh, C. C. 76
hubris syndrome 82–3
Hudson, J. 65
Hui, L. 72

identity 21, 27, 28, 39–54, 90–1
    bubbles 107
    conspiracy theories 147–9
    gossip 95
    modelling mistrust 164–6, 169
    negotiation 86
    protection 106–7
    resilience 39, 49–53, 54, 93, 106, 107, 133,
        148, 165–7
    shifting 86
    signalling 107
    social media 106–8
    theft 127–8
    threat 9, 20, 90–1
Identity Process Theory (IPT) 7–12, 20, 21,
    22, 25–6, 35, 44, 48, 49, 53
    conspiracy theories 147
    gossip 95

modelling mistrust 159
    social media 106
Igweze, Z. N. 64
informal leaders 73
information availability 21
information processing 15
Innes, H. 125–6
Innes, M. 125–6
institutions 64–7, 88
    blogs 109
    leadership 71–91
intergroup relations 58, 149, 159, 166
Internet 30–1
    see also social media
intersecting identities 85–6
intuition 35
Ipsos MORI 60–1, 87

Janssen, O. 95
Jaspal, R. 7, 8, 20, 27, 53, 85, 148–9, 155
Jodelet, D. 33
Johannesen-Schmidt, M. C. 84
Johnson, B. 87, 121
Jost, J. R. 88
judgement
    heuristics 15
    hindsight bias 24–5
Jurczak, A. 47
justification 40, 41, 43, 163

Kaakinen, M. 107
Kadvany, J. 15
Kahneman, D. 15, 17–18
Kark, R. 85
Kasperson, R. E. 11
Kay, J. 34–5
Kedmi, D. 24
Kennedy, J. F. 136–7, 142, 144
Keynes, J. M. 34
KGB Disinformation Agency 120
Khan, Q. R. 120
Khanday, A. M. U. D. 120
Ki Kim, 109
King, M. 34–5
Kirchler, E. 24
Klempe, S. H. 96
Knapp, R. A. 101–4
Knoll, M. A. 25
Kosfeld, M. 3
Kumar, S. 112

labelling 140, 141
Lahrach, Y. 139
laissez-faire leadership 74, 84–5
lame-duck leaders 88–9
Lantian, A. 147

Lasswell, H. D. 118
Lazer, D. 31
leadermatch 76
leadership 71–91, 170
    contingency model 75–6
    efficacy 75–7
    managed departure 89–90
    personality 27, 79–84
    Social Identity Theory 74, 85
learned helplessness 44
Lefcourt, H. M. 26
Liberman, Z. 94
life cycles 72, 86–90, 147
Lima, M. L. 21
locus of control 26
loss aversion 17
Lovric, D. 83
Lukito, J. 125
Lupton, R. N. 144
Luthans, F. 81
Luyten, P. 48
Lyons, E. 27

Maass, A. 119
McClelland, A. 16
McCombie, S. 112
Machiavellianism 80–1
machine learning techniques 120
McIntyre, L. 3
Macmillan, H. 87
Mahdavi, S. 25
Malaysia Airlines Flight 370 137
Maran, T. 81
Marková, I. 8
Martinescu, E. 95
Mashuri, A. 149
Mayer, F. 27
media
    conspiracy theories 146–7
    gossip columns 97–8
    modelling mistrust 162
    stereotypes 58
Melnyk, D. 58
memory
    hindsight bias 24
    reconstructive 102
Merkle, C. 24
Merrill, R. R. 72
meta-functions, rumour 104
Michelson, G. 99
Microsoft 89–90
Mileham, P. 73
military leaders 78
military propaganda 116, 118
Miller, P. 75
Miller, V. 20

minorities 118–19
misinformation 115
the mistrusted 43–4, 166–7, 170
    characteristics 55–69
    leaders 71–91
Mitchell, C. 78
Mittal, S. K. 25
Mitterrand, F. 85
Mlambo, O. B. 104
MMR vaccine 37, 145, 155
modelling mistrust 157–71
Molina, Y. 44
Montaudon-Tomas, C. M. 73, 75
Morgan, S. 127
Morisi, D. 88
Morrison, S. 112
Moscovici, S. 8, 10, 102, 118–19, 126, 139
motivation
    conspiracy theories 145
    fuzzy stereotypes 21
    optimistic bias 20
    rumours 103–4
Mouly, S. 99

Napier, J. L. 20
narcissism 80–1, 83
Nerlich, B. 27
Nestler, S. 24
neuroticism 80, 82, 129
New World Order 142–3
Nijstad, B. A. 95
Norman, S. M. 81

objectification 8, 9, 32, 33, 59, 140, 143
O'Brien, K. 41
OECD 65
Oliver, J. E. 138
online identities 107–8
openness 74, 76, 80
optimistic bias 20–3, 25
Orisakwe, O. E. 64
Ostroff, C. 73
Owen, D. 82, 83
Oxfam 109

Paine, R. 97
paranoia 47–9, 52–3, 145
Parent, J. M. 137
Parry, S. M. 22
participative leadership 74, 76
Pascua, E. 95
paternalistic leadership 74
Patev, A. J. 44
Paulhus, D. L. 80
Pearl Harbour 101
Pechar, E. 27

Pena-Rodriguez, A. 120
perceived cost 40, 41, 43, 163
perceived invulnerability 20
Perrin, A. 105
personal representations 9
personality 16, 26
    Big Five 26, 80, 144
    conspiracy theories 144–5
    'dark triad' 80–2, 83
    disinformation spreaders 129
    leaders 79–84
Personnaz, B. 119
persuasion processes 118–19
pessimism 21–2
    cognitive styles 27
    hindsight bias 24
Pew Research Center 87–8
phishing 127
Phong, L. B. 72
Pick, D. 24
Pickering, A. D. 141
Pidgeon, N. 11
Ping, H. 80
Pohl, R. F. 24
poison pen letters 93, 99, 100
polemical representation 10
popular culture, the mistrusted 62–4
post-traumatic stress disorder (PTSD) 47
post-truth 3
Postman, L. 103
Postmes, T. 3
Potter, P. B. 88
Powell, A. M. 46
Powell, R. 58
prejudice 57, 58, 144
propaganda 2, 101, 115–33, 169
Prospect Theory 16–19
prototypes 55–7, 59, 61–4, 74, 91, 114
psychosocial development 5

Rabani, S. T. 120
racism 58, 86
radical uncertainty 34–5
Rahimian, M. A. 25
random disinformation attacks 128
Rank, A. 75
rankings of untrustworthiness 59–62
rational economic man 35
rationality 27–8, 35
Rauthmann, J. F. 81
reconstructive memory 102
Redhead, K. 41
relationship-oriented leaders 74, 76
Remkes, M. 107
representativeness 14–16, 18
Reuters 132

revolutionary leaders 75
Richards, S. C. 80
risk 13–28, 41
    aversion 18, 19
    estimation bias 19–26
    modelling mistrust 160–3
    perception 34
    probability and effect 13–14
    social amplification 11
Ritzmann, A. 125
Rogers, E. M. 147
Ross, A. T. 46
Rothkopf, D. J. 124
Rothschild family 137
Roush, S. 45
Rowe, W. G. 78
Rowling, J. K. 110
Roy, D. 130
rumour 93, 100–5, 108–9, 114, 169
rumour cascades 130
Russell, B. 82
RussiaGate controversy 125

Sadler-Smith, E. 84
Saha, S. 41
Sales, S. 86
Sanders, K. 77
Sanders, S. 81
Saxton, G. W. 84
schemata 102
Schia, N. N. 125
Schlegel, L. 122
Schyns, B. 81
Sczesny, S. 84, 85
self-disclosure 74, 76
self-doubt 45–7, 48, 51, 54, 123, 165
self-efficacy 5, 8, 10, 20, 21, 22, 26, 27, 43–4,
    52, 54, 90, 165, 169
    conspiracy theories 147–8
    gossip 95
    propaganda 119
    social media 106
self-esteem 5, 8–9, 10, 21, 26, 27, 46, 51, 90,
    165, 169
    cancel culture 110
    conspiracy theories 147–8
    gossip 95
    propaganda 119
    social media 106
self-protection 106
self-serving bias 20, 25–6
servant leadership 74, 75
Severe Acute Respiratory Syndrome (SARS)
    epidemic 104
shared mistrust 19, 29, 36–7, 39, 46–7
shared uncertainty 29–37, 52

Shaw, A. 94
Shaw, G. P. 75
Shead, S. 110
Shinohara, A. 94
Shuper, P. A. 26
SIM splitting 127
Simmel, G. 5–6
Singer, P. W. 112
Singh, V. 88
Slind, M. 78
slogans 121, 140, 143
Slovic, P. 11, 26
Smallpage, S. M. 144
Smith, B. L. 118
soap operas 63
social amplification of risk 11
social cognition models 64
social constructions, risk 14
social context 41–2, 93–4
    modelling mistrust 158–63, 165–9
social exchange 95, 98
social identity 21
Social Identity Theory of Leadership 74, 85
social media 63, 93, 99, 100, 104–14, 125–6,
    128–30, 170
    conspiracy theories 146–7
    modelling mistrust 162
social media influencers (SMI) 109
social proofing 126
social representation 14, 28, 118–19, 126
    communication channels 93
    conspiracy theories 139–43, 147–8
    disinformation 133
    gender 84
    gossip 96–7
    institutional failures 66
    leadership 74, 90–1
    mistrusted images 59, 64
    modelling mistrust 160–3, 169
Social Representations Theory (SRT) 7–12, 32,
    35, 64, 119
    conspiracy theories 139–40, 146–8
    modelling mistrust 159
    schemata 102
social trust 65–6
societal crisis situations 143
sociometric networks 98
sock puppets 112
Son, T. T. 72
Sønderskov, K. M. 65
songs, the mistrusted 62–3
Sorrenti, L. 44
Sorrentino, R. 27
Spanish fascist party 120
Spitting Image 58–9
spoofing 126

Stephen, A. T. 107
stereotypes 57–8, 59, 61–4, 75, 91, 93, 114
    gender 84, 85
    gossip 94
    race 86
    salience 21
Stewart, A. E. 21
Stewart, W. D. P. 153
stickiness 11
subclinical psychopathy 80–1
subjective value 17–19
Suedfeld, P. 75
Sundermeier, J. 83
Surgevil, O. 85
surveys, method limitations 67–9
Sutton, A. L. 44
Sutton, R. M. 145, 146, 148
Swami, V. 145
Sweeney, P. J. 78
Sztompka, P. 3

Talwar, S. 113
Tang, W. 66
Tanis, M. 3
task-oriented leaders 74, 76–7
Taylor, P. M. 116–17
terrorism 63, 122, 125–6, 149
Thatcher, M. 85
Thorbjørnsrud, K. 113
Thornton, C. J. 46
Timotijevic, L. 9–10
Tomasello, M. 94
Tomljenovic, H. 148
Towler, C. C. 44
transaction costs 72
transactional leadership 73, 75, 84–5
transformational leadership 74, 76, 84
transition trust deficit 88
trolling 111–12, 125, 128, 146
Trumbo, C. 20
Trump, D. 87, 88, 113, 144, 152, 154
trust 3, 4–5, 158
truthing 126
Tsiring, D. 44
Tukachinsky, R. 130
Tversky, A. 15, 17–18
Tykocinski, O. E. 24

Uhlmann, A. J. 112
uncertainty 8, 12, 14–16, 19, 40–1
    absolute 34–5
    age of 29–30, 31
    modelling mistrust 160–3
    radical 34–5
    rationality 28
    shared 29–37, 52

tolerance 26–7
US conspiracy theories 144
US elections 57, 113, 125, 144, 154
US presidents 87–8, 154
Uscinski, J. E. 137

Vaccari, C. 130
vaccines 13, 140, 148, 155, 162
    MMR 37, 145, 155
    see also COVID pandemic
Vala, J. 33
van der Joop, P. 21–2
Van der Velde, F. 21–2, 27
Van Engen, M. L. 84
Van Kleef, G. A. 95
van Koot, C. 109
Van Prooijen, J.-W. 143
Vargo, C. J. 113
Veracity Index 60–1
Vergara, F. 44
Villejoubert, G. 24
Vinkenburg, C. J. 85
virtual environments 20
Voracek, M. 144–5
Vosoughi, S. 130

Walter, N. 130
Walumbwa, F. O. 74
Wang, D. S. 76
'War of the Ghosts' 102
Ward, P. R. 65
warnings 6–7, 162

watchwords 78
weaponising mistrust 115–33
wedge-driving rumour 101, 103
Weinstein, N. D. 20, 21
Wells, G. L. 24
Whalen, C. K. 21
Whaley, A. L. 46
Wilkes, R. 98
Williams, K. M. 80
Wilson, D. S. 94
Wilson, J. 118
Wilson, T. D. 16
wish/pipe-dream rumour 101, 103
Wisse, B. 81
Wittgenstein, L. 45
Womack, V. Y. 86
Wood, T. 138
Wozniak, L. 104
Wright, D. B. 67
Wynne, B. 14

Yang, Q. 66
Yin, Z. 99
Yu, H. 75, 99

Zabelina, E. 44
Zannettou, S. 125
Zawisza, E. 21
Zheng, W. 85
Zieliński, J. 47
Zimunya, C. T. 104
Zuckerman, M. 26